How to Do
Everything
with

Win
Me illennium
edition

How to Do *Everything* with Windows **Me**illennium edition

Curt Simmons

Osborne/**McGraw-Hill**

Berkeley   New York   St. Louis   San Francisco
Auckland   Bogotá   Hamburg   London
Madrid   Mexico City   Milan   Montreal   New Delhi
Panama City   Paris   São Paulo
Singapore   Sydney   Tokyo   Toronto

Osborne/**McGraw-Hill**
2600 Tenth Street
Berkeley, California 94710
U.S.A.

For information on translations or book distributors outside the U.S.A., or to arrange bulk purchase discounts for sales promotions, premiums, or fund-raisers, please contact Osborne/**McGraw-Hill** at the above address.

How to Do Everything With Windows Millennium Edition

234567890 CUS CUS 01987654321

ISBN 0-07-213039-3

Publisher:	Brandon A. Nordin
Vice President	
and Associate Publisher:	Scott Rogers
Acquisitions Editor:	Roger Stewart
Project Editor:	Jennifer Malnick
Acquisitions Coordinator:	Cindy Wathen
Technical Editor:	Tyler Regas
Copy Editor:	Sally Engelfried
Proofreader:	Carroll Proffitt
Indexer:	Valerie Robbins
Computer Designers:	Jani Beckwith, Tara Davis
Illustrator:	Michael Mueller
Series Design:	Mickey Galicia
Cover Design:	Joseph Humphrey and Tom Willis

This book was composed with Corel VENTURA™ Publisher.

Dedication

This book is dedicated to my wife, Dawn, who followed my chapters around, tested all the steps in this book on her Windows Me computer, and often said things like, "What you have said in this part makes no sense." Although aggravating at the time, she has helped make this book better and easier for you to use!

On a more serious note, writing is a lonely profession, and Dawn invariably has to share in some of that alone time as constant deadlines come my way. God has really blessed me with a wife who is always understanding, always loving, and always supportive when I have spend a little too much time in my "computer cave."

About the Author

Curt Simmons is a Windows expert who makes his living as a freelance author, trainer, and courseware developer. Curt has written more than a dozen high-level computing books about Microsoft technologies and related topics. He holds the Microsoft Certified Systems Engineer (MCSE), Microsoft Certified Trainer (MCT), and Chauncy Group Certified Technical Trainer (CTT) certifications. When he is not writing books, he and his wife spend their time constantly refurbishing their 100-year-old historical home. Curt and his family live in a small town outside of Dallas, and you can reach him on the Internet at http://curtsimmons.hypermart.net.

Contents at a Glance

Contents

Acknowledgements

Thanks to everyone at Osborne—it's been a real joy to work with you all. Special thanks to Roger Stewart, who rescued me (for a moment) from the land of Active Directory to do this really fun book. I also owe a big thanks to Cindy Wathen, who answered my nit-picky questions and kept the paper shuffle moving to the right people (I still owe you that Tex-Mex dinner!). Thanks to Jennifer Malnick and Sally Engelfried, who scrutinized my sentences and word choices—they have helped make this book really great. Also, thanks to Tyler Regis, the technical editor for this book, who brought his expertise to the table. Finally, as always, thanks to Margot Maley, my literary agent, who takes care of me.

Chapter 1

Exploring the Windows Me Desktop

How To...

- Start Your Computer
- Explore Your Desktop
- Examine Icons
- Manage and Configure the Recycle Bin
- Check Out the taskbar
- Use the Start menu
- Log Off, Restart, and Shut Down Your Computer

I've been telling my mother for the past few years that she needs to join modern society and get a computer (after all, it's embarrassing when a computer book author's own mother doesn't read his books). She always says, "I'm too far behind—I would never catch up." That's not exactly true. In fact, the opposite is true. Computers and software have become more complex during the past few years, but using computers and software has actually become easier. In the past, you had to know a thing or two about computer hardware and operating system glitches and problems. Obviously, Windows Me is not perfect, but it is easier to use than any operating system previously produced by Microsoft. This chapter gets your feet on solid ground by showing you around the Windows Me interface. If you're new to computing, this chapter is just what you need, and if you have some experience behind you, this chapter will help you get started.

Starting Your Computer

If you have just purchased a new computer with Windows Me preinstalled, your first task is to unpack it, attach your peripherals (which are your keyboard, mouse, printer, speakers, and so forth), then start the computer. Your computer comes with a booklet that explains how to attach your peripherals and start the computer. Most computers have a power switch on the back of the case that you must switch on to start the computer. Some models have an On switch on the back and also another button on the front of the case that gives you easy starting access. You have to check out your computer's documentation to find your On switch.

Once you flip the switch and your computer has power, you will most likely see a brand name screen—or maybe even a black screen with a bunch of information about your computer's hardware—and then you will see the Windows Me splash screen as your computer boots up. If this is the first time a new computer with Windows Me preinstalled is booting, it may ask you some questions to customize your computer and finish the install. See Appendix A for more information about installation. Also, you may see a Windows Logon dialog box where you can enter a password to logon to your computer. You can create a password at this time, or just click Cancel if you don't want to use a password.

TIP

Do you really need to use a password? That depends on your needs. Obviously, if you want to keep other people out of your operating system, then give yourself a password—but beware, Windows Me was not designed with security in mind, and a savvy computer user can get around your password. Most home users really do not need a password, and clicking Cancel will prevent the password prompt from being displayed during boot.

Did you know?

Here's the Geeky Boot Info

OK, do you want to know what *really* goes on when you turn on your computer? Your computer follows a boot process that loads Windows Me, called the boot or startup sequence. This process loads all of the operating system files so you can actually use Windows Me. Here's what happens:

1. When you first turn on your computer, a power on self test (POST) process occurs through your computer's Basic Input Output System (BIOS). Your computer checks its hardware and memory, then tells your system where to get the operating system (such as from the floppy drive or hard drive). Most BIOS configurations check your floppy drive first, then a section of your hard disk for a "bootloader," which can start the loading of the operating system.

2. Windows Me has a database of information called the Registry where information about your computer is kept. The Registry is loaded first so it can be read in order to boot Windows Me.

3. Windows loads a file called System.ini. System.ini is used to load older system configuration information.

4. Kernel32.dll is loaded. Kernel32.dll is the main operating system code used by Windows Me.

5. Gdi.exe and Gdi32.exe are loaded. These files give you the Windows graphical user interface (GUI).

6. User.exe and User32.exe are loaded. These files provide code necessary to manage the user interface, including your windows.

7. Resources and Fonts are loaded.

8. Win.ini is loaded, which provides older system programs and user support.

9. The Windows shell loads, which includes your basic graphical interface settings, and policies for your computer are also loaded.

10. The desktop components are loaded.

11. If you are connected to a network, a logon dialog box appears. Once you provide a valid user name and password, any network policies or logon scripts are applied.

12. All of the final information from any policies are loaded and you see your desktop. Fortunately, in Windows Me, all of this takes less time than ever before!

Checking Out Your Desktop

Windows Me, like previous versions of Windows such as Windows 95/98 and NT, uses a desktop for the standard user interface. The desktop is the place where you access your system components, applications you want to use, the Internet, and

1

basically everything else. Think of the desktop as, well, a desktop. The ideal desktop has everything you need within quick and easy reach. On your computer, the same idea holds true.

As you can see in Figure 1-1, the Windows Me desktop contains an open area, several icons (usually on the left side of the screen), and a taskbar at the bottom that contains the Start button, more icons, and your system clock.

Depending on your computer, the items you see on the desktop will vary, especially if you just bought a new computer with Windows Me preinstalled. If you are as old as I am (which isn't that old!), you remember when movies first became available for home viewing. You rented a video tape, popped it into

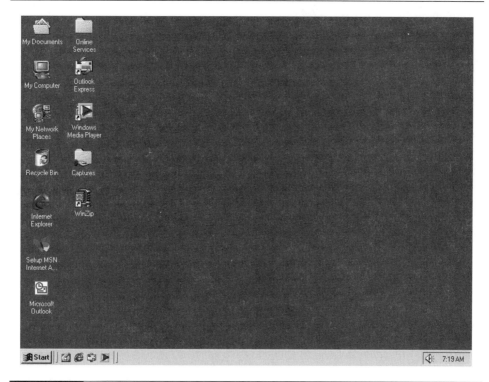

FIGURE 1-1   The Windows Me desktop

your VCR, and the movie started. However, when you watch a movie today, you usually have to wade through 10 or 15 minutes of advertisements for other movies or even products. Unfortunately, computers are following the same path. If you have a new computer, you may have a lot of...well, junk, on your desktop. Windows Me is no exception and includes several advertisements. You may see an icon to join MSN Internet (which Microsoft really wants you to do, by the way), a folder called Online Services, and you may have all kinds of other stuff, depending on your computer manufacturer.

You also have a number of shortcuts. Shortcuts are simply icons on your desktop that enable you to quickly and easily access some system component or application that you've installed without having to wade into the operating system and retrieve it. A shortcut icon appears on your desktop with a little arrow in the corner, as shown in Figure 1-2.

They can be helpful, but too many shortcuts clutter up your desktop and make it confusing. The good news is that you do not have to keep any advertisements or shortcuts on your desktop that you do not want. Simply delete them. When you delete a shortcut, you are not deleting the program, just the little icon on your desktop that points to the program. This feature lets you decide what should be on your desktop and what should not.

TIP *You don't have to worry about deleting icons that should not be deleted. Windows Me icons, such as My Computer and Recycle Bin, do not have the Delete option.*

FIGURE 1-2 A shortcut icon has an arrow in the corner

How to ...   Delete a Desktop Item

You can easily delete a desktop item, such as an advertisement or an unneeded shortcut, by following these steps:

1. Place your mouse on the icon you do not want and right-click it.

2. From the menu that appears, click Delete.

3. A message appears asking if you are sure you want to delete the item. Click the Yes button.

Did you know?   Mouse Keys

In case you are very new to computing, let me give you some quick tips about using your mouse. Your mouse has a right mouse key and a left mouse key. When you hold the mouse, you use your index finger to operate the left mouse key and your middle finger to operate the right mouse key (the wire connecting the mouse to your computer should be going away from your body if you are holding the mouse correctly). If you are left-handed, you can configure your mouse to operate correctly with your left hand—see Chapter 2 for details. When this book gives you mouse directions, here's what they mean:

■ Left-click—click the left mouse key with your index finger one time.

■ Right-click—click the right mouse key with your middle finger one time.

■ Double-click—click the left mouse key with your index finger two times very quickly.

Checking Out System Desktop Icons

Now that you have taken a look at your desktop, let's take a look at your standard system desktop icons. These icons are a part of the Windows Me operating system and are a permanent part of your desktop (in other words, you can't delete them). These icons are important to your work and play with Windows Me, and the following sections tell you about each of them.

My Computer

If you double-click the My Computer icon on your desktop, the My Computer window appears and displays some additional icons. The purpose of My Computer is to give you access to your computer's disk drives as well as Control Panel (which is explored in Chapter 2). In Figure 1-3, you see the floppy drive, your hard drive (usually labeled "Local Disk (C:)"), your CD-ROM drive, and you may see additional drive icons if your computer has them, such as an extra hard disk, or a Zip or Jaz drive, or even a hand-held device.

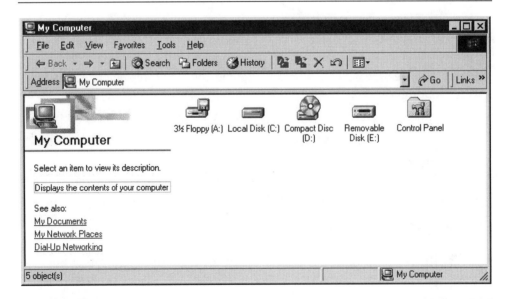

FIGURE 1-3   My Computer contains icons for your computer's drives and Control Panel

If you have previously used Windows 98, you may think some My Computer items are missing, such as your Printers and Dial-Up Networking folders. Don't worry—these items are still available in Windows Me, but they have moved to different locations. This book will teach you all about each of them.

You can double-click any of these icons to open the drives and see what is stored on each. For example, if you wanted to check out the contents of a floppy disk, you would put the disk in your computer's floppy disk drive and double-click the 3-1/2 Floppy icon to open the floppy disk. If you are new to Windows, spend a few minutes opening each of your available drives by double-clicking them. If you get an error message when trying to open your floppy or CD-ROM drive, this simply means you do not have a disk or CD in the drive.

You may notice that the My Computer window looks a lot like Internet Explorer. This is no mistake, as you might guess, because Microsoft wants your operating system to be streamlined with the Internet (Microsoft has big plans in the "operating system/Internet integration area." If you don't believe me, just wait until the next operating system releases next year!). However, you can completely customize how your windows look. See Chapter 3 for details.

My Network Places

My Network Places replaces Network Neighborhood, which was found in previous versions of Windows (My Network Places is also found on Windows 2000 operating systems). Why the change? My Network Places more accurately reflects networking today and includes Internet networking as well as home networking. If you double-click My Network Places, you see some standard icons, such as Add Network Place, Home Networking Wizard, and Entire Network, as shown in Figure 1-4. You can learn all about these in Part 2 of this book.

My Documents

If you have used operating systems in the past, you know that it is easy to save a document of some kind, and then to have trouble finding it. Windows Me makes this a lot easier with the My Documents folder, also found on the desktop. My Documents is a sort of catch-all folder and default storage location for anything you save. Most anything you choose to save, whether it is an application, a document,

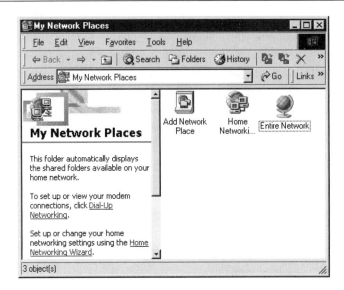

FIGURE 1-4 My Network Places enables you to set up networking for your computer

or even an Internet document, will be saved in My Documents instead of another folder on your computer. In short, this makes your stuff easy to find. As shown in Figure 1-5, My Documents contains a My Pictures folder, a My Videos folder, and a My Webs folder. As you can guess, documents you save that are pictures are automatically saved in My Pictures, videos are saved in My Videos, and so forth.

Recycle Bin

Want to know a secret? When you delete a file from your system (anything at all, a document, picture, shortcut—whatever), it isn't really deleted. It is sent to the Recycle Bin, where it waits to be deleted. The Recycle Bin is an excellent Windows feature. Why? You can recover deleted data that you actually want to keep. When you delete an item from your computer, it is removed from its current location and placed in the Recycle Bin. It stays in the Recycle Bin until you choose to empty the Recycle Bin or the Recycle Bin becomes too full. Only then is the item deleted forever.

I have given you only a brief overview of the other desktop icons because we will use them extensively throughout the book. However, Recycle Bin is only

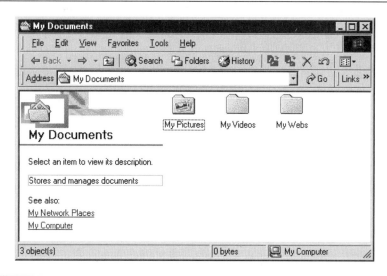

FIGURE 1-5   My Documents is the default storage location for all documents and related files

covered in this chapter, so I'll spend a little more time with it to make sure you know "how to do everything." Check out the following sections.

Using Recycle Bin

As mentioned previously, any time you delete an item it is sent to the Recycle Bin. You can open the Recycle Bin and see what is inside by just double-clicking the Recycle Bin icon on your desktop (you can also right-click the icon and click Explore). As shown in Figure 1-6, you can view the items in the Recycle Bin that are waiting to be deleted. You can see their names, original locations, the date and time they were placed in the Recycle Bin, the type of file, and the size of the file.

You see that you have two buttons available as well. One of these is the Empty Recycle Bin button, which you can click to permanently delete the items in the Recycle Bin.

 Once you choose to empty the Recycle Bin, all items in the Recycle Bin are permanently deleted from your computer. You cannot recover these items once they have been emptied from the Recycle Bin.

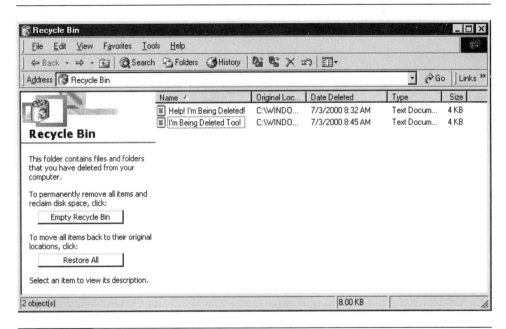

FIGURE 1-6 Deleted items reside in the Recycle Bin

You can also empty the contents of your Recycle Bin by simply right-clicking on the Recycle Bin icon on your desktop and clicking Empty Recycle Bin from the menu that appears.

You also have a Restore All button. What if you accidentally delete a file and it is moved to the Recycle Bin? No problem, you can use the Restore All button to move the file back to its original location on your computer. So, what if you delete 30 files and you only want to restore one of them? No problem—just select the file in the list by left-clicking it. The Restore All button changes to Restore. Click the button and the file is put back in its original location.

You can also move an item out of the Recycle Bin by just dragging it to the desktop. Put your mouse pointer over the file you want to take out of the Recycle Bin, then press and hold down your left mouse key. Continue holding down your left mouse key and drag the item to your desktop and let go of the mouse key. The item will now reside on your desktop. Do you want to know about an even easier way? If your accidental delete is the last thing you did on your computer, just hit CTRL+Z on your keyboard. The deleted item will return to its original location!

1

Changing the Recycle Bin's Properties

You can also change the Recycle Bin's properties, which basically changes the way it behaves. Right-click the Recycle Bin on your desktop and click Properties on the menu that appears. You see a Recycle Bin Properties window that has a Global and Local Disk tab (see Figure 1-7).

On the Global tab, there are two radio buttons that enable you to either configure your drives independently or use the same settings for all drives. This feature only applies to you if you have more than one hard disk in your computer. In most cases, the default setting that configures all of your drives the same way is all you need.

Next, there is a check box that tells your computer to delete items immediately instead of moving them to the Recycle Bin. As you can guess, this feature automatically deletes items when you click Delete. This provides you absolutely no protection in the event that you accidentally delete a file you want. Let's say you are writing your life story and you accidentally delete the document. If you have selected this check box, the document will immediately be gone from your computer—you will not be able to retrieve it. I strongly recommend that you

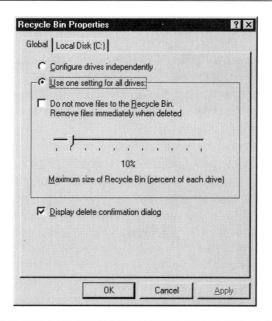

FIGURE 1-7   Access this window to change the Recycle Bin's properties

do not click this check box to enable this option. No matter how good your computing skills, you will make a mistake from time to time and accidentally delete something. Recycle Bin is your safety net so you can get that document back. By clicking this check box, you have no protection—so don't do it!

Next, there is a sliding bar that represents the maximum size the Recycle Bin can grow. Like everything else on your computer, the Recycle Bin stores items in a folder on your hard drive. The sliding bar enables you to set a limit to how big Recycle Bin can grow before it forces to you empty the contents and permanently delete items from your system. By default, this setting is configured for 10 percent. This means that 10 percent of your hard drive's space can be used before Recycle Bin tells you to empty it. That is, if you have a 10GB hard drive, you can store up to 1GB of deleted data in the Recycle Bin before it must be permanently removed and deleted from your computer. Under most circumstances, this 10 percent setting is all you need, but you can change it to a higher or lower percentage if you want. Just make sure you have a good reason for doing so.

NOTE   *Keep in mind that you do not have to wait until your Recycle Bin is full to empty it—and in fact, most people don't. Some people empty it every time they put documents in it, while others empty it on a weekly basis after they have reviewed its contents to make sure nothing was accidentally deleted. There is no right or wrong approach, of course—just find what works best for you.*

Finally, there is a Display Delete Confirmation Dialog check box. This tells Windows to give you that aggravating "Are You Sure?" message every time you delete something. This option is selected by default, and although the configuration message is sometimes a pain, it is a good safety check. I recommend that you leave this setting enabled.

In addition to the Global tab, there is a Local Disk Tab; you may have several of these tabs if your computer has more than one hard drive. You can't do anything on these tabs if you selected the Use One Setting For All Drives radio button on the Global tab. If you want each drive to have different settings and you selected that option on the Global tab, then you can configure each drive independently. The tabs have the same options, such as the slider bar for the percentage of the hard drive you want to use for the Recycle Bin. The real question is why would you do this? The answer is all about drive space.

Let's say your computer has two hard drives. One has 5GB, while the other only has 1GB. You can spare 10 percent of the 5GB drive for the Recycle Bin,

1

but what if your 1GB drive is already crowded? You might not want 10 percent of that drive used for Recycle Bin, so you can give it a lower percentage, such as 5 percent. Again, under normal circumstances and with most computers, you don't need to worry about any of this, but it's good to know the options are there in case you have some specific hard drive space issues.

Checking Out the Taskbar

The taskbar is the small bar you see at the bottom of your desktop and is shown in Figure 1-8.

The taskbar contains your Start menu, which is explored later in this chapter, and some built-in icons for Internet Explorer, Outlook Express, Windows Media Player, and Show Desktop. Any applications you open or any windows that you have minimized also show up on the taskbar. Just left-click any of these to open them or bring them up on your desktop so you can work with them.

There is also a separate box on the right side of the taskbar. This is called your System Tray, and it contains your clock, probably a volume control icon, and maybe several other icons, depending on what is installed on your computer. The System Tray is just an easy way to access some applications you may use frequently. If you right-click on any of the items in the System Tray, you can normally close or remove the item from the System Tray, or you can click Properties to configure it. For example, if you right-click your clock in the System Tray, you can click Adjust Date/Time. This action opens a simple window where you can change the current date and current time. These settings are easy and self-explanatory.

You can customize the taskbar in a number of different ways. See Chapter 3 for details and step-by-step instructions.

FIGURE 1-8   The taskbar is found at the bottom of your desktop

Minimizing Windows

Any window that is open on your desktop can either be maximized or minimized (or closed). If you look in the upper right-hand corner of a window, you see three buttons: an X, a square, and a flat line. The X button closes the window, the square button maximizes the window so that it takes up your entire desktop area, and the flat line minimizes the window so that it disappears from your desktop and appears on your taskbar. To maximize a minimized window on your taskbar, just left-click it and it will jump back onto your desktop as the active window. This feature enables you to have several windows open at one time without mass confusion on your desktop.

Exploring the Start Menu

If you have ever visited a theme park, you know there is typically one main entrance that leads you to all of the attractions the park has to offer. Windows Me is the same way with the Start menu. The Start button appears on your taskbar in the lower left-hand portion of your screen (see Figure 1-9).

Clicking this button brings up the Start menu, which is your gateway to most Windows components and the applications that you install. The Start menu is built on a folder hierarchy that begins with just a few top-level folders. From there, you can discover all that Windows has to offer.

If you click the Start button with your left mouse key, a pop-up menu appears, shown in Figure 1-10.

The following sections tell you about each of the Start menu items you see in Figure 1-10.

FIGURE 1-9   The Start button is located on your taskbar

FIGURE 1-10   Click the Start button with your left mouse key

Shut Down, Log Off, and Run

These Start menu options are explored later in this chapter, so see the sections "Using the Run Command," "Logging Off Your Computer," and "Restarting or Shutting Down Your Computer" for specific instructions.

Help

The Help option opens the new and improved Windows Me Help Files that contain information to help you resolve problems or answer questions. See Chapter 18 for information about Windows Help.

Search

The Search option on the Windows Start menu helps you locate a variety of information both on your computer and on the Internet. If you use your mouse

and point to Search on the Start menu, another pop-up menu appears, giving you
the option to search for the following items:

- For Files and Folders—This option opens a search window where you
  enter a search request (by name or keywords). Windows then attempts to
  find the file or folder you want on your hard drive.

- On the Internet—This option opens an Internet Explorer window and
  launches an Internet connection (or, if you have broadband "always-on"
  Internet connectivity such as DSL, Internet Explorer doesn't need to launch
  a connection). A window appears, as shown in Figure 1-11, from which you
  can search for people, a person's address, a business, a previous search, or a
  map. Just click the radio button you want, enter the requested information,
  and then click the Search button. Pretty cool, huh?

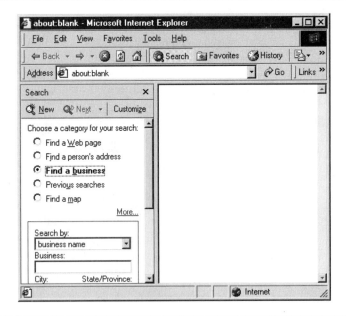

FIGURE 1-11   Use the Internet Search feature to find all kinds of information

- Find People—You can also choose the Find People option. This opens a simple dialog box in which you enter as much information about the person as you know, then use the drop-down menu to select an Internet search engine to attempt to find the person. For example, in Figure 1-12, I'm trying to find myself (I don't know where I am) on Bigfoot, an Internet search engine.

- Using Microsoft Outlook—If you use Microsoft Outlook for your e-mail, you can search your Outlook Address Book and find mail or people in that location.

Settings

If you point to Settings on your Start menu, another pop-up menu appears where you can open Control Panel, Dial-Up Networking, Printers, the taskbar, and Start menu. Several later chapters explore these items.

Documents

This option opens another pop-up menu that shows you what is in the My Documents folder on your desktop. This option is provided on the Start menu for ease of use and locating files you want to open.

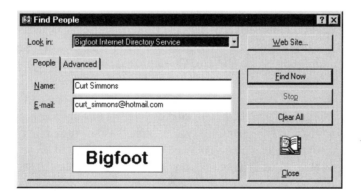

FIGURE 1-12   Look for people on the Internet using the Search feature

What Happened to Windows Explorer?

If you are prowling around the Programs menu, Windows 95/98 users will notice that Windows Explorer is no longer there. Is it gone? Not at all. It has simply been moved to the Accessories menu. Why? There are so many new wizards and folders that enable you to accomplish the same tasks that Explorer once did (and still does) that Microsoft sees it as an accessory now rather than as a major component. I don't see it that way and you probably don't either, but Microsoft thinks you would rather use the newer operating system tools instead of Windows Explorer.

Programs

This option opens yet another pop-up menu that lists all of the applications installed on your computer. There are also additional folders here, like Accessories, which we will explore in later chapters. Use the Programs menu to easily get to any of your programs.

Other Items

Above the Programs menu, you may have several other items, depending on what is installed on your computer. For example, in Figure 1-10 you can see that I have several Office icons as well as WinZip. One item that you do have here by default is Windows Update.

First introduced in Windows 98, the Windows Update Web site reads information about your computer and suggests downloads for you. For example, let's say Microsoft releases Windows Me and an operating system bug is discovered (What?! No way!). The Windows Update site can give you a "fix" that you can install on your computer and repair the problem. This is a cool feature and one that you should access every so often to see if there are updates that need to be downloaded from Microsoft and installed on your computer—besides, all of the updates are free of charge. Figure 1-13 shows you the Windows Update Web Site.

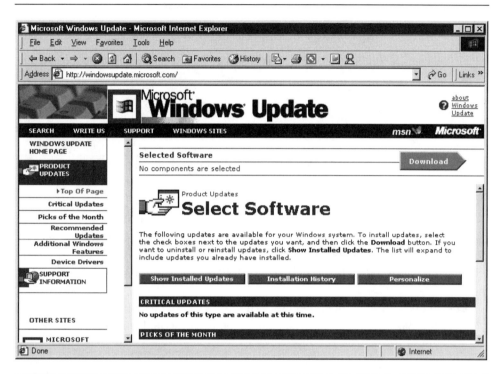

FIGURE 1-13   Windows Update enables you to download updates and fixes to your computer

   *If you are browsing the Internet and you want to check out the Update site, you don't have to use Windows Update on your Start Menu. Just type http://windowsupdate.microsoft.com in your browser, and your browser can take you directly to the site.*

Using the Run Command

There is a Run option on the Start menu. The Run command is a quick way to open folders, programs, documents, or even Internet sites on your computer. If you click Run on the Start menu, a simple dialog box appears (see Figure 1-14).

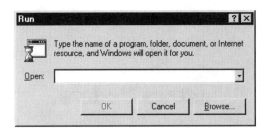

FIGURE 1-14   Use the Run dialog box to open items on your computer or a network

Just type what you want to open in the dialog and click OK to open it, or you can click the Browse button to find the desired item you want to open on your computer. You can open lots of things with the Run command, but it can be a little tricky. Here are some pointers on how to use it:

- To open a folder, document, or program, just type its name and click OK (but make sure you have the right name because the Run command doesn't "guess" for you).

- To open an Internet site, type the URL, such as **www.osborne.com**. Windows will open Internet Explorer and start an Internet connection (if necessary).

SHORTCUT
You don't have to type http:// when you want to use the Run command to open an Internet site, but you do need the www (or ftp, or whatever) so that the Run command can recognize the item as a Web address (this is unlike most Web browsers today, which do not require you to type the www).

- You can open any of your drives, such as your hard drive, CD-ROM drive, floppy drive, and so forth by simply typing the drive letter followed by a colon. For example, if you wanted to open your floppy drive, just type **A:**.

- You can open shared folders on your network by using the Universal Naming Convention (UNC) path. The UNC path is represented by *computername**sharename**filename*. For example, say I am on a network using a computer named Comp42 that contains a shared folder called Docs, and in that shared folder resides a file called Corp. If I want to open that document, I would type **\\comp42\docs\corp** at the Run line.

*If you don't know the name of a file or folder but you know the file or folder resides on a certain computer, just type **\\computername** to see all the shared folders on the computer for which you have permission to access. If you don't know the name of the computer, well, you're out of luck. However, you can use My Network Places to browse your network and perhaps find the computer that way. See Chapter 11 for more information.*

Logging Off Your Computer

Several people may use your Windows Me computer. For example, at home, you and some family members may share the computer, or at work, if your computer is on a network, several different users may access it. If you log on to Windows Me using a user name and password, Windows keeps track of the settings and changes you make to the system through your user name. If someone else uses your computer, Windows keeps track of that person's settings as well.

With all of this in mind, Windows Me enables you to log off the computer so that someone else can log on without having to restart the computer. To log off, just click the Start menu and click Log Off *user name*. A dialog box appears asking if you are sure you want to log off. Click Yes. You are logged off the system, and the username and dialog box window appears for the new user to log on.

Restarting or Shutting Down Your Computer

When you are finished using Windows Me, you can choose to shut down or restart the computer. Restarting is often called for in the case of problems or when something new is installed. To shut down or restart your computer, click the Start Menu, then click Shut Down. A dialog box appears that contains a drop-down menu, as shown in Figure 1-15. Click the drop-down menu, click Shut Down, Restart, or Standby, then click OK. Once the computer has shut down, you can turn off the power switch (if necessary—some computers do not require you to physically turn off the power switch).

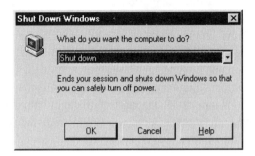

FIGURE 1-15   Use this menu to shut down or restart your computer

You should always shut down your computer or restart it using this command. Do not shut down or restart by turning the power off and on. While this method does work, it may damage your operating system. Always use the Shut Down command so that Windows can properly shut down and restart.

Chapter 2

Managing Your Computer with Control Panel

How To...

■ Access Windows Me Control Panel

■ Access Control Panel features

■ Use Control Panel features to configure your computer

Do you remember those old automobile radios? You know, the kind where you pushed the buttons and turned the dial to find the station you wanted, and then you simply adjusted the volume. Ah, the good old days...well, sort of. The radio/CD player in my truck now has so many buttons and controls that I still don't know how to work it very well, but the good news is that modern radios do all kinds of things they didn't do in the past. The result is a better product, but there are more controls that you must manage in order to operate that product.

Similarly, as computer systems become more complex, there's more to manage. Because of their complexity, there is a great potential that users will spend too much time trying to learn to use a system rather than actually using it. Microsoft understands this issue and has, for the most part, tried to make Windows Me very easy to configure. The major place you configure your system is in Control Panel. This chapter explores all of Control Panel's options, shows you what these options do, then shows you how, when, and what to configure and tells you why you might want to.

Accessing Control Panel

You can access Control Panel in two major ways. First, you can double-click My Computer on your desktop, then double-click the Control Panel folder. Or, you can click the Start button on your taskbar, point to Settings, then click Control Panel. Either way, the Control Panel opens, as shown in Figure 2-1.

Windows 95/98 users will notice in Figure 2-1 that Control Panel looks a little different. Windows Me conserves folder space and minimizes clutter by displaying only the Control Panel icons that are most commonly used. You can, however, view all of them by simply clicking the View All Control Panel Options link in the left side of the window. When you click this link, Control Panel changes to display all of the icons and looks the same as the Control Panel in Windows 95/98, as shown in Figure 2-2.

Now that you have opened Control Panel, the following sections of the chapter explore each feature and teach you how to use Control Panel to configure various components of your Windows Me computer.

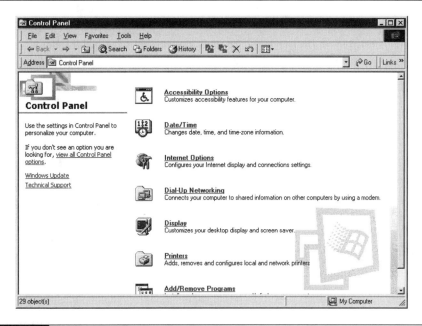

FIGURE 2-1   Windows Me Control Panel

 **Create a Shortcut**

In Chapter 1, you learned how to remove unwanted shortcuts from your desktop, but you can also easily create shortcuts to folders and applications that you use often. For example, you can create a shortcut on your desktop to Control Panel so that you have an icon directly on your desktop. To create a shortcut for Control Panel, or another folder or application, follow these steps:

1. Locate the folder or application icon on your computer. For example, to create a shortcut to Control Panel, double-click My Computer so you can see Control Panel.

2. Right-click the folder or application, then click Create Shortcut.

3. Windows Me asks you if you want to create a shortcut on your desktop. Click Yes.

An icon for the folder or application now appears on your desktop.

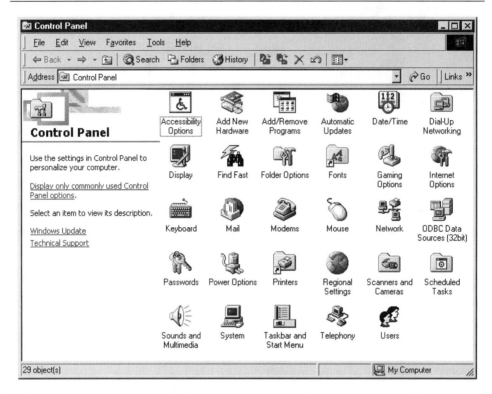

FIGURE 2-2 Control Panel now appears with all icons

Some configuration options are much more complicated than others and deserve their own chapters. In order not to repeat information in this book, some Control Panel features are briefly discussed in this chapter with a cross-reference to the part of the book where the configuration is thoroughly explored.

Accessibility Options

Accessibility Options enable you to configure your computer's input and output behavior for persons with certain disabilities. These accessibility options make computing much easier for these individuals. Windows Me provides excellent support for accessibility configuration, and you use this feature in Control Panel to configure most of them.

 *You can learn about some additional accessibility options in Windows Me in Chapter 5.*

If you double-click Accessibility Options in Control Panel, a Properties window appears with several different tabs that you can configure to your needs. The following sections tell you about each of these.

Keyboard

The Keyboard tab allows you to change the way your keyboard inputs information to the Windows Me operating system, as shown in Figure 2-3.

The Keyboard tab provides you with several options to make using your keyboard easier. The following sections tell you what those options are.

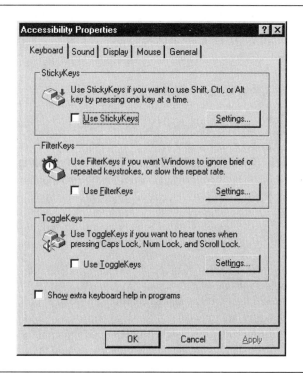

FIGURE 2-3   Use the Keyboard tab to change your keyboard's behavior

StickyKeys

StickyKeys are provided so that you do not have to hold down several keys at one time on the keyboard. For example, let's say that you want to press CTRL+ALT+DEL at the same time (which opens the Close Program window). Normally, you need to press these keys at the same time, but enabling StickyKeys makes the keys "stick" so that you can press CTRL, then press ALT, then press DEL, one at a time. This is an excellent feature for people who can use only one hand on the keyboard. To enable StickyKeys, just click the Use StickyKeys check box and then click the Settings button.

When you click Settings, a new Window appears with a few check boxes. First, you can enable the StickyKeys shortcut, which allows you to turn on StickyKeys by pressing the SHIFT key five times in a row. You can also select or deselect these options:

- Press Modifier Key Twice To Lock—This option specifies that the CTRL, SHIFT, or ALT key remains active if you press it twice (press it a third time to unlock it).

- Turn StickyKeys Off If Two Are Pressed At The Same Time.

- Make A Sound When Modifier Key Is Pressed (CTRL, SHIFT, or ALT).

- Show StickyKeys Status On Screen.

Once you enable or disable these as desired, you can then use StickyKeys by pressing the SHIFT key five times in a row. A message appears on your screen telling you that StickyKeys are enabled and a StickyKeys icon appears in your System Tray. Once you play around with StickyKeys, you'll see they are easy to use and very helpful.

FilterKeys

FilterKeys are provided in Windows Me to help your operating system "filter" keystrokes. If a user has difficulty using the keyboard, FilterKeys can be used to ignore brief or repeated keystrokes. To use FilterKeys, just click the check box on the Keyboard window, then click the Settings button.

Once you click the Settings button, click the Use Shortcut check box so that you can turn on FilterKeys by pressing the right SHIFT key. You can use the remainder of this window to determine how FilterKeys behaves by using (or not using) the following options:

■ Ignore Repeated Keystrokes—For example, if you hit the *T* key twice quickly, it will be filtered so that only one *T* appears on the screen. Click the Settings button to adjust the rate as desired.

■ Ignore Quick Keystrokes And Slow Down The Repeat Rate.

■ Beep When Keys Are Pressed Or Accepted.

■ Show FilterKeys Status On Screen.

As with StickyKeys, FilterKeys are easy to use. Play around with the settings to meet your specific needs.

ToggleKeys

ToggleKeys are a simple feature that tells the operating system to play a tone when you press the CAPS LOCK, NUM LOCK, or SCROLL LOCK features on your keyboard. To turn on ToggleKeys, just click the Use ToggleKeys check box. When you click the Settings button, a simple dialog box appears on which you can enable a shortcut to turn on ToggleKeys by pressing and holding down the NUM LOCK key for five seconds.

At the bottom of the Keyboard tab, there is a check box that enables additional keyboard help when using programs. This feature turns on keyboard help pointers that may be supported in some applications that you use.

Sound

The Accessibility Properties Sound tab gives you two quick options to enable Windows sounds to help you. This tab, shown in Figure 2-4, contains two check boxes.

The first option is SoundSentry. Depending on your Windows Me settings or what you do, certain warning or notice sounds are made. The SoundSentry option makes these warnings appear on your screen instead of as a sound. This feature is helpful to hearing impaired Windows Me users. To use SoundSentry, just click the Use SoundSentry check box. If you click the Settings button, you can decide what the screen should do to give you the warning (such as flash the active title bar, etc.).

Your second option on this tab is to use ShowSounds, which tells your programs to display text for any sounds or verbal speech cues they might give you. Enable this option by clicking the Use ShowSounds check box.

Display

The Display tab, shown in Figure 2-5, enables you to use high contrasting colors on your display that may be easier to read.

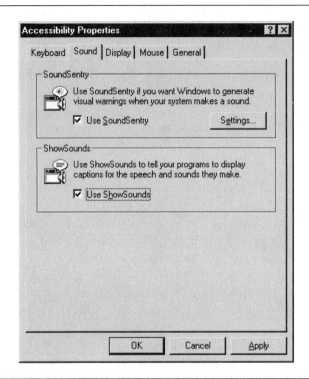

To enable this option, just click the Use High Contrast check box. If you click the Settings button, you can enable the shortcut, which is LEFT ALT+LEFT SHIFT+PRINT SCRN, by clicking the check box to enable the shortcut. You can also use this window to determine how high contrast should be used, such as white on black, black on white, or a custom combination. You can experiment with these settings to find which one works best for you.

Also notice on the Display tab that you can adjust the cursor settings. Use the slider bars to adjust cursor blink rate and width. These settings can make the cursor easier to see.

Mouse

The Mouse tab provides you with a simple check box that enables you to control the mouse pointer on your screen with the numeric keypad on your keyboard so that you do not actually have to use the mouse. Click the Settings button to enable

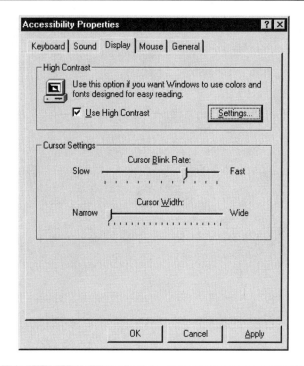

FIGURE 2-5   Use the Display tab to enable high contrast settings

the shortcut to this option, which is LEFT ALT+LEFT SHIFT+NUM LOCK. You can also use the Settings page to control how fast the mouse pointer moves and related settings, which are self-explanatory.

General

Finally, the General tab, shown in Figure 2-6, provides some basic control options for accessibility.

You have the following options:

■ Turn Off Accessibility Features After Idle For *x* Minutes—This feature turns off accessibility features if the computer is idle for a certain period of time. Use the drop-down menu to select the desired idle time.

■ Give Warning Message When Turning A Feature On.

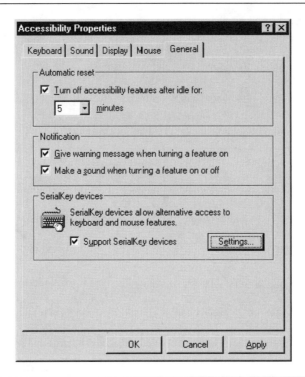

FIGURE 2-6 Use the General tab to configure standard options

- Make A Sound When Turning A Feature On Or Off.

- Support SerialKey Devices—SerialKey devices are additional input devices (also called augmentative communication devices) attached to your computer that are used by people who cannot use a standard keyboard and mouse. This setting tells Windows Me to support these devices.

Check Box Help

There are a lot of check boxes in Windows Control Panel pages that turn on or off certain features. Sometimes the explanation text isn't quite so easy to understand. Although this book explains all of these check boxes to you, you can get additional help in Windows Me by right-clicking any check box text and clicking What's This? Another dialog box appears that explains more about the check box item. Sometimes the help text that appears is great, and sometimes it's not so great, but it is good to know that this feature is available to you.

Add New Hardware

The Add New Hardware icon that appears in Control Panel is a wizard you can use to help you install troublesome devices on your computer. Although Windows Me typically installs new hardware automatically, this wizard can help if you have problems. The Add New Hardware Wizard is explored in detail in Chapter 6.

What Is a Wizard?

A wizard is a helpful program that walks you through a series of steps. Normally, the wizard collects some information from you in each step, then uses your information to accomplish a certain task. For example, the Add New Hardware Wizard walks you through a series of steps to help you install a new hardware device. The wizards provided in Windows Me make difficult configurations much, much easier.

Add/Remove Programs

Add/Remove Programs enables you to install new programs, remove programs, and install and remove Windows components. These features are explored in detail in Chapter 4, so refer to that chapter for step-by-step information. I will note here, however, that Add/Remove Programs contains a Startup Disk Tab. If you ever need to make a startup floppy disk that can boot Windows Me in the event of problem, here's where you make one. I know, this seems like an odd place to put the startup disk option. The best explanation I can offer is that you should make a new startup disk each time you install or uninstall programs, so the tab is here to remind you to make a new one (except this is kind of weird because no one really uses Add/Remove programs to install software—see Chapter 4).

Automatic Updates

Automatic Updates is a brand new, really cool feature in Windows Me. If you double-click the Automatic Update icon in Control Panel, you see a simple window, as shown in Figure 2-7.

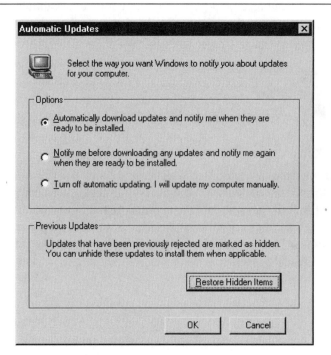

Automatic Updates in Control Panel

This feature enables your computer to periodically check the Windows Update Web site (see Chapter 1) for necessary updates to your computer. The Windows Update Web site can examine your computer and determine what downloads are needed for Windows Me. The downloads are free and the Microsoft site is safe for your computer to be talking to behind your back, so don't worry.

With the configuration option in Control Panel, you can enable your computer to automatically download needed updates and prompt you to install them, have your computer tell you that a download needs to occur and allows you to manually perform the download, or choose not to use automatic updating at all. Just click the appropriate radio button. Also, there is a Restore Hidden Items button at the bottom of the window. If Windows suggests an update and you tell it "No thanks," you can click this button to view the suggested updates again so you can install them.

Now, all this sounds great, and it is, but here is the caveat. Automatic Update works best for users who have "always-on" Internet access. This means that you have cable, ISDN, DSL, or satellite access and you do not have to dial an access number. In other words, your computer is always connected to the Internet. With always-on access, your automatic update can check the Web site and even download items without bothering you. If you don't have always-on Internet access, Automatic Update will need to launch a dial-up connection each time it needs the Internet, which, depending on your setup, can be annoying. You can always try out Automatic Update and turn it off later if you don't like the way it works.

You can also use Windows Update on the Start Menu to check for updates yourself. You don't have to enable this automatic functionality if you have Internet connectivity issues or problems.

Date/Time

As you might guess, the Date/Time feature in Control Panel enables you to set your operating system's clock. When you double-click the icon, you see a simple interface that contains a calendar noting the current date. You can change the date by simply using the drop-down menus. Likewise, you see a clock with a drop-down menu where you can change the current time as well as the time zone. As you can see in Figure 2-8, this interface is very easy to configure.

You can click the check box at the bottom of the Date/Time window so that your computer automatically adjusts the time for daylight savings time. If you live in an area that does not use daylight savings time, keep this box unchecked.

FIGURE 2-8   Use this interface to adjust your computer's date and time

 *If you need to adjust your computer's date and time, you don't have to use Control Panel. Just right-click the time in your System Tray and click Properties, or double-click the time itself. This action opens the same Date/Time window.*

Dial-Up Networking

The Dial-Up Networking feature in Control Panel enables you to configure connections so that your computer can access the Internet. As you might guess, there are a number of options, and the use of dial-up networking is explored in detail in Chapter 8.

Display

The Display feature in Control Panel enables you to configure your desktop and other display settings so that your computer looks the way you want. There are a number of things you can do, and you can learn all about using the Display features in Chapter 3.

Folder Options

Windows Me enables you to configure the appearance of your folders. You have several options available, and you can learn all about them in Chapter 4.

Fonts

The Fonts folder in Control Panel houses all of the possible fonts that your computer can use. When you open Fonts, you see a listing of all of the fonts available. There isn't anything you can configure here, with the exception of removing or adding fonts to the folder. In general, this is not something that you need to do since Windows Me and your applications handle the fonts that are used. If you want to change how fonts look within your display, you can use the Display feature in Control Panel to apply different schemes to your computer (see Chapter 3). Within the Fonts folder, however, you can double-click any font to learn more about the font and to see a sample of how the font looks.

Game Controllers

The Game Controllers feature in Control Panel provides you with a location to manage any gaming devices attached to your computer, such as joysticks and other playing devices. You can learn all about the Game Controllers features in Chapter 13.

Internet Options

Internet Options in Control Panel enables you to configure, as you might guess, Internet Explorer. You can also access these properties from within Internet Explorer itself; these options are explored in Chapter 9.

Keyboard

The Keyboard feature in Control Panel enables you to configure how your keyboard operates. When you double-click this icon, you see two tabs, which are explained in the following sections.

Speed

The Speed tab allows you to configure how fast your keyboard responds to keystrokes. As you can see in Figure 2-9, the Speed tab gives you a few simple options for adjusting your keyboard's speed.

First, there are two slider bars for Character Repeat. The first, repeat delay, determines how much time passes before a character repeats when you hold down a key. If you are a fast typist, you will probably want this setting moved to Short.

There is a also a Repeat Rate slider bar. The Repeat Rate slider bar determines how fast a character repeats when you hold it down. The repeat delay determines how fast the initial repeat begins while the repeat rate determines how fast the characters are actually repeated. A medium setting (between slow and fast) is typically all you need.

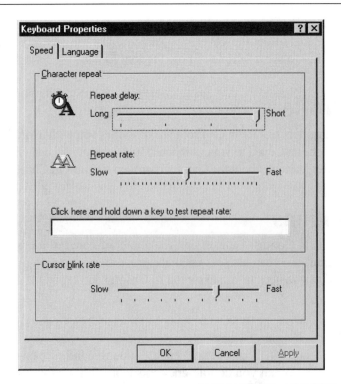

FIGURE 2-9   Use this tab to configure the speed of your keyboard

2

At the bottom of the window, there is a Cursor Blink Rate slider bar. Use it to change the cursor's blink rate; the cursor blinks on the tab as you change the rate for test purposes. The best setting is typically toward the fast end of the slider bar.

Language

The Language tab, shown in Figure 2-10, enables you to use several different languages with your keyboard. The default language is selected for you based on your input during installation. You can, however, use this tab to add more languages that you want your computer to support.

To add a language that you want to use, simply click the Add button and select the desired language from the drop-down menu. Likewise, you can use the Remove button to remove any languages that you do not want to use. The Set As

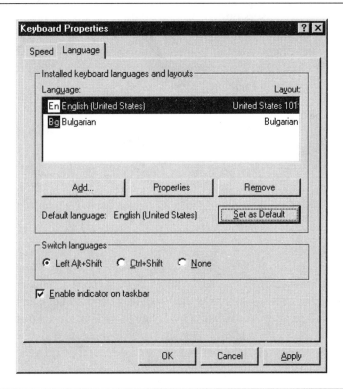

FIGURE 2-10   Use the Language tab to manage languages used by Windows Me

Default button sets the default language that your keyboard will use. To do this, just select the language in the list and click the Set As Default button.

In the second part of the window, you can choose a radio button to select a keyboard stoke to change to a different language (these options are grayed out if you are only using one language). And, if you click the Enable Indicator On taskbar check box, the taskbar will display whether you are using multiple languages. When multiple languages are used, this option is selected by default.

Mail

The Mail feature in Control Panel enables you to configure your Windows Me computer to receive e-mail from some type of e-mail server service, such from a Microsoft Exchange Server. This icon only appears if you upgraded from Windows 95/98. If you have purchased a new computer with Windows Me preinstalled or performed a clean install yourself, this icon will not appear.

You use this feature to create different profiles in case you use several different e-mail accounts. Home users don't need to use this feature because you can set up Windows Me to send and receive e-mail over the Internet using the mail client of your choice (see Chapter 10). If you are using Windows Me on a corporate network, you should follow your company's networking procedures for configuring the mail option in Control Panel, if necessary.

Internal Mail Servers

The primary purpose of the Mail feature is to configure Windows Me to send and receive e-mail through a particular mail server. A mail server is a computer that handles e-mail for a public or private network. For example, let's say that your computer resides on a corporate network of thousands of users. The network contains server computers that handle the e-mail coming in and flowing out of the network. Windows Me has to be configured to communicate with this mail server in order to receive e-mail on the network. For home use, none of this is necessary since you access the Internet to send and receive e-mail instead of a private mail server on a local area network.

Modems

The Modems feature in Control Panel provides a place where you manage modems attached to your computer. In the past, modems were painfully difficult to setup and troubleshoot, but Windows Me makes modem configuration much easier. As you might guess, modem setup and configuration is a lengthy topic, and you learn how to do it all in Chapter 8.

Mouse

The mouse is a universal input device that lets you point and click your way into Windows oblivion. The mouse itself is a simple device, but surprisingly, there are a number of configuration options for it that you can access by double-clicking the Mouse icon in Control Panel to display the Mouse Properties dialog box. You have a few tabs and several different options, and the following sections show you how to configure your mouse so that it operates and behaves in a way that is useful to you.

Buttons

The Buttons tab, shown in Figure 2-11, lets you determine how your mouse buttons or keys work.

First, you can click the appropriate radio button so that your mouse functions as either a right-handed mouse or a left-handed mouse. The right-handed mouse buttons provide:

■ Left Button—Normal Select and Normal Drag

■ Right Button—Context Menu or Special Drag

If you choose the left-handed option, the mouse buttons provide:

■ Left Button—Context Menu or Special Drag

■ Right Button—Normal Select and Normal Drag

As you can see, selecting the left-hand option simply reverses which button performs which action from the right-handed option.

Next, you can use the slider bar to speed up or slow down your mouse's double-click speed. Most people use a medium setting (where the slider bar is in the middle), but you can choose the setting that works best for you.

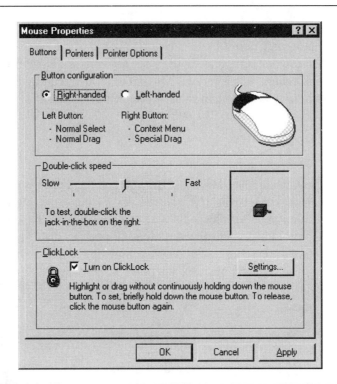

FIGURE 2-11
Use the Buttons tab to configure how your mouse buttons work

Finally, at the bottom of the window there is an option called ClickLock. This option enables you to drag items around your desktop without having to continuously hold down the drag button (the left mouse button for right-handed users). Click the Turn On ClickLock check box to use it, then click the Settings button. The settings window gives you a slider bar so you can determine how long you have to hold down the left mouse button before it locks into place and you can drag items without holding it down.

You'll need to play around with the slider bar setting for ClickLock to find which setting works for you, but short ClickLock settings are usually more aggravating than helpful. This setting causes your left mouse key to lock very quickly every time you press it, so don't start out with a short setting when you are configuring ClickLock.

Pointers

The Pointers tab, shown in Figure 2-12, provides a place for you to configure the way your pointer appears on your Windows Me computer. Depending on what you are doing, your mouse pointer will change. For example, a typical pointer is simply an arrow. If your system is busy, your mouse pointer changes to an hourglass, and so forth. You can use the Pointers tab to customized the pointers as you wish.

At the top of the window, there is a Scheme drop-down menu that enables you to select preconfigured Windows schemes. Scroll down and select some of them. You'll see the various pointers change in the Customize window. Just select the scheme that you want and click Apply to use that scheme.

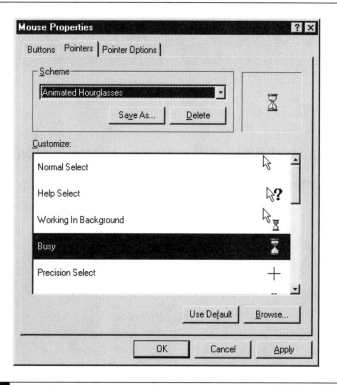

FIGURE 2-12   Use the Pointers tab to select desired pointer appearances

Did you know?

Scheme Options

The basic Windows Me schemes provide several different appearances for your pointers. One of the best options, however, is the large pointer support that some of the schemes provide so that your mouse pointers are larger on your display than normal. These settings are very helpful to people with vision problems. As with many Control Panel settings, you can play around with the Pointer Schemes and find one that you like best.

Aside from using the standard Windows Me pointer schemes, you can also create your own schemes by modifying the desired pointers. If you click the Browse button, you can choose to use a different cursor file, such as one you have downloaded from the Internet or obtained from a CD. You can then select a desired pointer and save your scheme as a custom pointer scheme.

 **Create a Custom Pointer Scheme**

To create a custom pointer scheme, just follow these easy steps:

1. Use the drop-down menu and select a scheme that is close to your desired scheme options.

2. Select the option in the Customize window that you want to change.

3. Click the Browse button and locate the desired pointer file you want to use.

4. Select the desired file and click OK.

5. On the Pointers tab, click the Save As button and give the scheme a name. Click OK.

 **Mouse Pointer Files**

If you want to use different pointer files for your custom configuration, you can use one of two types of files. First, you can use a standard cursor file, which ends with the .cur extension. Also, you can use an animated cursor file, which ends with an .ani extension. When you choose to browse for a different pointer file, Windows Me only looks for files with either a .cur or .ani extension.

Pointer Options

The final mouse configuration tab is Pointer Options, as shown in Figure 2-13. This simple tab gives you a series of check boxes or slider bars with which you can configure how your mouse pointer moves around the screen.

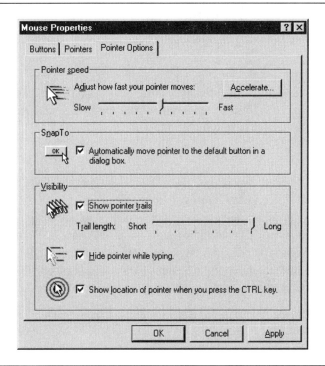

FIGURE 2-13   Use Pointer Options to configure how your mouse pointer moves around the screen

You can play around with these settings to determine which (if any) of them you would like to use. The options are as follows:

- Pointer Speed—Use the slider bar to determine how fast your pointer moves when you move your mouse. You can try different adjustments to find the speed you like. If you click the Accelerate button, you can also select how fast your pointer moves when you begin moving your mouse.

- SnapTo—This option automatically moves your mouse pointer to the default button in any given dialog box. You can try this option to see if you like it, but many users find SnapTo more aggravating than helpful (myself included).

- Visibility—The visibility options control how your pointer looks when in motion. There are three check box options. First, you can choose to use a mouse trail, which leaves a disappearing trail when you move your mouse. Some people like this settings, some don't (it gives me a headache), but you can experiment with it. Next, you can choose to hide your mouse pointer when you type. This just makes your mouse pointer disappear when not in use. Finally, you can choose to make your mouse pointer appear when you press the CTRL key.

Network

The Network feature in Control Panel enables you to configure networking components so that Windows Me can participate on a local area network. You can learn all about networking with Windows Me in Chapter 11.

Passwords

As you are aware, you can log on to Windows Me using a password. This feature enables different people to use the same computer. You can also use different profiles so that each user can set their own system settings. For example, let's say that Susan uses Windows Me, and her son, Tom, uses the same Windows Me computer. Susan and Tom can use different passwords and profiles so they can each use the same system without interfering with each other. To configure these options, you use the Passwords and Users feature in Control Panel. The Users feature is explored later in this chapter.

When you double-click the Passwords icon in Control Panel, you are presented with the Passwords Properties dialog box, which has three tabs with different password options. The following sections show you what is available on each tab.

Change Passwords

As you can guess, the Change Passwords tab, shown in Figure 2-14, lets you change your current Windows Me password.

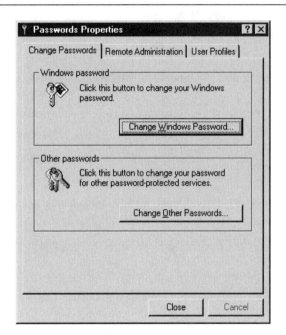

FIGURE 2-14   Use the Change Passwords tab to alter Windows passwords

You have two different options. First, you can change your Windows Me password by clicking the Change Windows Password button. When you click this button, another window appears that enables you to select other services for which you want to alter the password. For example, my Windows Me computer is connected to my own Microsoft network. When I begin to change my Windows Me password, I can choose to change it for my local computer as well as my network service at the same time. This enables me to have the same password to log on to both my network server and my local computer. At that point, all I have to do is type the old and new passwords and confirm the new password again.

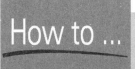 **Change Your Password**

To change your Windows Me password, just follow these easy steps:

1. Click the Change Windows Password on the Change Passwords tab.

2. In the Window that appears, select any additional network services for which you want to change the password. If you don't want to change any of these or if none are available, click OK.

3. In the dialog box that appears, enter your old password, then enter your new password twice in the provided dialog boxes.

4. Click OK to the confirmation message that appears.

5. Log off Windows Me and log back on using your new password.

2

The next option you have is to change other passwords. This option provides the same functionality as changing your Windows Me password and a networking service password at the same time. Here's the difference. Let's say that you need to change your network password but you do not want to change your Windows Me password. In this case, you would use this option since you do not want any changes to your local computer's password.

The other password options are only necessary for computers connected to networks where servers and network security is in use. For your home use or even your home network, you don't need to worry about this option.

Remote Administration

The Remote Administration tab is a simple tab where you can enable remote administration. This means that if your computer is connected to a network, you can let other users on the network use and manage the files and printers on your computer by accessing them with a user name and password. However, Windows Me has to be configured to share files and printers, and if your Windows Me isn't configured to do so, this tab will not appear. Chapter 11 explores networking with Windows Me, so refer to that chapter for more information.

User Profiles

The User Profiles tab enables different users to use the same computer and manage their own settings without interfering with each other, as shown in Figure 2-15. This feature enables Bob to have an orange desktop while Cindy, who uses the same computer, has a desktop that displays a picture of her cats.

There are two standard user profile options. The first one lets all users access the same desktop area. In this scenario, if Bob changes the desktop color to bright orange, Cindy will see the same bright orange desktop (although she can change it to something else, which will probably infuriate Bob). The second option enables each user to configure his/her own settings, which is really your best bet if you,

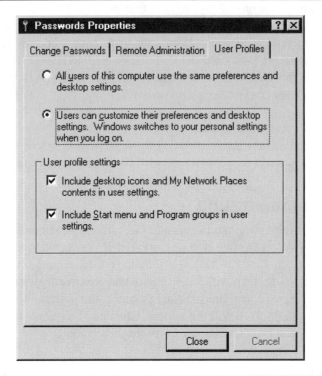

FIGURE 2-15 You can enable user profiles on your computer with this tab

your family, and your family pet all use the same Windows Me computer. If you choose the second option, you have two other options you can select:

- Include Desktop Icons And My Network Places Contents In User Settings—This enables both local customization and network and Internet customization for the computer.

- Include Start Menu And Program Groups In User Settings.

As you might guess, there is no right or wrong setting; these settings are all about degrees of freedom when multiple users access the same Windows Me computer.

2

Power Options

Windows Me is equipped to save energy by using power schemes that you can configure. These options can automatically turn off your monitor or hard drive after a certain period of inactivity. The Power Options in Control Panel is also available within Display properties, and Chapter 3 explores this option.

Printers

The Printers folder, which was available in My Computer in Windows 98, is now located in Control Panel. As you can imagine, printing can be a complex topic, so check out Chapter 7 for all the details.

Regional Settings

Regional Settings in Control Panel provides you a place to configure your computer to use different language symbols, currency, and other specific regional options. For example, let's say that you are using Windows Me in France and you want Windows Me to calculate money in French currency. You can enable this option by using Regional Settings. When you open Regional Settings, you see a standard Regional Settings tab, Number tab, Currency tab, and a Time and Date tab. Each tab contains drop-down menus so you can select the desired regional settings. The options presented to you are self-explanatory.

Scanners and Cameras

Due to the popularity of scanners and digital cameras, Windows Me includes a Control Panel feature to help you manage these hardware devices. You can learn about the installation and management of scanners and cameras in Chapter 7.

Scheduled Tasks

The Scheduled Tasks folder in Control Panel contains three wizards you can use to set up a variety of PC maintenance utilities to run in the background. These options are all covered in Chapters 16 and 17.

Sounds and Multimedia

The Sounds and Multimedia feature in Control Panel lets you make some basic configuration changes to the way your Windows Me computer handles default Windows sounds and multimedia and sound devices attached to your computer. If you double-click the Sounds and Multimedia icon in Control Panel, the properties page appears with four tabs, which are explored in the following sections.

Sounds

On the Sounds tab, shown in Figure 2-16, you can use different sound schemes to determine which sounds Windows Me plays for different events that occur. For example, when you receive an e-mail, Windows plays a sound. The default sounds are applied when Windows Me is installed, so you do not have to configure anything here, but there are a number of sounds to choose from, and you can make changes to suit your personal taste.

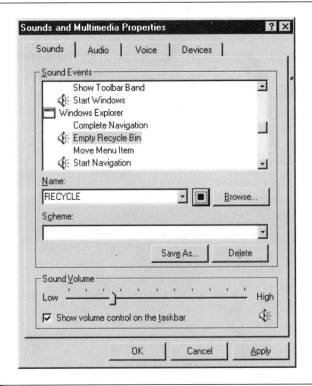

FIGURE 2-16　Use the Sounds tab to change Windows Me sounds

2

You can use the drop-down menu to select a Windows scheme, such as Windows Default, then you can select each sound in the Sound Events window, click the Browse button, and change the sound as desired by selecting a different one. You can then save this new scheme using the Save As button.

At the bottom of the Window, there is a slider bar with which to adjust the sound volume and a check box that enables the volume control to be displayed in your System Tray. I recommend that you keep this check box selected so you can easily control the volume from your taskbar (you can learn more about the taskbar in Chapter 3).

Audio

The Audio tab presents you with three different types of audio input and output: sound playback, sound recording, and MIDI music playback, as shown in Figure 2-17.

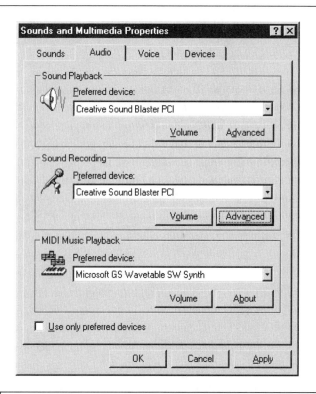

FIGURE 2-17   Use the Audio tab to configure different types of input and output

For each type, you can use the drop-down menu and select the preferred device. This means that a particular device on your computer should be preferred over other devices for that type of input or output. For example, say I want Sound Playback to use my computer's sound card to play sounds. This means that my sound card is the preferred device, as you can see in Figure 2-17. If you have multiple sound cards or devices that can be used, just use this drop-down menu to select the preferred device.

For each device, there is a Volume button. Click this button to change the volume as desired. The Volume Control windows present simple slider bars that you can adjust as needed.

With the Sound Playback and Sound Recording options, there is also an Advanced button. The Sound Playback Advanced window has two tabs, Speakers and Performance. The Speakers tab enables you to use a drop-down menu to select the speaker type that should be used, such as desktop speakers, headphones, etc.

The Performance tab also appears in the Sound Recording Advanced window. This tab, shown in Figure 2-18, has two slider bar options: Hardware Acceleration and Sample Rate Conversion Quality. The default settings are Full for Hardware Acceleration and Good for Sample Rate Conversion Quality. You don't need to change these settings under normal circumstances. If you do change them, you may experience some performance problems.

 *The sound card, microphone, and other sound devices on your computer should have come with instructions about any special settings that need to be made. Check your computer documentation for details.*

One final note about the Audio tab: there is a Use Only Preferred Devices check box at the bottom of the window. This check box makes sure that only the preferred devices that you selected can be used. Should you enable this option? If your programs require a certain sound card or device, then yes. If not, don't worry about this check box.

Voice

The Voice tab works just like the Audio tab, except you can configure voice playback and voice capture options.

Devices

Finally, there is a Devices page. This window lists all the sounds and multimedia device categories for Windows Me. By clicking on a category, you can see the

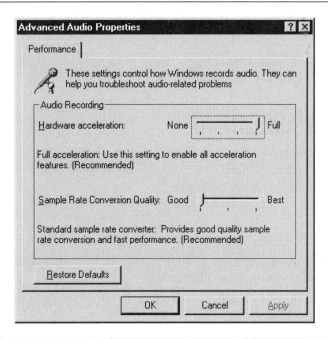

FIGURE 2-18   It's best to use the default settings on the Performance option

actual device or software installed to manage that category. There isn't much you can do here, but if you select a device and click the Properties button, a window appears with these three options:

- Use Audio Features On This Device—This option is enabled by default.

- Do Not Use Audio Features On This Device—This option allows you to effectively disable the device.

- Do Not Map Through This Device—This option prevents a program from accessing the device unless the program specifically requests it. Do not use this option unless you are certain of the ramifications to your programs that may need to indirectly access the sound device.

System

The System feature in Control Panel contains four different tabs: General, Device Manager, Hardware Profiles, and Performance. These tabs manage different components of your Windows Me system, and they are explored in various other chapters throughout this book.

 *You can also quickly access the Devices page Properties window by right-clicking My Computer on your desktop and clicking Properties.*

Taskbar and Start Menu

The taskbar and Start Menu feature enables you to configure the items that appear on your taskbar and Start Menu to suit your needs. You can learn about taskbar and Start Menu configuration in Chapter 3.

Telephony

The Telephony feature gives you a place to configure dial-up rules and options. You can learn all about these in Chapter 8.

Users

The last feature in Control Panel is Users. This feature gives you a simple window where you can create new user accounts so that different people can log on to your Windows Me computer. If you have enabled the Passwords option, different users cannot log on without a valid user name and password. When you double-click the Users icon, the User Settings window appears, as shown in Figure 2-19.

As you can see in the figure, I have a user account for Mom that I have created using the New User button. You can create as many different accounts as you need so that different people can use your computer (like your family, friends, and all the people in your neighborhood who don't own a computer).

When you click New User, a wizard appears that asks you some questions. Once you answer the questions, the new user account is created and appears in your list. Once the new account is created, you can manage the account by simply selecting it and using the available buttons, such as Delete, Make A Copy, Set Password, or Change Settings. The Make A Copy option copies the account and starts the New User Wizard again so that you can enter a new user name. This is faster then using the New User Wizard over and over if you have several accounts to create. The Change Settings option lets you make changes to the options you selected when you created the account.

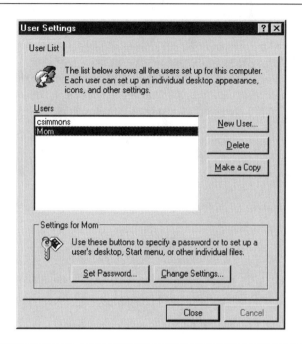

FIGURE 2-19   Use the User Settings window to manage user accounts

How to ... Create a New Account

To create a new user account, just follow these steps:

1. In the User Settings window, click the New User button.

2. At the Welcome screen, click Next.

3. In the dialog box, enter a name for the user. You are limited to 128 characters. Click Next.

4. Enter and confirm a password, if desired. Click Next.

5. Choose the items you want to personalize for the user by selecting the check boxes. Your options are Desktop Folder and Documents Menu, Start Menu, Favorites Folder, Downloaded Web Pages, and My Documents Folder. Once you select the options, choose one of the radio button options presented. You can either create a copy of the existing settings for the user account, or tell Windows Me to create new items so that the new users have completely new folders and settings. Make your selections, then click Next.

6. Click the Finish button. Windows creates the new account and it appears in your list.

Chapter 3

Configuring System Settings

How To . . .

- Customize the Appearance of the Windows Me Desktop
- Customize Your Folders
- Customize Your Start Menu and Taskbar
- Use Windows Me Desktop Themes

For the past year, my wife and I have spent a lot of time remodeling and refurbishing our 100-year-old historical home. We have spent hours examining wallpaper and paint samples and choosing lighting fixtures for our walls and rugs for our hardwood floors. It can be a tough job because there are so many options available, and after all, we want our home just right. In many ways, Windows Me is the same—there are lots of options you can choose to make your desktop, folders, taskbar, and Start menu appear just the way you want. Finding what you like best is half the fun though, and this chapter shows you how to configure these items so that your Windows Me operating system looks just the way you want.

Configuring Your Display

One of the major places you configure the way your Windows Me system looks is through your Display properties. If you remember from Chapter 2, Display is an icon in Control Panel that you can open, then configure various settings that affect the appearance of your Windows Me display. Just click Start, point to Settings, click Control Panel, then double-click the Display icon to open the Properties window. Once you open Display Properties, you see several tabs, all of which are explored in the following sections.

The Display icon officially resides in Control Panel, but you don't have to open Control Panel to access the properties window. Just find an empty area on your desktop (a place where there is no folder), then right-click the desktop and click Properties. The same Display properties window appears.

Background

The first tab you see on the Display Properties window is the Background tab, as shown in Figure 3-1. The Background tab lets you decide how your Windows Me desktop area should look. In other words, the background lets you decide what color, style, or even picture appears on your desktop.

3

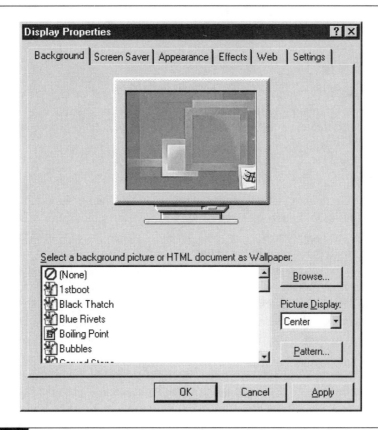

FIGURE 3-1 The Background tab lets you choose a desired desktop background

Windows Me gives you several built-in options that you can choose for your background in the list on the Background tab.

Using a Background Pattern

If you scroll through the list on the Display tab, you see that each file has a name and an icon next to it. Some files give your desktop a background pattern while others give your desktop a background picture (called wallpaper); you can tell which is which by the type of icon (usually).

Background patterns are Windows bitmap files. For example, in the following illustration, you can see the Blue Rivets file uses a bitmap icon, which means this file is a pattern file you can apply to your desktop background.

What Is a Bitmap?

A bitmap is a very common type of graphics file that can be created using a variety of programs, including Windows Paint. A bitmap is made up of tiny bits, or pixels, that each take on a certain color and shade in order to create the desired picture.

To give your desktop a background pattern, on the Background tab, select one of the bitmap files. When you select a file, you will see a picture of it in the test screen on the Background tab. The odds are good that when you select a pattern, you'll see a small piece of it in the center of the test screen. This is because your Picture Display setting is set to Center by default. To change this, go to the Picture Display drop-down menu on the right side of the Background tab, click it, and then choose Tile. This causes the pattern to fill the entire test screen so you can see how it looks before you decide to use it. You can also choose Picture Display's Stretch option to stretch the pattern across the test screen, which will give you a different look.

If you like what you have selected, click the Apply button at the bottom of the window, and the new background pattern will be applied to your desktop. If you don't like it, pick something else on the Background tab. You can look at all of the patterns and even reapply different patterns until you find the one you want.

Using Wallpaper

Before making a decision about your Windows Me background, you should also consider using a background picture, or wallpaper. Windows Me supports the use of pictures, such as JPEG and even HTML documents, for use as wallpaper.

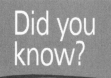

What are JPEG and HTML Files?

JPEG (as well as GIF) files are standard file types for pictures and graphics used on the Internet. When surfing the Net and looking at pictures or graphics, you are usually looking at JPEG and GIF files. HTML files are Web pages. You can display an entire Web page as your background if you like, and you'll see how to do that later in this chapter. In a nutshell, virtually any picture on the Internet can be used on your Windows desktop as long as it is a BMP, JPEG, GIF, DIB, or HTML file or document.

Just as you can select a pattern from the list on the Background tab, you can select one of the wallpaper options provided. When you select a wallpaper, a sample appears on the test screen. You can tile and stretch wallpaper too, but this usually has a distortion effect, so it is not recommended.

If you leave the Picture Display default at Center for your wallpaper, there will be an area of your desktop still showing on the test screen. Windows Me allows you to alter the remaining desktop area to your preference by using a pattern in this leftover background space so it looks the way you want.

TIP

In order to access the Pattern window after you choose a wallpaper, the Picture Display setting must be set to center. Windows Me will not allow you to set a pattern when your existing wallpaper takes up the entire screen (the Pattern button will be grayed out). It is also important to note that some wallpaper pictures automatically take up the entire desktop area, in which case you don't need to (and can't) use an additional pattern since there is no empty space on the desktop.

Once you click the Pattern button, a small window appears, as shown in Figure 3-2. A list of patterns is displayed in the left side of the window; simply select one to see a sample of it in the right side. When you find one you like, click OK.

What if you find a pattern you almost like but is not quite right? You can edit it by clicking the Edit Pattern button. This option opens another window with a greatly enlarged sample of the pattern. Use your mouse and click inside of the pattern to change its shape. This can be a little tricky, but just play around with it until the pattern looks the way you want. When the pattern is right, click the Change button, then click Done.

TIP   *Do you have to use an additional background pattern? No. It is important to remember that all of this stuff is optional. Windows Me gives you a basic background upon installation, and if you are happy with that background, you don't have to change anything. However, all of the options explored in this chapter are provided so you can configure your Windows Me computer to look the way you want it to.*

Once you have finished your background pattern and selected anything else from the Background tab you want to use for the main pattern, click Apply and then OK. As you can see in Figure 3-3, I set a background picture in the center of

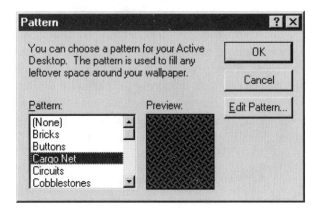

FIGURE 3-2   Use the Pattern window to select an additional pattern to fill in extra desktop space

FIGURE 3-3   You can use a background picture and pattern to customize your desktop

my desktop and added a background pattern to fill in the empty space (hey, I had to get a picture of my daughter in this book somewhere!).

Installing Other Wallpaper

Windows Me provides you a limited set of wallpaper options when you install it in order to conserve disk space. You can install additional wallpaper using Add/Remove Programs in Control Panel. When you double-click the icon, the Add/Remove Programs Properties sheet opens with three tabs. Click the Windows Setup Tab, as shown in Figure 3-4.

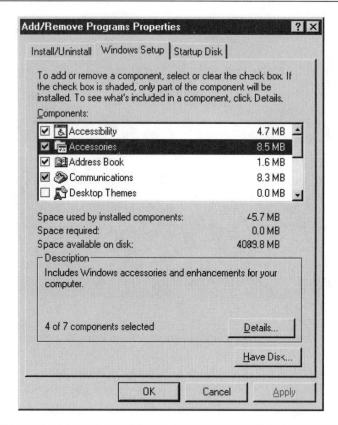

FIGURE 3-4 Use the Windows Setup Tab to install more wallpaper

You can use this tab to install additional wallpaper to your system. You'll need your Windows Me installation CD-ROM for this operation; if you need step-by-step instructions, refer to the How To box.

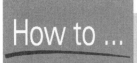 **Install Additional Wallpaper**

To install additional wallpaper, just follow these steps:

1. Open Add/Remove Programs in Control Panel, then click the Windows Setup tab.

2. In the Components window, select Accessories, then click the Details button.

3. In the list that appears, click the Desktop Wallpaper check box so that a check appears in the box.

4. Click OK to close the window, then click OK on the Add/Remove Programs Properties window.

5. Windows Me scans your Windows Me CD-ROM and installs additional wallpaper. You will see the additional wallpaper on the Display Properties Background tab.

NOTE *Some wallpaper cannot be displayed unless the Active Desktop is enabled on your computer. To learn more about the Active Desktop, refer to the "Web" section later in this chapter.*

Using Your Own Wallpaper

Windows Me provides you with several wallpaper options, but you can use your own picture files or Web files as wallpaper as well. This feature allows you to display family pictures—or any other picture you like—on your desktop. If you currently have picture files stored on your computer (such as GIF, JPEG, or BMPfiles), you can simply browse and select the desired picture. See the How To box for step-by-step instructions.

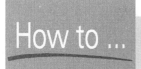

How to ... Browse for Pictures

To browse and select a personal picture to use as wallpaper, follow these steps:

1. On the Display Properties Background tab, click the Browse button.

2. In the Browse window that appears, navigate to the location on your computer where your picture files are kept (such as the My Documents or My Pictures folders).

3. Once you locate the desired picture, select it, then click the Open button on the Browse window.

4. The picture will appear in the test screen on the Display tab. Click OK for your picture to be displayed on your computer's desktop.

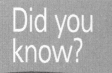

Did you know? Getting Wallpaper from the Internet

You can use any pictures or even Web pages as your wallpaper. If you are using Internet Explorer, just right-click the picture you want to use as wallpaper and click Set As Wallpaper. That's all there is to it! If you want to use an entire Web page, use Internet Explorer's File menu, save the Web page, then use the Browse button on the Background tab to browse and select it for display.

3

Screen Saver

The Screen Saver tab provides two functions: it allows you to configure a screen saver for your computer and to configure power management options. A screen saver is a simple program that runs once your computer has been idle for a certain period of time. The screen saver protects your monitor from "screen burn." When a monitor is left unattended for too long and one continuous picture or window is displayed, the image can burn itself onto your monitor and always be sort of floating in the background regardless of what you are doing. The screen saver provides enough activity for your screen so that this will not occur.

Using a Screen Saver

The Screen Saver tab is easy to use, as you can see in Figure 3-5. Just use the drop-down menu to select a screen saver and a sample of it will be displayed in the test screen. Once you find one you like, just click the Apply button.

Once you select a screen saver that you want to use, you have a few other options as well, including:

- Settings—The Settings button opens a small window specific to the screen saver. Click this button to configure the screen saver. These settings are easy and self-explanatory; play around with them to find the settings you want.

- Preview—If you click Preview, your screen goes blank, and then the screen saver begins so you can see if you like it. Just move your mouse to get control of your system again.

- Password Protected—This check box enables password protection. If you select this option, once your screen saver begins, you must reenter your password to access the system. This is a simple security feature to use if your computer is in a place where others might access it when you are away from the PC. Click the Change button to change the password.

- Wait—This scroll box enables you to set the amount of time to pass before the screen saver comes on. The default time is 14 minutes. There is no right or wrong setting, but to protect your screen, keep the setting under 30 minutes, and do not set the time setting so low that it comes on after 1 minute of activity—you'll find that setting very aggravating!

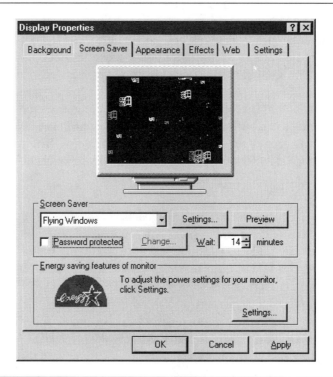

FIGURE 3-5 Use the Screen Saver tab to configure screen saver and energy saving options

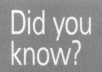

Using Your Pictures for a Screen Saver

Windows Me offers a My Pictures screen saver. This feature lets you use any pictures on your computer as a screen saver. To do this, select the My Picture screen saver from the list, and click the Settings button to set it up. The Settings options are self-explanatory and easy to use. You designate a folder the program accesses, such as My Pictures, where the pictures are stored. All of the pictures in the designated folder will be used for the screen saver. You can then set transition effects as desired, which are simply graphical transitions used to merge pictures together.

 *Several 3D screen savers are available on the Screen Saver tab. While these are cool and perfectly safe to use, 3D graphics are much more CPU-intensive for your computer to run. If you want to conserve energy and CPU work, don't use the 3D screen savers.*

Using Energy Saving Options

You can also access energy savings options on the Screen Saver tab by pressing the Settings button in the bottom of the window. The Power Options Properties window appears (the same properties window you see if you click Power Options in Control Panel), as shown in Figure 3-6.

On the Power Schemes tab, you have a few options to manage how your computer conserves energy when it is idle. First, there is a drop-down menu called Power Schemes. There are three basic schemes:

- Home/Office Desk—When using this scheme, your monitor is automatically turned off after 15 minutes of inactivity, hard disks are turned off after 30 minutes, and your system goes on standby after 20 minutes.

- Portable/Laptop—This scheme uses the same settings as Home/Office Desk.

- Always On—This scheme automatically turns your monitor off after 30 minutes and your hard disks after one hour of inactivity, and your system never goes on standby.

OK, here's the deal. You can use a particular scheme and change any of the settings you want by simply using the drop-down menus. For example, say I want to use the Home/Office Desk scheme, but I do not want my monitor to turn off until there have been 30 minutes of inactivity. No problem: just use the drop-down menu for the monitor and change it to 30 minutes. You can also change all of the settings and click Save As to create your own scheme. Just give the scheme a name and it will appear in your scheme list.

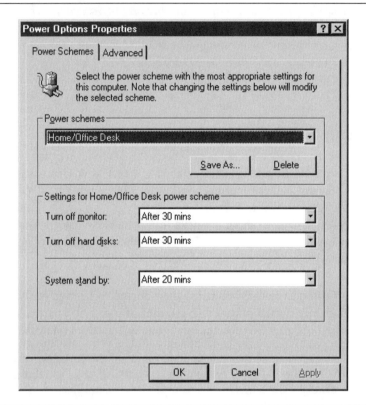

FIGURE 3-6 Use Power Options Properties to manage the power used by your computer

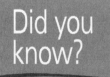

Which Settings Should You Use?

Now that you see what options you have, which scheme should you use? There are no exact answers, but for the typical home user, I recommend the Home/Office Desk scheme with the default settings. This ensures that your computer is using the least amount of energy once the computer becomes inactive for 15 to 30 minutes. This setting makes the best use of energy.

Power Options Properties also has an Advanced tab (which really isn't that advanced). There are only two check box options that you can enable here if you want to:

- ■ Always Show Icon On The Taskbar—This option puts a power icon on your taskbar so you can easily access your power options.

- ■ Prompt For Password When Computer Goes Off Standby—This option requires you to reenter your password when your computer goes off standby before you can use the system again. This helps prevent someone from gaining access to your system when you are away from it.

Appearance

The Appearance tab, shown in Figure 3-7, allows you to pick an appearance scheme for your Windows Me computer.

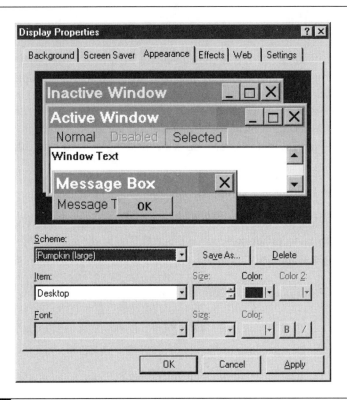

FIGURE 3-7   Use the Appearance tab to pick an appearance scheme

If you click the Scheme drop-down menu, you see that you have a lot of different appearance schemes to choose from. These schemes affect the way your windows appear as well as the colors and fonts that are used in your Windows Me windows and various property pages. When you select a scheme from the drop-down menu, a sample of it is displayed in the test screen. As you can see in Figure 3-7, I selected the Pumpkin (large) scheme, and a sample of that scheme is displayed. Once you find a scheme that you want to use, just click OK. If you decide you don't like the scheme, you can always return to this tab and change it to something else.

As you work with Windows Me, you'll see both Apply and OK buttons on tabs where you can make configuration changes. The Apply button enables you to make a change without closing the configuration window. OK also applies the changes, but the window is closed. You don't have to use Apply to make a change—you can just click OK—but if you want to preview any changes you make before committing to them, use Apply.

You can also customize a scheme and save it so that you have your own scheme. Just use the scheme drop-down menu to select a scheme that is close to what you want, then use the Item drop-down menu to change individual components. For example, if you wanted to use the Pumpkin scheme but wanted the desktop background to be purple, you would click the Item drop-down menu, select Desktop, then use the color drop-down menus to change the color. You can use these options to alter color, font, font size, and even bold or italic. Again, there are no wrong settings. Just play around with these options to find the settings that you like best.

Effects

The Effects tab has just a few simple configuration options. First, you can change your desktop icons to different icons if desired. To do this, select the icon and click the Change Icon button. The trick here is that you do not have a lot of alternative icons to pick from anyway (unless you have Themes installed, which you can learn about later in this chapter), so you probably will not want to change your icons.

There is also a series of check box options on this tab:

- Use Transition Effects For Menus and Tooltips—This option (which is enabled by default) allows Windows to use color changes to windows as they are opened and closed.

- Smooth Edges Of Screen Fonts—This option helps smooth out jagged font edges. You may need to use this option, depending on what appearance scheme you are using.

- Use Large Icons—This option changes your icons to larger icons, which are easier to see but take up more screen room.

- Show Icons Using All Possible Colors—This option (which is enabled by default) gives you the best icon color resolution

- Show Window Contents While Dragging—This option shows the contents of the window while you are dragging it. Without this option enabled, only the window's outline is visible while you drag it.

Web

The Active Desktop in Windows Me is a way for you to view Web content right on your desktop. You can add interactive items to your desktop and Windows Me can automatically update those items from the Web as they change. First introduced in Windows 98, the Active Desktop was supposed to be the way of the future. It didn't gain that much popularity, but it still has some cool features that you may want to use on your Windows Me computer.

The Web tab simply contains a Show Web Content On My Active Desktop check box. Once you click this check box, you can begin adding content to your desktop by clicking the New button. Any items you add to the Active Desktop are listed on the Web tab so you can delete them later if you do not want to use them any longer.

When you click the New button, the New Active Desktop Item window appears, as shown in Figure 3-8.

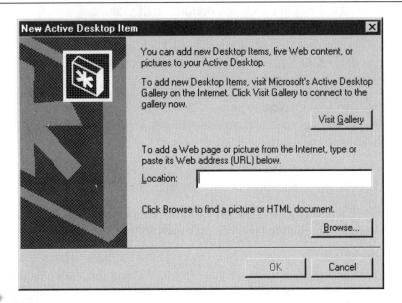

Use this window to add new Active Desktop items

This window allows you to add items in two different ways, and both of them require an Internet connection. First, you can click the Visit Gallery button to access the Microsoft Active Desktop Gallery on the Internet. When you click this button, Internet Explorer is launched (as well as an Internet connection, if necessary) and you are taken to the gallery Web site, which is located at **www.microsoft.com/windows/ie/ie40/gallery**. Once you access the gallery, you will see different categories, such as news, sports, entertainment, etc. By clicking a category, you can see what downloadable content is available. If you want to add something to your Active Desktop, just click the item you want, then click the Add To Active Desktop button that appears.

The second way you can use the New Active Desktop window is to simply enter a Web address in the Location text box and click OK. This opens an Internet connection and retrieves the Web page for display on your Active Desktop.

Once you obtain items, you can select them in the Web tab and click the Properties button to configure the item. For some items, the Properties window will just give you information; for others, it will enable you to configure a schedule for Internet updates. These options are easy to configure and self-explanatory.

Settings

The final Display Properties tab is the Settings tab. You use this tab to manage the actual video card hardware that resides within your computer. As you can see in Figure 3-9, there are a few basic options.

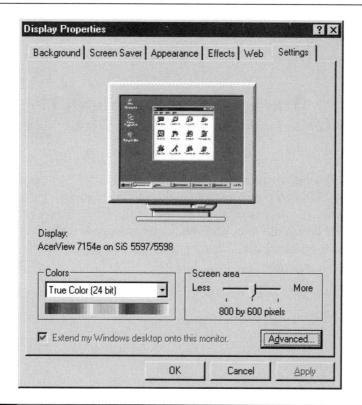

FIGURE 3-9   Use the Settings Tab to configure your video adapter card

First, the Colors drop-down menu enables you to select the number of colors Windows Me can use to generate all of the graphics and pictures that appear on your monitor. True Color (24 bit) is the highest color scheme that you can use, and depending on the quality of your video card, you may only have a few color options available. The highest resolution provides the best color performance.

To adjust the size of your desktop area, use the Screen Area slider bar. By sliding this closer to either Less or More, your desktop area (including your icons) gets either smaller or larger.

The Advanced button opens the Properties window for your video card. In general, the default settings found on these pages are all you need, and you really should not change any of them unless your video card documentation tells you to do so.

Multiple Monitor Support

Windows Me, like Windows 98, supports the use of more than one monitor. This means you can use two monitors and have your desktop appear across both screens. The multiple monitor feature can also be effective if you need to use two different applications but view them at the same time. You can put each application on a monitor. Multiple monitor usage is not widely adopted, but if you do want to use multiple monitors, just access the Windows Help files for easy setup instructions.

Configuring Folder Views

Aside from using an appearance scheme so that your folders appear with a certain color and font, Windows Me also includes several capabilities that enable you to customize your folders. Keep in mind that a folder is simply a storage location. Windows Me has several folders it creates and uses, and you can create your own as well (see Chapter 4).

You can configure folder options from either one of two places: from Control Panel, double-click the Folder Options icon, or, from within any Windows folder, click the Tools drop-down menu, then click Folder Options. This opens the same folder options you see when you open the Control Panel icon.

 *If you change your folder options from within a folder, you are making changes to the appearance of all of your folders. In other words, you cannot individually configure folder options for each folder—one setting applies to all folders in Windows.*

 *Folder options do not affect folder toolbars, but you can change folder toolbars; you will learn how to do this later in this chapter.*

Once you open Folder Options (regardless of from where you open it), you see a simple interface with two tabs.

General

You can make major appearance changes to your folders on the General tab, which presents you with a list of radio buttons, as shown in Figure 3-10.

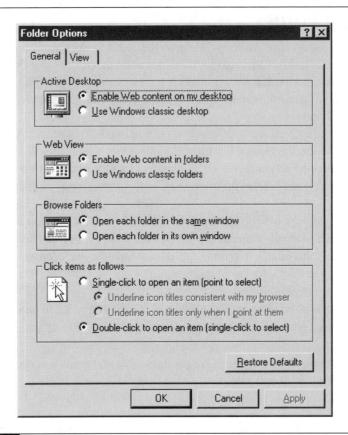

FIGURE 3-10   Most folder configuration is performed on the General tab

As you can see in Figure 3-10, there are four different categories from which you can choose a radio button option:

■   Active Desktop—This category allows you to choose to display Web content on your desktop by choosing the option Enable Web Content On My Desktop. This is the same option that you had in Display properties, but it is also provided here for your convenience.

3

■ Web View—This category allows you to choose to display Web content in your folders by choosing Enable Web Content In My Folders. The Web Content option gives you the blue hyper-links you have seen in the left side of your folders (which jump to another location when you click them). Choosing this option also enables your folders to display HTML documents and graphics files. For example, say you have a picture file called My Dog. When you select My Dog by clicking on it once, a small sample of the picture will appear in the left side of your folder.

> **NOTE**
>
> *My Computer and Control Panel are always displayed in the Web page view, even if you do not select this option.*

> **TIP**
>
> *When using the Open Each Folder In The Same Window option, use the Back button on the folder's tool bar to return to a previous window, just as you would do when surfing the Internet. For example, if you open My Computer and then Control Panel, just click the Back button to return to My Computer.*

Did you know?   Your Folders and the Internet

One of the design goals Microsoft had for Windows Me was to make the operating system more integrated with the Internet. Notice that when in Web View, your folders look a lot like the Internet Explorer browser. This is by design, and as you might guess, you can jump from a local folder to the Internet without even changing to a different window. In the folder's address bar, just select what is currently listed, hit your keyboard's backspace or delete key, then type the Internet URL you want and press ENTER. You computer will launch an Internet connection if you are not currently connected and take you the Internet site (very cool!).

- Browse Folders—This category allows you to choose how your folders are displayed when you are browsing through a folder structure. For example, say you open My Computer and then you open Control Panel. If you choose Open Each Folder In The Same Window, opening Control Panel will replace the My Computer window. If you choose Open Each Folder In Its Own Window, Control Panel will open in a separate window on top of the My Computer window. There is no right or wrong option, but if you work with a number of windows at one time, you may find the Open Each Folder In The Same Window option less cluttering to your desktop.

- Click Items As Follows—This category allows you to choose how your mouse clicks work. If you choose the Single-Click To Open An Item (Point To Select) option, you simply click your left mouse key to open any item, just as on the Internet where a single-click on a hyperlink connects you directly to Web pages and other Internet sites—this means no more double-clicking! This option does take some getting used to, but feel free to experiment.

Which Folder Options are Best?

As I have mentioned, all of the configuration options in this chapter are provided so you can customize Windows Me—there are no right or wrong settings. However, I do recommend that you enable the Active Desktop and Web Content in your folders. These options provide help links and links to other portions of your operating system. You may rarely need the links, but they may be useful from time to time, and it certainly does not hurt anything for them to be enabled.

View

The View tab in the Folder Options window contains a number of check boxes that enable you to make a number of different decisions about files and folders. These options concern the display of certain file types, folder views, and other lower level settings. Windows Me does a good job of configuring the common settings for you, and changing some of these settings can cause you problems. I recommend that you do not make any changes to the View tab unless you have a very specific reason to do so. Because you don't need to use these, I'm not going to discuss them all, but the following list does point out some of the more common options and whether those options are enabled by default:

- **Display All Control Panel Options And All Folder Contents**—Do you remember how Control Panel displays only the most common icons? If you don't like that feature, click this check box to turn it off (this option is not selected by default).

- **Do Not Show Hidden Files And Folders and Hide Protected Operating System Files**—These two separate options, both of which are enabled by default, do not show hidden files and folders in Windows Me. Windows Me hides many of the files and folders that hold operating system files that make Windows Me run. Obviously, you don't need to do anything with these files, and Windows Me hides them to help prevent tampering or accidental deletion. You should leave these settings as they are so that Windows Me continues to hide system files and folders.

- **Hide Extensions For Known File Types**—This hides file extensions. For example, if you type a Microsoft Word document called Cat, the document's official name is Cat.doc. The Hide Extensions option hides the .doc extension and all other extensions for files that Windows recognizes. This makes your folder files cleaner and easier to read. This option is enabled by default.

- **Remember Each Folder's View Settings**—You can use the view menu in a particular folder to determine how the folder appears and what you can view (you can learn about these options later in this chapter). This setting tells Windows to remember each folder's view settings. This option is enabled by default and you should keep it enabled.

Configuring Folder Views and Toolbars

Once you make some decisions about how you want your folders to appear using the Folder Options, you can also make some decisions about your folder views and toolbars. When you open a folder, there is a View menu, as shown in Figure 3-11.

Most of the options you see on this menu are self-explanatory, and you can try the different setting options to determine what you like best. The following sections explore your major options.

Toolbars

First, when you hold your mouse over the Toolbars item, a submenu pops out. This submenu allows you to select the toolbar items you would like to use. Some of these are enabled by default, but you can enable or disable them by clicking them with your mouse. You have these options:

■ Standard Buttons—Enabled by default, this option provides you with the standard toolbar buttons, such as Back, Forward, Up One Level, Search, and so forth. You need these, so keep this option enabled.

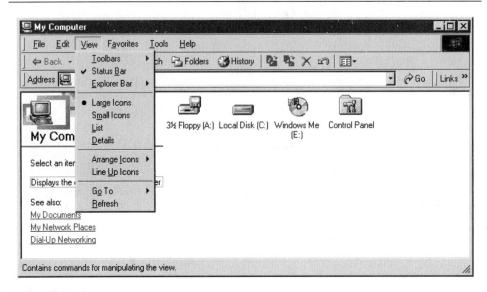

FIGURE 3-11   Use the View menu to make changes to your window's appearance

3

■ Address Bar—Enabled by default, this option gives you the address bar so you can move to different areas of your computer or even the Internet. For example, you could access a folder on your computer by simply typing the path to the folder (such as C:\My Documents) or an Internet address.

■ Links—Enabled by default, this option gives you a Links button on your toolbar so you can use links or resource locations that you commonly access.

■ Radio—Radio? That's right, you can add a radio toolbar so you can play your Internet radio from any folder. See Chapter 14 to learn more!

Aside from these standard options, you can also click Customize. This option opens a Customize Toolbar window, shown in Figure 3-12, where you can add and remove various toolbar buttons and options. This feature allows you to configure your folder toolbars so they are exactly what you want!

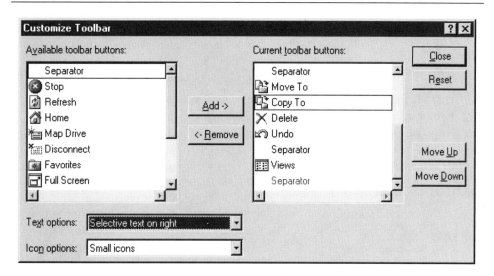

FIGURE 3-12   Use the Customization Options to create custom toolbars

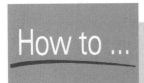 **Create a Customized Toolbar**

Follow these easy steps to create a customized toolbar:

1. In the desired folder, click View, click Toolbars, then click Customize.

2. In the Customize Toolbar window, select any item in the left portion of the window that you want to add to your toolbar, then click the Add button. Continue this process until you have moved all options that you want.

3. In the right portion of the window, select any item that you do not want to use on your toolbar, then click Remove. Continue this process until you have removed any options you do not want.

4. In the right portion of the window, select an option and use the Move Up or Move Down buttons to adjust the order of the toolbar as desired.

5. Click Close when you are done.

Status

The Status bar is the small bar that runs along the bottom of your window. It tells you what is going on when you are trying to use or connect to other resources. This bar works just like the Status bar in Internet Explorer, and you can choose to use it or not by clicking Status Bar on the View Menu so that a check appears by its name.

Explorer Bar

This option has an additional drop-down menu that lists various Explorer items you can select, such as Search, Favorites, and so forth. If you select one of these items, an additional pane appears in your window that provides the Explorer option. For example, if you select the Search option, the window provides a search section, as shown in Figure 3-13. You can experiment with these settings to find ones that are useful to you.

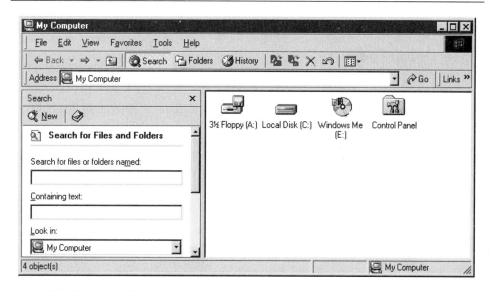

FIGURE 3-13   Explorer Bar options provide additional features in your windows

Icon Appearance

The remainder of the View menu contains a number of different icon and list options
to determine how the contents of a folder are displayed. For example, you can use
large icons, small icons, a list, and so forth. Just click these options to experiment
with them until you find the appearance that you like best.

*You can also learn more about files and folders and how to use folder
menus in Chapter 4.*

Customizing Your Start Menu and Taskbar

As with many other Windows Me options, you can customize your Start menu and
taskbar by accessing the appropriate icon in Control Panel. You can also open their
properties pages by right-clicking the taskbar on your desktop and clicking
Properties. Either way, you reach the Taskbar And Start Menu Properties window,
which contains a General and Advanced tab.

General

The General tab, shown in Figure 3-14, contains a series of check box options that you can choose to use.

You have the following easy options:

■ Always On Top—This option keeps your taskbar visible on the screen, even when a program is run in full screen mode.

■ Auto Hide—This feature hides your taskbar if you are not using it. If you want to use it, just move your mouse to the bottom of the screen and the taskbar reappears.

■ Show Small Icons In Start Menu—By default, the icons in your Start menu are large icons. Choose this option is you want small ones.

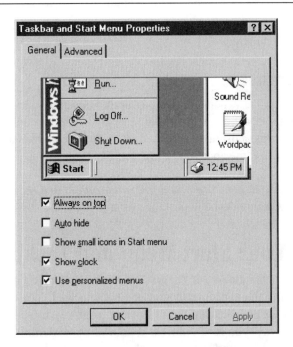

FIGURE 3-14   Use the General tab to enable taskbar and Start menu configuration options

- Show Clock—This gives you a clock in your system tray. If you don't care what time it is, you can clear the check box to remove it.

- Use Personalized Menus—Personalized menus are new in Windows Me. Essentially, Windows Me remembers what programs and folders you most often access, and it hides the ones you don't use very often. For example, say you click Start | Programs. You may have a lot of programs installed, but Windows Me reduces the list that's displayed by only presenting the programs you most frequently use. The menu gives you an arrow so you can make them all appear if you prefer. Personalized Menus is a simple feature that was added to Windows Me to make your computer system easier to use.

Advanced

On the Advanced tab, shown in Figure 3-15, there are some additional customization options for your Start menu.

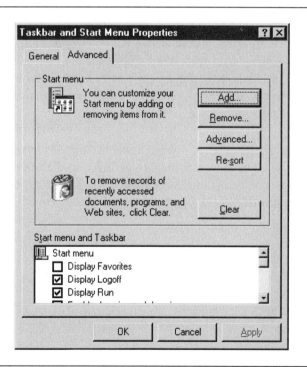

FIGURE 3-15   Use the Advanced tab to customize your Start menu

The items in your Start menu are essentially shortcuts to where the items actually reside on your operating system. You can add items to your Start menu that you access frequently so that you can get to them easier. Just click the Add button and type the location of the item (or click Browse) to find it. Windows Me will create an internal shortcut and put the item in the Start menu so you can access the item faster and more easily. By the same token, you can use the Remove and Resort buttons to remove or reorganize your Start menu. If you click the Advanced button, an Explorer window opens that displays all of your Start menu items so you can add or remove items through the Explorer interface.

In the middle of the window, there is another option: To Remove Records Of Recently Accessed Documents, Programs, and Web Sites, Click Clear. This refers to the list of all of the files you have recently used that appears when you click the Start button and choose Documents, which is a quick way to access a file you have recently worked on without going to the file's folder. However, the Documents list can become long and cluttered; you can use the Clear button to clear all of the file markers. Keep in mind that this operation just clears the Documents list of the files; in no way does it delete or move any files on your system.

NOTE   *The Documents list can be a little misleading. Actually, only documents that are directly opened from within Windows appear here. For example, say you are using Microsoft Word. If you use the File menu to open another Word document, the document you just opened will not appear in the Documents list because you opened it from within an application, not Windows itself.*

Finally, you have a list of check boxes at the bottom of the window. These check boxes tell you all of the items that are included in the Start menu and list several that are not. You can choose to remove or include items by just selecting or clearing their respective check boxes. That's all there is to it!

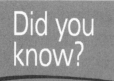

Expandable Start Menu Items

Windows Me includes a feature that can help you make your Start menu usage easier: expandable Start menu items. For example, one way to access Control Panel is by clicking Start, pointing to Settings, and then clicking Control Panel. Once you do this, the Control Panel window opens and you can click on an icon to open any Control Panel item. However, another way is to use an expandable menu so that when you point to Start | Settings | Control Panel, an additional menu pops out that lists all of the Control Panel items. From there, you can just click the item you want to open without ever having to open the Control Panel window. These features are available at the bottom of the Advanced tab in the Start Menu And Taskbar check box options list. Check them out!

Using Windows Me Themes

First introduced in Windows 98, themes are very cool overlays that you can put on your operating system to make your desktop, icons, screen savers, and even folder appearances follow a particular theme. They're fun and easy to use, and the following sections tell you all about them.

Installing Themes

Themes are not installed by default when you install Windows Me, but you can easily install them using Add/Remove Programs in Control Panel. You'll need your Windows Me installation CD to do this, so once you have your CD in your hand, just follow these easy steps:

1. Insert your Windows Me CD-ROM into your CD-ROM drive.

2. Click Start | Settings | Control Panel.

3. Double-click Add/Remove Programs in Control Panel.

4. Click the Windows Setup tab.

5. In the provided list, find Desktop Themes. Click the check box next to Desktop Themes to select it, then click OK.

6. Windows Me installs the themes on your computer.

Setting Up Themes

Once the themes are installed, you'll find a Desktop Themes icon has been added to your Control Panel.

 *If you had Control Panel open while you were installing the themes, you may need to click the View menu and click Refresh so that the new icon will appear.*

Double-click the icon to open the Windows Me Themes options, as shown in Figure 3-16.

At the top of the window, there is a Theme drop-down menu. Click the drop-down menu to select a theme that you want and a sample of the theme appears in the main portion of the window. For example, Figure 3-16 displays the Underwater theme. The desktop picture, icon changes, and window appearances are displayed in the test screen.

 *Each theme is followed by the display resolution requirement. For example, the Underwater theme must use High Color. If your computer cannot support the display resolution requirement, you cannot use the theme.*

On the right side of the Window, there is a Screen Saver button and a Pointers, Sounds, Etc. button; there is also a series of check box options. You can use these check box options to prevent the theme from changing some portion of your system. For example, if you want to use a theme but you do not want the theme to change your desktop icons, just clear the check mark by the Icons option in the check box list. If you make changes to the list, click Save As to save your custom theme by giving it a name—this action keeps your setting options for later use.

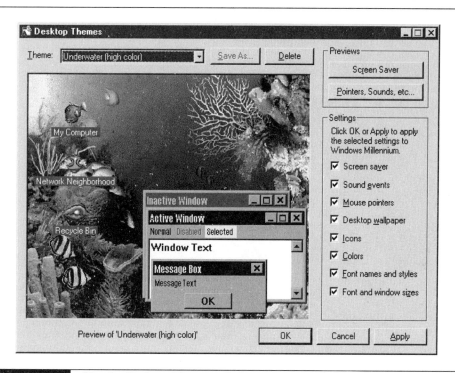

FIGURE 3-16   Use the Desktop Themes window to set up a desktop theme

TIP   *Some theme screen savers also play music, which can be rather annoying (they're not exactly studio quality). If you want to use a screen saver but don't want to hear the music, go to the Display tab, select the screen saver you want, and click the Settings button. For the screen savers that play music, there will be a Mute check box. Just click the check box to kill the music.*

Once you find a theme you like, just click Apply to see it come to life on your desktop. Now, what happens if you do not like the theme? No problem—access this window and choose a different theme. What happens if you don't like themes at all and you want your old settings back? No problem again, just click the Theme drop-down menu and click Previous Windows Settings. This option returns all of your original settings—no harm done!

Chapter 4

Managing Components, Programs, Folders, and Files

How To...

■ Install and Remove Windows Me Components

■ Install, Manage, and Remove Programs

■ Create and Configure Folders and Files

When you boil it all down, a major reason for owning a computer with an operating system is so you can install and use applications that you need (or just want). Applications, additional Windows components, and even your files and folders enable you to both work and play with Windows Me, and to make the most of Windows Me, you need to know a thing or two about managing applications, components, and folders. Once you master these items, you can use Windows Me to meet your needs and run a variety of applications to make your work and life easier (or at least more interesting).

Managing Windows Me Components

If you poked around in Chapter 3, you learned that you can install additional wallpaper and Windows Me themes. These items are found on your Windows Me CD-ROM, but they are not installed by default when you first install Windows Me. Why? Windows Me only installs the most regularly used components to save space on your hard disk. This way, you don't end up with a bunch of operating system junk that you'll never use. However, when you need these components, you can easily install them and even remove them later. The following sections show you how to install and remove additional Windows Me components.

What Additional Components?

Windows Me contains a number of additional components you may find very helpful, interesting, and weird, or totally unnecessary, depending on your point of view. You can install additional Windows Me components by double-clicking Add/Remove Programs in Control Panel, then clicking the Windows Setup tab. Here you see a number of different categories of components, as shown in Figure 4-1.

The good thing about the Windows Setup tab is that it gives you some much needed information about any component you select. Notice in Figure 4-1 that I have the Accessories category selected. The remainder of the window tells me

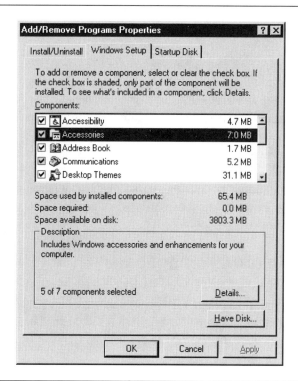

FIGURE 4-1   Use Windows Setup to add or remove Windows components

how much space is required to install all of the accessories and how much space I currently have on my disk. For example, in Figure 4-1, I need 65MB of disk space to install all of the accessories, and I have 3803MB of disk space, so I have plenty. Because I have not actually selected a specific item to install, the Space Required field is at 0, but it will change when I select something (see the next section).

Also, notice that a brief description of the category or item is provided in the window, and if you have a category selected, you are told how many items (if any) are actually installed. As you can see in Figure 4-1, I have five of the seven accessory options installed on my computer. All of this information can help you make decisions about what you want to install and if you have enough room on your hard disk to install it.

You can select any category in the window and click the Details button to find out exactly what is available to install. For example, if you select Accessories and click Details, an Accessories window pops up with a list of all accessories available, such as Briefcase, Calculator, Desktop Wallpaper, etc.

If you select a category and the Details button is grayed out, then there are no additional items to choose from.

Some category items even have additional subitems. If you select an item and the Details button appears on the next window too, you know there are additional items. For example, if you select Screen Savers under the Accessories category, you see that additional screen saver options are available by clicking the Details button.

There are a number of different options available to you, and this book will direct you to certain ones in various chapters. You may want to spend a few minutes at this time, however, to get familiar with your options—and you may even want to install or remove a few of them!

Installing Windows Components

Installing Windows components is very easy. In order to install a component, just select the check box next to it and verify that you have enough disk space to complete the installation. Setup will need your Windows Me installation CD-ROM as well. For step-by-step instructions, see the following How To box.

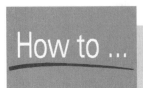 **Install Windows Components**

To install Windows Components, just follow these steps:

1. Locate your Windows Me installation CD-ROM and insert it into your CD-ROM drive.

2. Open Control Panel, then double-click Add/Remove Programs.

3. Click the Windows Setup tab.

4. In the list on the Windows Setup tab, locate the item you want to install. You may need to use the Details button to reach the item.

5. When you locate the item you want to install, click the check box next to the item in order to select it for installation.

6. Note the hard disk space requirements to ensure you have enough room.

7. Repeat steps 4–6 to select other items as desired.

8. When you're done selecting items, click OK. Setup installs the components and may prompt you to reboot your computer. You may also need your installation CD-ROM to install some items. If you are prompted to reboot, click Yes so that installation can complete.

Removing Windows Components

Just as you can install any Windows Components you want to use, you can uninstall components that you do not want. This action frees up more disk space on your computer that can be used for other purposes. In order to remove a component, just uncheck the selected check box so that Windows will remove it. You may need your installation CD-ROM for this action as well; see the following How To box for specific steps.

 **Uninstall Windows Components**

To uninstall Windows components, follow these steps:

1. Locate your Windows Me installation CD-ROM and insert it into your CD-ROM drive.

2. Open Control Panel, then double-click Add/Remove Programs.

3. Click the Windows Setup tab.

4. In the list on the Windows Setup tab, locate the item you want to install. You may need to use the Details button to reach the item.

5. When you locate the item you want to uninstall, click the check box next to the item in order to select it for uninstallation.

6. Note the hard disk space you will free up by removing the component.

7. Repeat steps 4–6 to select other items as desired.

8. When you're done selecting items, just click OK. Setup uninstalls the components and may prompt you to reboot your computer. If you are prompted to reboot, click Yes so that installation can complete.

Managing Programs with Windows Me

Programs are pieces of software that you install on Windows Me in order to perform some task. Programs can come in many forms, such as applications, games, utilities, and so forth. The purpose of a program is to give you some functionality that is needed. For example, Windows Me does not ship with an advanced word processing application. So, in order to perform advanced word processing functions on Windows Me, you need a program that provides you with a word processing application, such as Microsoft Word. You install the application on Windows Me using the program's installation CD-ROM, and then you can use the application on your Windows Me computer.

If you purchased your computer with Windows Me preinstalled, you probably have a number of programs that are installed on your computer already. These programs are sold as a bundle and are preinstalled with Windows Me. Just click Start | Programs to see all of the programs that are currently installed on your computer.

Of course, you may purchase additional programs and install them on your computer. Before you purchase a program, you should first make certain that it is compatible with Windows Me. Check out the label on its box—it should tell you right there that the program will work under Windows Me. The odds are also very good that applications that functioned well under Windows 95/98 will work just fine too.

Once you are sure your program will work under Windows Me, you simply need to install the program. There are two ways to do this, which are explained in the following sections.

Using a Program's Setup Feature

Programs that you purchase are placed on a CD-ROM for easy installation. In fact, most programs today have an auto-start file to help you get the program installed. For example, when you place the CD-ROM into the CD-ROM drive, the disk spins, then a dialog box appears on your screen asking if you want to install the application. This varies from manufacturer to manufacturer, so you'll need to check out and follow the documentation that came with the program you purchased.

   If you put the CD-ROM into the CD-ROM drive and nothing happens, you can manually start the setup program by opening My Computer, then double-clicking the CD-ROM icon. You'll probably see some folders and files once you open the CD. Find an icon called Setup, as shown in Figure 4-2. Double-click the Setup icon and this should start the installation.

CAUTION   *You should always examine the setup instructions that come with any program. Programs are different from one another, so be sure to follow the manufacturer's instructions for installing the program on your computer.*

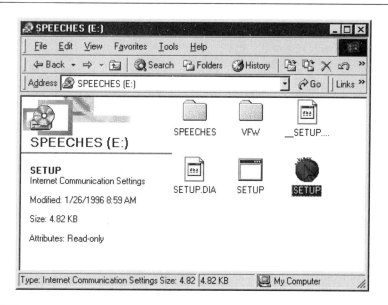

FIGURE 4-2   Double-click Setup.exe to start an installation

Once the installation process starts, just follow the instructions that appear.

Installing Programs Using Add/Remove Programs

As you might guess, you can also use Add/Remove Programs in Control Panel to install a program. Double-click the Add/Remove Programs icon, and on the Install/Uninstall tab, you see an Install button, as shown in Figure 4-3. You can use this button to help you get programs installed on Windows Me. Essentially, the Install option found here tells you to insert the CD-ROM or floppy disk and it will find Setup.exe and launch it for you. To use this option, see the step-by-step instructions in the next How To box.

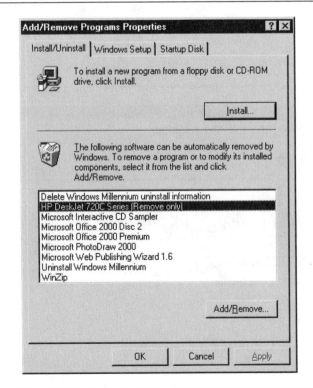

FIGURE 4-3   Use the Install button to let Windows Me help you install a program

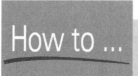 ## Use Add/Remove Programs to Install a Program

To install a program using Add/Remove Programs, follow these easy steps:

1. Click Start | Settings, then click Control Panel.

2. Double-click the Add/Remove Programs icon.

3. On the Install/Uninstall tab, click the Install button.

4. The window that appears tells you to insert the CD-ROM or floppy disk that contains the program you want to install. Insert the CD-ROM (or floppy) into your computer, then click the Next button on the window.

5. Windows Me looks for an installation program on the media. If it finds one, a window appears telling you what it found and asking if you want to install the program. Click the Finish button to continue.

6. Follow any additional instructions presented to you by the setup program.

 ## Which Way Is Correct?

Should you install a program using its setup icon or using Add/Remove Programs? In truth, there is no difference. Add/Remove Programs just launches the Setup.exe program for you instead of starting it yourself. In reality, most programs today have an auto-start file so all you have to do is put the CD-ROM into your computer, and the disk will tell you what to do next. In the event this does not happen, you can start setup yourself by double-clicking Setup.exe or using the Install option in Add/Remove Programs. You will find that Windows Me often provides more than one way to accomplish a task, and there is no right or wrong way—it's just a matter of preference.

Uninstalling a Program

Just as you can install a program on Windows Me, you can uninstall the program as well. For example, let's say that you've been using a particular application but you decide to purchase a different application to replace the older one. If the application you purchase is not an upgrade to the old one, you may want to remove the old application from Windows Me. After all, the application takes up disk space, and since you're not going to use it any longer, you don't need it cluttering up your system.

Once you remove an application from your system, you will not be able to use any of the files generated by that application. For example, if I remove Microsoft Word from my computer, I will not be able to open and read any of my Word documents. Make sure you no longer need an application before removing it from your computer.

There are two ways to remove a program from your computer, which are explained in the following two sections.

Using a Program's Uninstall Option

Some programs come with their own Uninstall option. You can just put the CD-ROM into the CD-ROM drive, let it automatically begin, and a window appears that allows you to install additional components or remove existing components—or the entire program. Microsoft Office is an example of this feature. Some programs also have an Uninstall routine built right in. You can click Start | Programs, point to the program's folder, and a menu pops out with an Uninstall option. Not all programs have this feature, so don't worry if you do not see this option.

Using Add/Remove Programs

If you have a mean program that doesn't help you with the uninstall, you can, once again, use Add/Remove Programs in Control Panel. When you open Add/Remove Programs, you see a list of programs on the Install/Uninstall tab. The programs listed on this window are installed on your computer. To remove one of them, just select it and click the Add/Remove button that appears.

Only Windows-based programs appear on this tab.

What Happens When You Uninstall a Program?

When you choose to uninstall a program, Windows Me takes a look at the program and all its components, then deletes the files from your computer in an organized manner. When programs are installed, various files are used so the program can communicate with Windows Me and interact with it. In some cases, files are present that help the program function with other programs on your computer. Windows Me makes certain all of these files are deleted properly so that an uninstall of one program does not damage another program or Windows Me itself.

If All Else Fails...

Sometimes, you end up with a program that really likes you and does not want to leave your computer. There is no Uninstall option on the CD-ROM, and the program is not listed in Add/Remove Programs with an option to uninstall it. Although this normally does not happen, you can still remove the program by deleting its folder. This is not a recommended action since you may experience problems by forcing an application to delete itself. However, this option can be used when absolutely necessary. See the following How To box for step-by-step instructions.

CAUTION   *Under no circumstances should you delete a program's folder if you can use the CD-ROM or the Add/Remove Programs option. Deleting the folder does not allow Windows Me to properly delete and clean up after the application, so this should be considered a last resort option. Also, before using this option, check your program's documentation for specific information about uninstalling the program from Windows Me.*

TIP   *If trying to install or uninstall a program on your computer has left you with a bunch of problems, Windows Me offers a "rollback" feature that can help you get things sorted out. See Chapter 18 for details.*

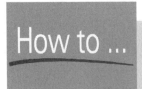

Forcefully Remove a Program

In the event that you cannot use Add/Remove Programs or the program's Uninstall option, you can forcefully remove a program by following these steps:

1. Open My Computer, then double-click your C drive icon.

2. Locate a folder called Program Files, then double-click it. You may need to click the View All Contents link as prompted.

3. Look through the folders and find the one that holds the program you want to install. Typically, the name of the folder will say the program's name or the manufacturer's name.

4. When you have found the folder, right-click it and click Delete to remove it from your computer. Make sure you are deleting the correct folder before completing this action.

Downloading Programs from the Internet

The Internet contains a wealth of applications that you can download and use on your computer, and many of them are free. For those that are not free, you can download an evaluation version of a program to see if you like how it works on your computer before actually purchasing it. There are also all kinds of different utilities for Windows and games you can download.

When you choose to download an application from the Internet, you click a link on the Web site that starts the download to your computer. When this happens, a dialog box, such as the one shown in Figure 4-4, appears so you can choose whether to run the application from its current location or save it to disk. If you choose to run the application from its current location, the setup files are downloaded to your computer and setup begins. If not, the files are all saved to a place that you specify on this window (such as your desktop or My Documents folder). You can then start setup yourself when you are ready. There is no right or wrong here; it's just a matter of preference.

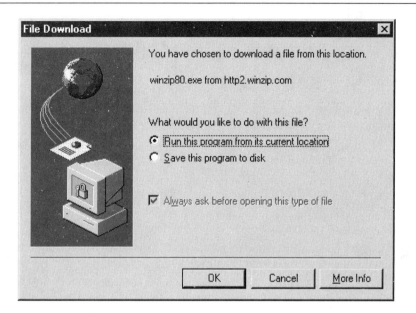

FIGURE 4-4 This dialog box appears when you begin to download a program from the Internet

Starting Setup

If you choose to save a program to disk when you start the download, the program is downloaded to your computer in a compressed format. This saves time when downloading. Usually, the application will appear as a simple icon. Double-click the icon to uncompress and start the installation. Windows Me includes compression software so you can open and use compressed folders (see the Folder Compression section later in this chapter). For specific installation steps, refer to the Web site where you downloaded the program.

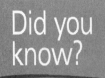

About Downloaded Programs and Viruses

Internet programs are a great way to get utilities, applications, and games for your computer—and a great way to get a computer virus as well! Computer viruses are made up of code that often hides within other code—such as in a setup program for an application. In order to protect yourself, I highly recommend that you purchase some antivirus software for your Windows Me computer. This type of software watches for viruses, identifies them, and kills them on your computer. Visit your local computer store or an Internet store to shop for antivirus software.

Aside from using antivirus software, another great way to keep from getting a computer virus resides right in your own head—common sense! Be wary of downloading programs from Internet sites that do not appear to be on the up and up. Your best bet is to download software from respected Internet sites and companies. When in doubt, don't!

Managing Folders and Files

As you have indirectly learned in the first few chapters of this book, Windows Me manages data by using various folders to store that data. Just as you would not want to dump a bunch of single papers into a filing cabinet and hope to find what you need later, you don't want to do that on your computer, either. Windows Me uses folders to keep operating system files, program files, and even your own files organized. In this section of the chapter, you learn how to manage your files and folders.

 Before we begin, I would like to offer a big warning. You can manage your own folders and files, but you should never make changes to any of the folders and files found in C:\Windows. These folders and files are used by the Windows Me operating system to function. Tinkering with them can —and probably will—cause Windows Me to stop working. So, manage your own files and folders, and let Windows Me manage its files and folders.

Creating, Renaming, and Deleting Folders

You use folders in Windows Me to store data, such as documents, pictures, spreadsheets, you name it—any type of file or application can be stored in a folder. Depending on your needs, you may not need additional folders. After all, Windows Me automatically tries to place files in your My Documents folder or one of its subfolders such as My Pictures. However, you may need to create your own folders to manage data. For example, each time I begin work on a new book, I create a folder on my computer in which I store all of the files for the book. Within that folder, I then create additional folders for each chapter. This way, each chapter document, as well as the graphics files for that chapter, has a specific folder so I can keep it all organized. You can create folders within folders and within those folders to as many levels as you want or need.

> TIP *Although folders are great, don't get too wild with folder creation. Too many folders can be more confusing than helpful, so keep your folder structure in check to make sure that it actually meets your needs.*

The good news is that you can easily create, rename, and delete folders as needed. To create a new folder, open the folder you want to create the new folder in, such as My Documents, or simply your C drive. Click File | New | Folder. A new folder appears. Hit the BACKSPACE key on your keyboard and type a name for the new folder.

> TIP *If you want to create a new folder directly on your desktop, just right-click an empty area of your desktop, point to New, and click Folder.*

At any given time, you can rename a folder by simply right-clicking the folder and clicking Rename. Then hit your BACKSPACE key, type a new name, and press the ENTER key. This feature makes it easy to keep your folders organized and move your folders from place to place as needed.

Finally, you can delete any folder by right-clicking the folder and clicking Delete. This moves the folder to the Recycle Bin. However, do keep in mind that anything in the folder is deleted as well. This includes files, applications, other folders—anything at all.

Using Folder Menus

Windows Me folders contain a standard set of menu options at the top of the folder, which are File, Edit, View, Favorites, Tools, and Help. You can use these different menus to perform various actions on the folder and on the files within the folder. Though many of the options are self-explanatory, this section describes the most commonly used menu features.

File Menu

First, the File menu enables you to manage files and folders within the folder. Aside from using the File menu to create a new folder, you can also select a file or folder, click File, then perform any of the following options:

- Open With—This feature opens a window that allows you to select an application with which to open the file. You can use this option if you are having problems opening a file.

- Send To—This feature enables you to send a folder or file to a particular location, such as a floppy disk or as an attachment to an e-mail message. (You can also right-click any folder or file to get this option.)

- New—This drop-down menu enables you to create yet another folder. You also see a list of files you can create, which varies depending on the applications installed on your system. This feature enables you to start a new file of your choice directly from this location.

- Others—In the lower part of the menu, you can perform basic other tasks, such as create a shortcut for the item, delete it, rename it, and even close the item.

Edit Menu

The Edit menu provides you with several features so you can manage the folders or files within the folder. These features are easy to use, and the following list points them out to you:

- Undo Delete—Accidentally delete something? No problem. Just click this option to restore what you deleted (if you have performed no other operations since you deleted the item, that is).

■ Copy, Cut, and Paste—You can copy, cut, and paste items from one folder to another using these commands. Let's say you want to cut a document from one folder and place it in a different folder. Just select the document, click Edit | Cut, then open the folder where you want the document and click Edit | Paste.

> **TIP**   *You can use keyboard shortcuts to accomplish the Copy, Cut, and Paste actions as well. See Appendix B for a list of helpful keyboard shortcuts.*

4

■ Move or Copy to Folder—You can move or copy items to another folder by using these options. When you click one of them, a window appears that lets you choose where to move or copy the file or folder.

> **TIP**   *Do you need to copy or move several items to the same target folder? You can do them all at the same time! Just select the first item, then hold down the* CTRL *key on your keyboard and click the remaining items you want to move or copy. All of the items you click will be selected. Then just click Edit and select the option you want. This moves or copies all items at the same time. You can perform this same operation when cutting, deleting, moving, or copying items manually.*

■ Select All and Invert Selection—Use Select All to select all items in the folder. This feature is helpful if you want to copy or cut all items in a particular folder. You can also use invert selection to give you the exact opposite of what is currently selected. For example, let's say you have five files in a folder. Two of the files are selected. If you use Invert Selection, the two previously selected files will not be selected, and the three previously unselected files will be selected. As you can imagine, this feature is helpful if you tend to do things completely backward from time to time.

View Menu

The View menu enables you to configure the appearance of your folder, and you can learn about this option in Chapter 3.

Favorites Menu

For Web-enabled folders, the Favorites menu works just like Favorites in Internet Explorer (and is, in fact, exactly the same). See Chapter 9 for details.

Tools Menu

The Tools menu contains just a few folder items you should know about:

- Map Network Drive—For computers connected to a network, you can use this item to map a network drive. This feature enables you to use a network folder and still have an icon on your computer so that it looks like the folder is local to your machine. To map a network drive, just click the option in the Tools menu. A dialog box appears, shown in Figure 4-5, where you can select a drive letter that is not in use, then enter the network UNC path to the shared folder you want to map to.

- Disconnect Network Drive—If you no longer want to use a particular network drive, use this option to disconnect it permanently from your computer.

- Synchronize—The Synchronize option enables you to have a folder on a network server and the same folder on your computer. Using the Synchronize option causes the data in the network folder to change when you change the data in the folder on your computer. To use the synchronization feature, click the option, then click the Setup button to set up the folders you want to synchronize. This option even allows you to automate the process by setting up a synchronization schedule.

Did you know?

What Is a UNC Path?

A UNC (Universal Naming Convention) is a method used to connect to network folders or files on Windows networks. The UNC path is represented by two backslashes (\\) followed by the name of the computer you want to connect to, followed by the share name and the file name. Each portion of the path is connected by a single backslash. For example, if I want to connect to shared folder named Fishing on a computer named Curt123, and I want to access a particular file named Bass, then the UNC path is `\\curt123\fishing\bass`.

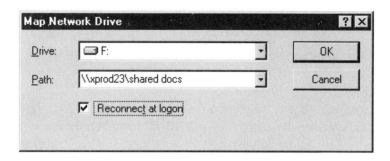

FIGURE 4-5   Use this option to map a connection to a network folder

Help Menu

The Help menu gives you a quick and easy way to open Windows Me Help Files.

Folder toolbars contain a number of icons that essentially repeat what is available in the menus. The difference is they give you an icon you can press for easy access. For example, you can cut items, undo a delete, copy to a folder, etc. all by clicking buttons on the toolbar. You can also create customized toolbars, which you can learn about in Chapter 3.

Sharing a Folder

Windows Me contains networking capabilities so that your computer can share folders and printers on a network. It is important to note here that you cannot share individual files—you can only share folders, which give access to files. For example, let's say I have a Word document called My Dog. I can't share My Dog by itself, but I can put My Dog in a shared folder so that others on the network can access the document.

You can share any folder in Windows Me by right-clicking the folder, clicking Properties, then clicking the Sharing tab.

If the folder you want to share resides within another folder, you can just right-click the folder you want to share and click Sharing.

 *It is important to note here that Windows Me must have its networking components configured before any folders can be shared. If you don't see the sharing option, you do not have your networking components configured. See Chapter 11 to learn how to set up Windows Me for networking.*

The Sharing tab, shown in Figure 4-6, is very easy to configure. Just click Shared As and enter a share name for the folder. Remember, the name you give the folder is how the folder will appear to other users, so make the name easily understandable—something like Shared Documents, not SHDC765, which no one will be able to decipher.

Next, you determine the level of sharing you want to give. You can choose to give one of the following options:

- Read-Only—This access option enables users to read the items in the folder. Users cannot add or delete items to the folder.

- Full—With Full access, users can do anything they want to with your folder: add items, delete items, move items, or even delete the entire folder. Obviously, you should be careful about giving out this permission.

- Depends On Password—If you click this option, two password blanks appear so you can enter both a read-only password and a full access password. This way, some users have read-only access while some have full, depending on the password you assign. If you want to use this option, enter the desired passwords—and make sure you remember them!

Using Folder Compression

Windows Me includes a very cool feature to help you conserve disk space: folder compression. Compression shrinks the normal size of a folder and its contents in order to free up more disk space that you can use for other purposes. Compression also helps you use zipped files that are downloaded from the Internet. Compression in Windows Me is quick and easy to use.

Installing Compression

The compression feature is a Windows Me component that you can install by using the Windows Setup tab of Add/Remove Programs in Control Panel. The compression option is found under System Tools and is called Folder Compression. Select this option and install it so that compression will be available

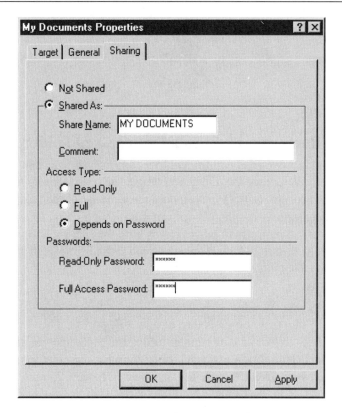

FIGURE 4-6   Use this window to share a folder on a network

to you. For specific steps on how to use the Windows Setup option, see the section at the beginning of this chapter.

Creating a Compressed Folder

You can create a compressed folder just as you create any other folder. In the folder where you want to create the new compressed folder, click File | New, but then click Compressed Folder instead of just Folder. If you want to create a compressed folder on your desktop, just right-click an empty area of the desktop, point to New | Compressed Folder. Either way, a new compressed folder appears. Compressed folders have a zipper on them so you can identify them, as shown in the next illustration.

MADV

Adding and Removing Items to a Compressed Folder

You can add and remove files and folders to a compressed folder just as you do in
any other folder in Windows Me. Once you drag a file or folder into a compressed
folder, the item is compressed. Once you drag the item out of the folder, it is
automatically decompressed—there's no configuration you have to worry about.
Additionally, you can perform all other actions with the file, such as opening,
renaming, deleting, and so forth just as you would if the file were in a regular folder.

Using Extraction

Compressed folders in Windows Me use the WinZip technology to compress
folders. A part of that technology is the "extraction" option. This feature enables
you to pull every item from a compressed folder and place the item in a folder that
is not compressed. This action extracts—or decompresses—the items so they are
no longer compressed. If you right-click on a shared folder, you will see the
extraction options. You can extract the folder to a different folder or location, or
you can even choose to e-mail the compressed folder. No matter what option you
choose, the WinZip utility opens to help you with the procedure. If you choose the
Extract All option, a wizard begins that lets you choose where you want the folder
extracted to.

Along with extraction, you also see an Encryption option when you right-click
a compressed folder. This option enables you to assign a password for the folder.
For example, you can encrypt a folder and e-mail it to a friend who uses Windows
Me, and your friend would have to enter the correct password in order to open the
encrypted, compressed folder. Pretty cool!

Removing Compression from a Folder

So what do you do if you have a compressed folder that you do not want to be compressed any longer? You simply right-click the folder and click Extract All, which essentially recreates the folder and all data, without the encryption.

Although anything residing in a folder can be compressed, you should not compress a folder that contains a program. Compression may prevent the program from operating correctly.

4

About Files

As you have already learned, files are placed in various folders on your computer for safekeeping and organization purposes. Files are created by various programs you have installed on your system, and they have different file extensions. For example, a Microsoft Word document has the .doc (document) extension, while a document you create with Paint might have the .bmp (bitmap) extension. In short, there has to be some kind of program to create a file of any kind. The good news about files is that you really do not have to manage them individually. You can right-click any file and see the same options you get with a folder, such as Sent To, Copy, Cut, etc. You can also drag and move files around to different locations on your computer without damaging them.

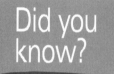

Solving File Extension Mysteries

Due to a number of different factors, a file may not get an extension or may not have one. For example, have you ever received a file in an e-mail that you could not open? This is caused by one of two problems: you either do not have an application that can read the file, or the file extension is missing. This causes your computer to say, "I don't know what this file is or which application to open it with." In this case, you normally get an Open With window asking you to pick an application to attempt to open the file. If you have a file that does not have an extension, and you know which application is supposed to open it, you can easily fix the problem by right-clicking the file, clicking rename, and giving the file a name with the extension, such MyDog.doc. This helps your computer know which application to use so the file can be opened.

Chapter 5

Using Windows Me Accessories

How To...

- ■ Access Windows Accessories
- ■ Use Windows Accessories
- ■ Configure Windows Accessories

Windows Me, like its predecessors, includes a category of mini programs called Accessories. Accessories, as the name implies, gives you the capability to accessorize Windows Me so that you have more computing functionality within the operating system. For the most part, your Accessories options are quite easy to use, with just a few being detailed and complex. This chapter shows you how to use them and why you would want to use them.

As you might guess, a few of the accessories or accessory categories deserve their own chapters, or naturally belong in a different chapter. For example, Windows Media Player, which is new—and very cool, by the way—has its own chapter, as does Windows Movie Maker, so I'll direct you to other places in the book where necessary. Also, if you read about an accessory in this chapter that does not seem to appear on your computer, then you probably need to add it to your system using the Windows Setup tab of Add/Remove Programs (see Chapter 4). Not all accessories are installed by default, but you can add them using Windows Setup. You can locate the accessories on your Windows Me computer by clicking Start | Programs | Accessories. You see a drop-down menu listing the accessory programs.

Accessibility

In Chapter 2, you learned about the Accessibility options found in Control Panel. There are a few other accessibility options in your Accessories menu as well. Accessibility refers to a number of Windows Me tools that make Windows Me easier to use for people with certain disabilities. If you point to Accessibility, an additional drop-down menu appears, which provides three additional options.

Accessibility Wizard

The Accessibility Wizard is a Windows Me feature that helps you set up and make decisions about the appearance and functionality of your computer so that it meets your needs. The wizard is easy to use and understand—just follow these steps:

1. Click Start | Programs | Accessories | Accessibility | Accessibility Wizard.

2. On the Welcome screen, click Next.

3. On the Text Size screen, use your mouse to select the size text you want Windows Me to use. Make your selection and click Next.

4. On the Display Settings screen, you see some check box options that enable you to select how your display appears. You can choose to change the font size, use Microsoft Magnifier, or disable personalized menus, as shown in Figure 5-1. You may also be able to use a lower screen resolution, depending on your video card. Make your selection and click Next.

You can also configure your own Display settings to meet your personal needs. See Chapter 3 for details.

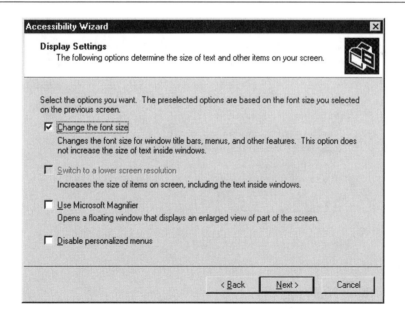

| FIGURE 5-1 | Use this window to select Accessibility display setting options |

5. Next, the Set Wizard Options screen appears. This screen gives you a series of check boxes where you can select the type of disability you have so the wizard can help you select some options. For example, if you select the I Am Blind Or Have Difficulty Seeing Things On My Screen check box, the wizard enables you to select various scroll bars, icons, display settings, and so forth. The other options available, shown in Figure 5-2, provide different options, depending on your needs. Select the check box that best describes your needs and click Next.

6. Depending on your selection in step 5, your Accessibility Wizard options will vary, but they are self-explanatory. Continue to follow the wizard steps until you reach a summary screen. Review your settings, and then click the Finish button to complete the wizard. The options you selected will then be configured on your computer.

Magnifier

The Accessibility options in Accessories also include the Magnifier. The Magnifier gives you a window at the top of your desktop that magnifies whatever you point at with your mouse so that the options are very large, as you can see in Figure 5-3.

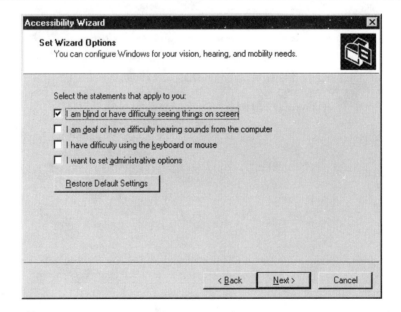

FIGURE 5-2   Select the option that best describes your needs

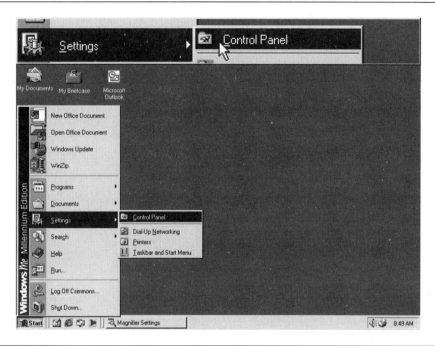

FIGURE 5-3   Use the Magnifier option to help you see large images

If you choose to use the Magnifier option, click Magnifier in the Accessibility window, and the Magnifier Settings window appears. This simple window, shown in Figure 5-4, gives you a few options about the operation of the Magnifier. You can choose from the following:

- Magnification Level—The default setting is 2. You can try different settings to find the one that is right for you.

- Follow Mouse Cursor—Also selected by default, this option has the Magnifier show whatever you are pointing to with your mouse—this setting is recommended.

- Follow Keyboard Focus—If you begin using your keyboard, the Magnifier follows what you do on the keyboard. This setting is enabled by default and is also recommended.

■ Follow Text Editing—This option follows any text editing that you are doing. As with the other options, this one is selected by default and is recommended.

■ Invert Colors—This option inverts, or reverses, the colors in the Magnifier. It is not selected by default, but you may find this setting easier to see if you have certain vision problems.

■ Use High Contrast Mode—This option turns on high contrast colors. You can try this setting out and see if it helps you.

■ Start Minimized—This option tells the Magnifier to start as a minimized option on your computer (rather than maximized, as it is in Figure 5-3).

■ Show Magnifier—This option is selected by default, and it automatically shows the Magnifier at the top of your screen.

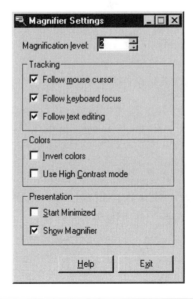

FIGURE 5-4   Use this window to configure your Magnifier settings

On-Screen Keyboard

The final Accessibility option in Accessories is the on-screen keyboard, which gives you, well, an on-screen keyboard! The keyboard appears, and you can use your mouse to click the keys, just as you would do on a regular keyboard. The on-screen keyboard is a limited version, however, but you can learn about other options available to you at **www.microsoft.com/enable**.

Communications

The Communications option in Accessories provides you with a drop-down menu in which a variety of different communications tools are present. Use this menu to access Dial-Up Networking, Home Networking Wizard, Internet Connection Wizard, ISDN Configuration Wizard, and so forth. As you might guess, these options are explored in the Internet and networking chapters of this book, Chapters 8 and 11, so refer to those chapters for more information about these very cool options.

Entertainment

Want to have some fun with Windows Me? You access some fun options here, such as your CD Player, Sound Recorder, and Windows Media Player. You can learn all about these options in Chapters 13 and 14.

Internet Tools

The Internet Tools menu (which actually only contains one tool, the Web Publishing Wizard) helps you publish files to a Web or FTP site. You can learn how to use this easy wizard in Chapter 9.

System Tools

The System Tools menu gives you several tools that can help your Windows Me computer run better and solve problems. As with the other major menu sections, these tools deserve their own chapter, and you can learn how to use them in Chapter 16.

5

Address Book

The Address Book found in Accessories is actually the same Address Book that's built into Microsoft Outlook Express, which is a part of your Windows Me operating system. The Address Book feature is very easy to use and is a great way to keep track of phone numbers, e-mail addresses, and such. You can learn more about it in Chapter 10.

Calculator

Windows Me provides you with a quick, on-screen calculator, which you can access at any time using Accessories. Your on-screen Calculator works just like any other calculator. Use it to count your money, pay your bills, or figure out how much you owe the IRS (what fun).

A quick note about the Calculator: you can use the View menu to see a standard calculator or a scientific calculator or both, as shown in Figure 5-5. Other than this option, use your mouse or the numbers keypad on the keyboard to use the calculator just as you would a desktop version.

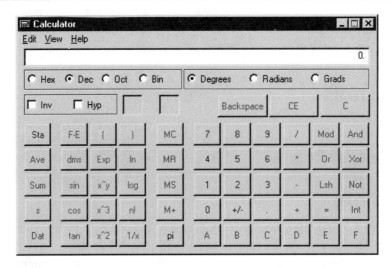

FIGURE 5-5   The Calculator—you can use the regular or scientific option or you can see both at the same time

Imaging

Imaging is a lower-level image editor that enables you to open or create bitmap, TIFF, or AWD (Fax) files. When you choose to open an existing image file of one of these types, the Imaging utility automatically opens so you can view the file. From this point, you can choose to perform some lower-level editing of the image if you desire.

Because Imaging is not an advanced image editor, you can perform only basic image editing tasks, and we will not spend a lot of time on them here. When you open a file with Imaging, the picture opens in a window surrounded by a number of buttons on the Imaging toolbar, as shown in Figure 5-6.

Once you open an image, you can use the toolbar to make some changes. There are quite a few buttons, but they are simple options. For example, you can rotate the image, save it, cut and paste, view a thumbnail of the image, insert text onto the image, and so forth. The best way to get familiar with the buttons is to open an image and play around with the button options. This will help you see what you can and cannot do with an image.

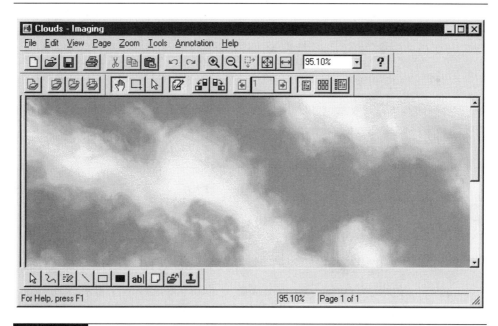

FIGURE 5-6   Imaging is a lower-level image editor

Placing Text on Images

You can place text on any image that you open by clicking the Annotation Selection button on the toolbar (it looks like a mouse arrow) and then using the Annotation menu to select the type of annotation you would like to add. Your options include, among several others, typed text, freehand, notes, and rubber stamps. Experiment with them to learn what is available to you.

If you access the File menu, you see that you can save the open file, open new files, and create new ones. If you choose to create a new file, you can essentially use the annotation option and create various text-based pictures. For example, you can use the freehand annotation, draw your name, apply styles to it, then save it as a bitmap, TIFF, or AWD file. You can also use the File menu to print a file, manage the color options, and even send the file to someone else in an e-mail.

As you can see, your options are limited with the Imaging utility, but it can be useful in a variety of ways. One of those ways is to view images that you put into your system with a digital camera or scanner and to make notes (annotations) directly on the images. You can then save the picture with the annotation. You may find other uses for the Imaging utility as well, and it is a good extra included in Windows Me.

 *If you are interested in real image editing and generating graphics files, there is plenty of software for sale. Check out the graphics software section of your favorite computer store or Internet reseller.*

MS-DOS Prompt

The Windows Me operating system will be the last Microsoft operating system to support MS-DOS. MS-DOS can be used with Windows Me to perform some tasks, and most often will be used to try and fix Windows Me problems. This feature bypasses the Windows Me operating system and enables you to perform command line configuration. The DOS commands available in Windows Me are much more restricted than they were in Windows 95/98, but they are still available. Obviously, you have to know a thing or two about MS-DOS to use the DOS window that appears. Also, as a general rule, anything that can be done in DOS can also be done using Control Panel and other Windows tools.

MS-DOS was used more extensively in the past by different programs and those good old MS-DOS games (which caused a lot of nasty system crashes, by the way).

*You can also access the MS-DOS prompt by clicking Start | Run and typing **command** in the dialog box and pressing OK.*

Paint

Like Imaging, Windows Paint is a lower-level graphics creation program that enables you to generate or open various graphics files and save a created graphics file as a bitmap or JPEG. You are limited in what you can do with Paint, but it is a utility with moderate functionality that you may find useful in a variety of ways.

Like Imaging, the best way to learn to use Paint is to simply open it up and play around with the toolbar and menu options. You can spend about half an hour playing with Paint and you'll know almost all there is to know; I'll use this section to get you on your way.

First, you can use Paint to open any standard graphics file, such as a BMP, TIF, JPEG, GIF, and so forth, as shown in Figure 5-7. Once you have the graphics file open, you can click on any of the toolbar buttons to make changes to the graphic. Your toolbar options include Paintbrush, Pencil, Spray Can, Text, and various line shapes.

Aside from using the Paint tools to draw or change an existing file, you can create your own file by clicking the File | New. This opens a blank document window on which you can try your own artistic skills.

As with Imaging, your options are limited, but Paint is a useful accessory to view and change image files, save them, and change file types. Spend some time playing with Paint and experimenting with its features.

Notepad and WordPad

Accessories also include two text editor programs, Notepad and WordPad. Notepad is a simple text editor. You can open any kind of text-based document in Notepad and make changes to it. Advanced computer users often use Notepad to make text based changes to Windows configuration (which is not something you

FIGURE 5-7 Paint enables you to edit and generate graphics files

 **Adjust an Image**

As with Imaging, you can use Paint to make adjustments to an image, such as flip, rotate, invert colors, and other appearance options. Just open the image you want to make changes to, then click Paint's Image menu and select a change you would like to make. You can experiment with these options to find one that meets your needs.

should try on your own!). You can use Notepad to simply type a message of some kind and send it via e-mail or print it on your printer.

Notepad, as shown in Figure 5-8, enables you to open, create, and save text files. You can use the edit menu to perform cut and paste operations and choose the font you would like to use. Also, you can use the Search menu to find specific words or phrases within the text document.

However, Notepad is simply a text editor. You cannot perform any formatting functions, such as paragraph formatting, text formatting (such as italic and bold fonts), and you cannot create any tables or use other word processing features. Notepad simply does text, nothing else. Also, Notepad has a limit of 64K, so any document larger than this must be used in another application, such as WordPad.

Your second Accessories text editor option is WordPad. WordPad is also a text editor, but it functions more like a word processing application. Keep in mind, however, that WordPad does not by any stretch contain the functionality that most major word processing applications, such as Microsoft Word, do, but it does contain enough functions to be very useful. With WordPad, shown in Figure 5-9, you can edit and create text just like Notepad, but WordPad supports major formatting features, such as various fonts and text formatting. Also, when you save a WordPad document, the formatting is maintained as well. You can use WordPad for all kinds of documents. You can use tabs and different paragraph schemes, but you cannot create tables or spreadsheets within the documents. However, for a free text editor, this one is certainly not bad at all.

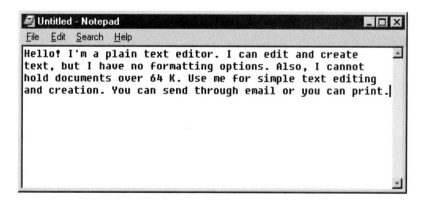

FIGURE 5-8   Notepad is a text editor

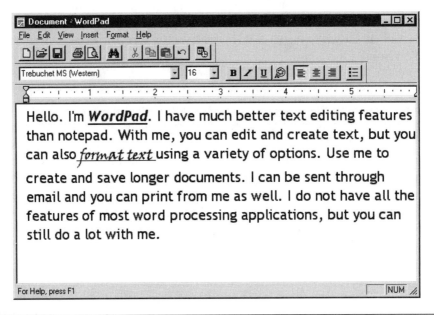

FIGURE 5-9   WordPad supports major formatting features

Windows Explorer

Another accessory you find in the Accessories menu is Windows Explorer. If you read Chapter 1, you endured my brief soapbox about Windows Explorer now being considered an "accessory" in Windows Me. In Windows 95/98, Windows

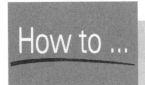 **Format Text in WordPad**

You can easily format text in WordPad. Just type the text you want, then highlight the text using your mouse. You can use the WordPad toolbar to select a format button, such as bold, italic, font changes, etc. You can also click the Format menu to see a list of other options.

Explorer was a major operating system feature, something you used all the time. However, with Windows Me's Internet integrtion and easy folder configuration, Microsoft now thinks of Windows Explorer as an accessory—something extra you can use if you want. Depending on your point of view, this may seem rather aggravating, but nevertheless, Windows Explorer is now found in the Accessories menu.

If you're kind of new to Windows computing, you may be wondering what the big deal is. Well, Windows Explorer provides you with a single interface with which you can view all of the folders on your computer and make additions to or delete them. As you can see in Figure 5-10, Windows Explorer presents all of your folders in a hierarchy. You simply click the plus box next to what you want to expand and continue to click the plus boxes until you reach the folder you want. Once you reach that folder, just select it to see all of its contents in the right Windows Explorer pane.

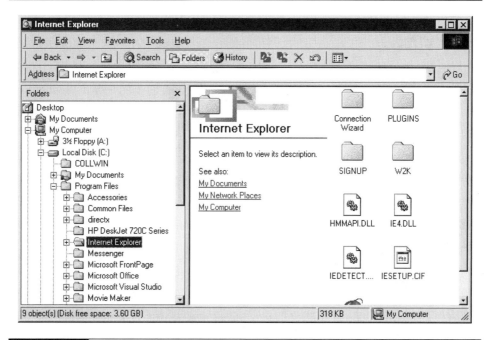

FIGURE 5-10   Windows Explorer provides a hierarchical view of your folders

As you can see in Figure 5-10, Windows Explorer is a great way to browse through your folders, especially for those folders in a folder in a folder in a folder... (you get the picture). So, from this single interface, you can find what you need and even make changes to it. Essentially, everything on your computer's hard drive, CD-ROM, floppy, and other data storage devices can be viewed from Windows Explorer.

Windows Explorer is actually just a folder in Windows Me. If you click on any of the Windows Explorer menus, such as File, Edit, Tools, etc., you notice that the options are the same as any folder in Windows Me (see Chapter 4). The good thing about Windows Explorer is that you can create and remove folders and files on your computer from a single location. Also, Windows Explorer is a good tool to use because it helps you visually examine the folder structure on your computer. You can then make decisions about any changes that need to be made. Without this view, it is sometimes hard to keep an accurate picture in your mind of what data is stored where on your computer. Of course, in Windows Me you can also gain this view directly from any open folder by clicking on the folder's button on the toolbar. In fact, that is the primary reason that Windows Explorer is now seen as an accessory.

My Briefcase

The final accessory is My Briefcase. My Briefcase first appeared as an icon on the Windows 95 desktop, and Microsoft seemed to think it was very important. However, no one ever used My Briefcase, so it has now retreated into the background as an accessory. In fact, My Briefcase is not even installed by default—you have to use Windows Setup to install it. As I said, no one really uses it, but in today's society, where many people use more than one PC, My Briefcase may come back from the dead.

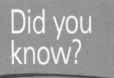

Folder Functions

In Windows Explorer, you can right-click on any folder in the hierarchy and perform the same actions on the folder as you would in any other place in Windows Me. You can also use the right-click menu to access the Search feature so you can search through various folders for a particular item you can't seem to find.

So what is My Briefcase? My Briefcase is an application that enables you to work on the same document or file on two different PCs. For example, let's say you are writing the great American novel. You have the documents in your My Briefcase folder on your home PC, but while you are away, you take the same documents on your laptop so you can write. Upon returning home, you can network the two computers together (or put My Briefcase on a floppy and move it to your PC), and your files will synchronize with each other to ensure that each copy is up-to-date. It's a little confusing, and most people would rather just copy and paste new files instead of going to all the trouble to use My Briefcase.

In reality, My Briefcase works well if you are constantly switching from one computer to another. The following sections show you how to use My Briefcase.

Putting Items in My Briefcase

If you double-click My Briefcase (once you install it, it will appear on your desktop), you see that it is essentially just a folder. It gives you the same folder menu options as any other folder, but there's also a Briefcase menu. All you need to do is drag any items into the Briefcase window that you want keep there so they can be synchronized, as shown in Figure 5-11.

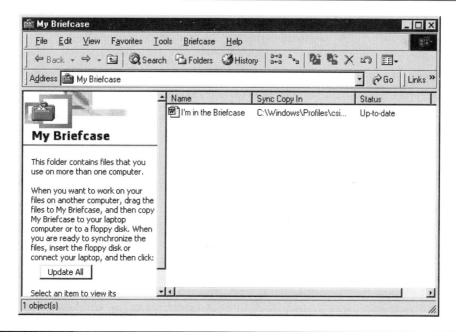

FIGURE 5-11   Drag items into the Briefcase

Using My Briefcase with a Removable Disk

If your computers aren't networked together, you can use a removable disk, such as a floppy or Zip disk, to keep items on different computers synchronized with each other. Here's how you do it:

1. Open My Briefcase, then drag and drop the items that you want in the briefcase. Close My Briefcase.

2. Insert a removable disk into your computer, then drag My Briefcase to the removable disk so that it is copied onto the disk.

3. Remove the disk and put it in your other computer. Open the disk drive and work on the files in My Briefcase from the removable disk.

NOTE   *You do not have to work on the files from the removable disk. You can always copy My Briefcase to your desktop, work on the files, then recopy My Briefcase back to the removable disk. Just choose which option works best for you.*

4. When you want to synchronize the files, put the removable disk back into the primary computer. Open the disk drive, then open My Briefcase.

5. Click the Briefcase menu and click either Update All to update all of the files, or Update Selection to pick which files you want to update.

Using My Briefcase on a Network

If your computers are networked together, you can also use My Briefcase to keep files synchronized. Let's say you have a small home network with a primary PC. You also have a laptop you use when you're away from home. You can use My Briefcase to keep your work files synchronized. Just follow these steps:

1. When your two computers are connected, copy the files from your primary computer to My Briefcase on your secondary computer.

2. Use the secondary computer to work on the files as needed.

3. When you are ready to update, make sure the two computers are networked together, then open My Briefcase on the secondary computer, click the Briefcase menu, and select either Update All or Update Selection. The updates will travel over the network to your primary computer.

 *Your computers only need to be networked together to initially copy the files and to perform the update. Your computers do not need to be connected together when you are working on the files.*

Separating Copies

My Briefcase works well to keep two files completely synchronized. However, consider this scenario. Let's say you are working on a file on a laptop computer while you are away on a trip. Major changes are made to the file while you are gone, but you want to keep the original document on the home PC. In other words, what began as one file has now become two files. How can you keep My Briefcase from synchronizing them? The answer is simple. You simple choose to "split" the two files so they become separate files. Just open My Briefcase, select the file you want, click the Briefcase menu, and then click Split. This separates the file from its counterpart so that the file becomes a "new original."

 Once you use the Split option, you cannot reconnect the two files using My Briefcase. Make sure you want the two files split before using this option.

5

Chapter 6

Managing Hardware with Windows Me

How To...

■ Install New Hardware

■ Manage Hardware with Device Manager

■ Install New Hardware Drivers

■ Use Multiple Hardware Profiles

■ Troubleshoot Hardware Problems

In the not-so-recent past, computer hardware problems and configuration issues were enough to send even the most savvy computer user into fits of rage. No question: hardware problems were among the most common help desk calls and a major complaint of end users. After all, no computer user wants to spend his/her time trying to get a modem, sound card, printer, or some other device working—they want to actually *use* the device. Fortunately, both Windows 98 and Windows Me made great improvements in hardware configuration and support. I'm sorry to say that Windows Me is not perfect, so hardware problems still may plague you, but the odds are quite good that you won't have any hardware problems when using Windows Me (especially if you play by the "rules," which I'll explain in a bit). This chapter shows you hów to install, configure, and troubleshoot hardware problems in Windows Me.

The Hardware Basics

If you are like me, it's usually helpful to understand a potential problem before you try to solve it, so this section tells you a bit about hardware—why it has been a problem in the past and what Windows Me does to reduce those problems.

In the past, computer operating systems were "dumb" in that you had to tell them what hardware devices were installed or connected to your computer. You had to specify which sound card, video card, printer, modem, and other hardware devices were installed on your computer. You then had to provide a driver for those hardware devices.

NOTE *A driver is a piece of software an operating system uses to communicate with a particular device. For example, in order for your operating system to communicate with your modem, there has to be a driver present so that the operating system can manage and use the modem.*

Each hardware device has its own driver, which is usually provided by the hardware device manufacturer. To make the hardware work, you had to install it and provide a driver, and then you usually had to configure the operating system to work with the device and vice versa (as well as keep the device from interfering with other devices). As you can imagine, this process all became very maddening for even the experienced user.

All of this began to change with Windows 95. Windows 95 introduced a technology called Plug and Play (which was nicknamed Plug and Pray). The idea was that it would be an operating system that was "aware" of its environment. The operating system would automatically detect when new hardware was added and attempt to install it. You might have to provide a driver for the hardware, but Windows 95 also had its own database of generic drivers that could be used for typical pieces of hardware.

This sounded wonderful, but if you used Windows 95, you know that Plug and Play was not perfect. It still didn't work well with some hardware, and some hardware didn't work well with Plug and Play.

Windows 98, Windows 2000, and Windows Me all use a more grown-up version of Plug and Play. Windows Me has an extensive driver database so that it can automatically detect and install most devices without your help at all. This is a great feature, since most of us would rather do something other than tinker with hardware installation. Most of the time, Windows Me can take care of the entire process without any intervention from you.

So, Plug and Play in Windows Me is designed to install and remove devices from your computer without any intervention from you. Then how does it work? This is what happens when you install or connect a new device to Windows Me:

1. Windows Me detects that a new hardware device has been added to the system. You will usually see a message stating this.

2. Windows Me installs the new device and finds a generic driver for the device in its database.

3. Windows Me assigns computer resource access to the device so the device can work with your computer.

When you remove a device from your computer, Windows Me does the following:

1. Detects that a hardware device has been removed

2. Removes the device from the system and uninstalls the device's driver

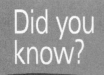

Plug and Play Grows Up

Want some extra details about Plug and Play? Then here they are. Windows 95 achieved Plug-and-Play operation through the Advanced Power Management (APM) Basic Input/Output System (BIOS), or a Plug-and-Play BIOS. APM BIOS allowed the system to detect when devices were installed or removed from the computer. Plug and Play in later versions of Windows, such as Windows 98, Windows Me, and Windows 2000, uses an OnNow design called Advanced Configuration and Power Interface (ACPI), which provides better Plug-and-Play capabilities as well as power management. Because of ACPI, Windows Me contains a number of Plug-and-Play features:

- Automatic detection of hardware changes. Windows Me knows if a device is added or removed from your computer without any input from you. When a change is detected, Windows Me tries to automatically install or remove the device from the system.

- Automatic resource allocation. Each hardware device on your computer uses resources, such as Interrupt Request Lines (IRQs), input/output ports, DMA channels, and a number of other boring items. Windows Me manages all resource allocations for hardware devices to ensure that devices have the resources they need and do not interfere with the operation of other devices.

- Automatic driver. Windows Me contains an extensive driver database. When a new device is detected and installed, Windows Me tries to install a driver for the device without any help from you.

The Rules of Windows Me Hardware

Remember how I told you that Windows Me should give you little hardware trouble, provided that you play by the rules? The rules you should follow are very simple, but they do get overlooked by many Windows users.

First of all, if you have purchased a new computer with Windows Me preinstalled, your existing hardware will work fine with Windows Me. The computer manufacturer works with Microsoft to ensure that your computer's hardware is compatible, so you have no worries if you fall into this category.

However, what happens if you want to upgrade to a different device later? What if you want one of those new awesome video cards or a new modem? No problem. You can purchase a new device and add it to your computer. However, this is where the "rules" apply, and here they are:

1. Only buy Plug-and-Play compliant hardware. How do you know if it's Plug-and-Play compliant? The new hardware device will say "Plug and Play" right on the box. There is little hardware out there these days that is not Plug and Play, but if a device doesn't say "Plug and Play" on the box, keep moving—don't buy it!

2. Look for a Microsoft seal of approval or a "compatible with Windows Me" statement on the box as well. If you can't find a statement like this, it doesn't mean the device will not work, but take it as a warning sign. Approved, well-tested hardware will tell you on the box that it is definitely compatible with Windows Me.

3. Stick to recognizable brand names. Remember, as with most things in life, you get what you pay for. If you choose to purchase FlyByNight's Jiffy Modem on the Internet for $9.95 (with a set of steak knives), don't be surprised if it doesn't work well.

Installing a Plug-and-Play Device

Now that you know about the rules for purchasing a new hardware device, installing it is rather anticlimatic. If the device is Plug and Play and supported by Windows Me, installing it should be very easy. Just follow these steps:

1. Shut down Windows Me and turn off your computer. Attach the new device to the correct port or slot in the back of your computer. If the device is an internal device, unplug your computer from the power outlet and follow the manufacturer's instructions for removing the computer's case and installing the device in the correct slot.

 You absolutely MUST unplug your computer from the power outlet before removing the case. Just because your computer is turned off does not mean that power is not flowing to some of its components. Play it safe and unplug the computer!

 *Always check the device manufacturer's documentation that came with the hardware device for instructions. Most hardware manufacturers include specific installs that tell you exactly what to do in order to install or attach the device to your computer.*

2. If the device is an internal device, replace the cover and plug the computer back in. If the device is external, make sure it is attached to your computer correctly, then turn on the device.

 *In some cases, you should not turn on the external device before booting Windows Me. Check the device documentation to make sure.*

3. Turn on your computer and boot Windows Me. Windows Me will automatically detect the device and install it on your computer. Depending on the type of device you are installing, other instructions may appear. Just follow them as directed.

Removing a Plug-and-Play Device from Your Computer

If you want to remove a Plug-and-Play device from your computer, Windows Me will automatically detect the change and remove the internal software and driver. Just shut down Windows Me and remove the device. If you are removing an internal device, remember to unplug the computer from the power source. Once you are done, reboot Windows Me. Windows Me will detect that the device is missing and uninstall the driver for the device.

 *You can also manually remove a device from Windows Me without physically removing it from your computer. See the "Using Device Manager" section later in this chapter.*

Installing a Non-Plug-and-Play Device

As I mentioned, virtually all hardware devices sold today are Plug-and-Play compliant. However, it is possible for a hardware device to work under Windows but not support Plug and Play. Or you may have an older device that you want to use that does not support Plug and Play. In order to accommodate these needs, Windows Me includes an Add New Hardware Wizard in Control Panel. This wizard is designed to help you install non-Plug-and-Play devices and troublesome Plug-and-Play devices.

 **I Can't Find a Windows Me Device**

It takes a little time for device manufacturers to catch up with operating system releases, so you may have a hard time finding the "Windows Me compatible" device logo at first. The odds, however, are really good that devices that work under Windows 98 will also work under Windows Me. I did say the *odds* are good—they're not perfect. You can also visit the Microsoft Web site and check out the Hardware Compatibility List (HCL) at **www.microsoft.com/hcl**. This list will tell if a particular hardware device has been tested by Microsoft and if it is compatible with Windows Me.

NOTE   *You should use Plug-and-Play hardware if at all possible. You'll see the best performance and experience the least problems if you use Plug-and-Play hardware that is compatible with Windows Me.*

If you do need to use devices that are not Plug and Play, you can install them with the Add New Hardware wizard. To use the Add New Hardware Wizard, follow these steps:

1. Click Start | Settings | Control Panel.

2. Double-click the Add New Hardware icon.

3. Click Next on the Welcome screen.

4. The wizard tells you that Windows Me will now search for any Plug-and-Play devices on your computer. Click Next.

5. Once Windows has finished searching, a window appears with a list of devices (if any) and two radio buttons, as shown in Figure 6-1. If your device is in the list, click the Yes button and select the device, then click Next. If your device is not in the list, click No, then click Next (and skip to step 7).

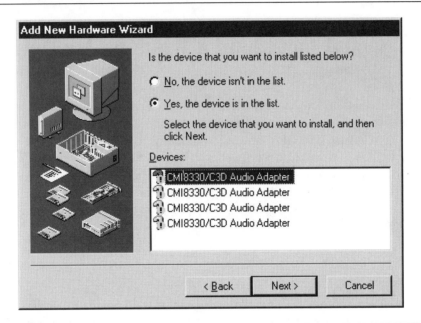

FIGURE 6-1   Select the device in the list

6. Windows installs the device, or if it has problems, tells you that the device is installed but has a problem. Click Finish.

7. If your device was not in the list and you selected the No radio button, Windows provides you with the option to search again or to pick the device from a list. The recommended option is to allow Windows to search again, but if you know the hardware device is not Plug-and-Play compliant, you'll need to pick it from the list. Select the radio button you want, then click Next.

8. If you chose to pick the device from a list, a window appears from which you can select the type of hardware you want to install. For example, in Figure 6-2, I have selected a modem from the list because I want to use an

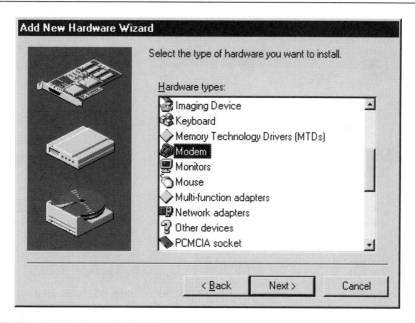

FIGURE 6-2   Select the device you want to install from the list

old non-Plug-and-Play modem (hey, maybe I like things to move very, very slowly). Just select the device you want to install, then click Next.

9. Depending on the hardware device you want to install, Windows Me may prompt you again to allow it to search for the device. If the device is not found, you end up with a screen from which you can select the manufacturer and the model, as shown in Figure 6-3. Select the manufacturer and the model, or click the Have Disk button to install from a disk or CD-ROM. Click Next.

10. Once you select the manufacturer and model (or use the Have Disk option), the wizard may ask you for a little more information, depending on the type of hardware device. Follow the remainder of the onscreen instructions and click Finish.

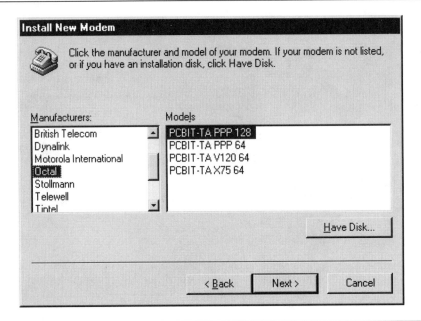

Select the manufacturer and model of the device

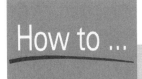

Use the Have Disk Option

You may have a floppy disk or CD-ROM for your device. These were
commonly provided when a hardware device was not Plug and Play. Check
your documentation for instructions about using a disk or CD-ROM to install
the device. If you have a disk or a CD-ROM, you can click the Have Disk
button within the wizard, point the way to the disk (such as to your floppy
drive), and the wizard can install the device using the disk or CD-ROM.

Using Device Manager

Once you install devices on your computer, you can manage them in a few different places. For certain devices, such as printers, scanners, cameras, and modems, there is an icon in Control Panel. These devices require more management than others, so Windows Me helps you by giving them a specific Control Panel option (these options are explored in additional chapters). Also, all devices installed or attached to your computer can be managed from a tool called Device Manager.

 *Some gaming devices may not show up in Device Manager, but there is a Gaming Options icon in Control Panel you can click to manage these devices.*

6

Device Manager is located in System Properties. You can double-click the System icon in Control Panel to reach the Properties windows, or just right-click My Computer on your Desktop and click Properties. Either way, System Properties appears. Click the Device Manager tab to see Device Manager, as shown in Figure 6-4.

As you can see, Device Manager provides an interface similar to Windows Explorer. You see different categories of hardware devices, each with a plus sign next to it. Click the plus sign to expand the category to see the actual devices. For example, in Figure 6-4, you can see my Rockwell Modem and my AcerView monitor.

Notice at the top of the window that you can choose to view devices either by type (which is the view in Figure 6-4) or by connection. This option shows you how different hardware devices are connected and the resources on your computer they use. This view option can be helpful when troubleshooting.

At the bottom of the window, you see a few other button options:

- Properties—You can view a device's properties by selecting the device in the list and clicking this button. See the next section for details.

- Refresh—If something has changed on your system, click this button so that Device Manager can refresh itself.

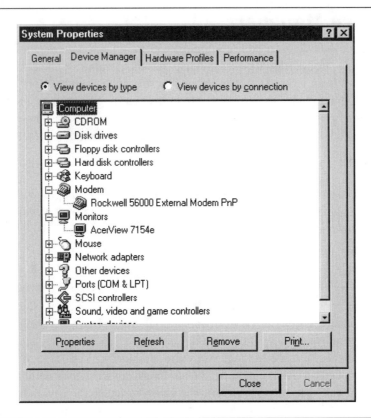

FIGURE 6-4 You can manage your devices with Device Manager

- Remove—This action removes a device from your system. When you click the button, the software for the device, such as the driver, is removed.

- Print—This option prints information about your system configuration. You'll see a summary of resources used on your computer, including which device is using which IRQ.

 *You can also get to these options by right-clicking on any device in the Device Manager list.*

Did you know?

What Is an IRQ?

Devices installed on your computer use Interrupt Request Lines (IRQ) to gain access to the processor. Your computer's processor is the brain of the computer; it performs all computations and calculations. Most system components use the processor to accomplish tasks. The IRQ enables the device to get to the processor. The IRQ prevents two different devices from trying to access the processor at the same time and conflicting with each other (although certain devices can share an IRQ). IRQ conflicts were very common device problems in the past, but Windows Me automatically handles these settings for you and IRQ conflicts are now quite rare.

6

Exploring a Device's Properties

As I noted in the previous section, you can use Device Manager to examine specific properties for a device. Just select the device in the Device Manager list and click the Properties button (or right-click the device icon and click Properties). Once you access the Properties window, you see several tabs for the device. What you see may vary according to the device, but there are typically three basic tabs: General, Driver, and Resources. The following sections explore each of these tabs.

General

The General tab gives you information about the device, and one piece of information can be particularly helpful. Along with the type of device, manufacturer, version number, and other information, in the middle of the window you'll also see a message about the status of the device, as shown in Figure 6-5.

As you can see in Figure 6-5, the device is working properly. If it were not working properly, you would see a message here telling you what might be wrong (such as a bad driver).

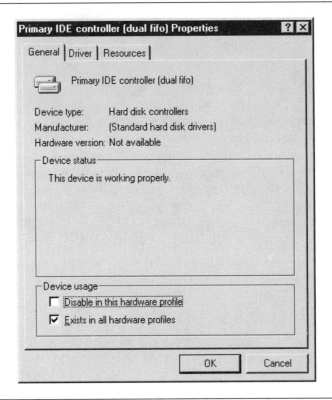

FIGURE 6-5   The General tab gives you information about a device's status

At the bottom of the window are the only two configurable options, in the form of two check boxes:

■ Disable In This Hardware Profile—If you check this box, the device is disabled and Windows cannot use it (the driver is not loaded for the device). This device is still physically installed or attached to your computer, but it is disabled within the operating system. This setting is often used for troubleshooting purposes.

■ Exists In All Hardware Profiles—This option, which is enabled by default, allows the device to exist in all hardware profiles configured on your computer. This means that the device is available to all users.

See the "Using Hardware Profiles" section later in this chapter to learn more about hardware profiles.

Driver

As you might expect, the Driver tab, shown in Figure 6-6, gives you information about the device's driver. You can use this tab to see the publisher of the driver, the date, and whether the driver is digitally signed. A digitally signed driver means that the publisher has included a digital signature to ensure the driver is authentic. Microsoft recommends that you only use signed drivers to ensure compatibility with Windows Me.

6

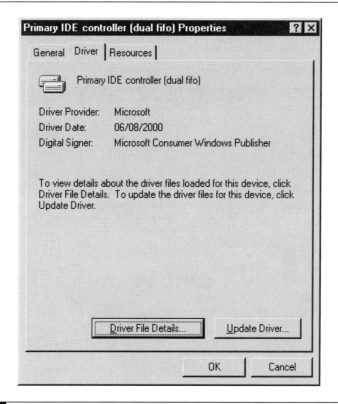

FIGURE 6-6   Use the Driver tab to inspect the device's driver

If you click the Driver File Details button, a window appears that gives you more information about the driver. This is not information that you will typically need, but it may be useful to Microsoft support personnel should you ever need to get telephone or Web support from them. If you click the Update Driver button, you can install a new driver for your device. See the "Installing New Drivers" section later in this chapter for details.

Resources

The Resources tab, shown in Figure 6-7, tells what computer resources the device is using. For some devices, you can use this tab to manually change the resource allocation that Windows Me has established for the device. As you can image, you must know what you're doing before tinkering with these settings, and I do not advise you to make changes here without qualified assistance.

 Making incorrect changes on the Resources tab can cause the device to stop functioning and may cause other devices to stop functioning as well.

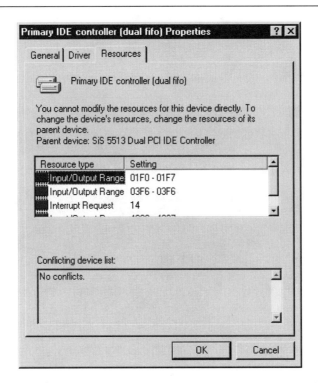

FIGURE 6-7   The Resources tab tells you what computer resources the device is using

The best thing about this tab is that it tells you if there are any conflicts with other devices. As you can see in Figure 6-7, there are no conflicts with this device. However, if there were conflicts, this dialog box would tell you the kind of conflict and the other device with which it was conflicting. Again, this information is very helpful when troubleshooting a device that is not working properly.

Installing New Drivers

I mentioned earlier that a driver is a piece of software that enables Windows Me to interact with a hardware device. If you purchase a new computer with Windows Me preinstalled, the drivers are all set up and are included on your installation CD-ROM. You don't have to worry about them in this situation, but if you purchase a new device to add to your computer, you should probably use the manufacturer's driver, which is normally included in the box on a floppy disk or a CD-ROM.

When you install a new device, Windows Me uses its driver database to install a generic driver for the device. This generic driver may be all you need; however, the generic driver may not enable all of the device's functionality. Your best bet is to use the manufacturer's driver.

6

NOTE *The previous advice assumes you have purchased a hardware device that is Plug and Play and compatible with Windows Me.*

Also, keep in mind that drivers are constantly being updated. Let's say you buy a new video card for your computer so you can play some 3D games. As you use the card, check the manufacturer's Web site from time to time to see if there is a new driver. When a new one becomes available, download and install it for your video card. New drivers make your hardware work better and often solve hardware problems with specific operating systems (at least, it hopefully does—as with all products, you can get a bad driver, too).

If you are upgrading Windows 95/98 to Windows Me, you should gather all of your driver disks and do a little Web surfing for updated drivers before you install Windows Me. This will help reduce the likelihood of encountering hardware problems during installation. If new drivers are not available, the Windows 98 drivers will probably be fine—probably.

TIP *Check out Appendix A for more information and complete steps for installing Windows Me.*

When you need to install a new driver, you simply access the device's
properties in Device Manager, click the Driver tab, then click the Update Driver
button. The wizard helps you get the new driver installed, and you can use the
following steps as a guide:

1. After obtaining the new driver, access the Driver tab on the device's
    Properties window. Click the Update Driver button.

2. The Update Driver window appears. On this window, you have the option
    of allowing Windows Me to search for a better driver, or you can specify
    the location of the driver. If you allow Windows Me to search, it will look
    for a disk in your floppy drive and check your CD-ROM drive. If the
    search finds a better driver, it will report what it finds. (You may want to
    specify the driver location. In this case, click the Specify A Location radio
    button and click Next.)

3. If you chose to specify a location, a window appears in which you can
    enter the location of the driver, as shown in Figure 6-8. For example, you
    can select the Specify A Location check box and then browse to the correct

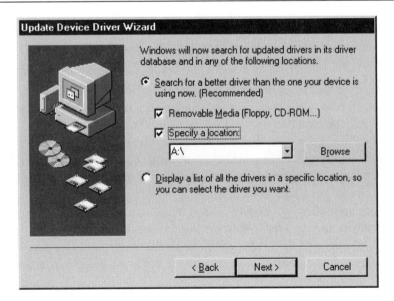

FIGURE 6-8   Specify the location of the driver.

location, such as a floppy drive or to a folder (if you have downloaded a driver from the Internet). Enter the desired location and click Next.

4. Windows searches for the driver. When it locates it, a Window appears listing the driver. Click the Finish button to install the new driver.

Using Hardware Profiles

Hardware profiles allow your computer to provide different hardware configurations. For example, let's say that you want a laptop computer to load all devices in one profile but to load only a few necessary ones when you are traveling. You can create two different hardware profiles. When you start your computer, you will be prompted for the hardware profile you want to load.

Under most circumstances, you probably will not need different hardware profiles. The most common example of needing them is when using a laptop computer, although some people also choose to use different hardware profiles for different users. For example, let's say you are teaching your five-year-old how to use your computer. You can create a hardware profile that disables the CD-ROM drive, printer, modem, etc. so that the child can't do anything damaging to these devices.

Creating a New Hardware Profile

Windows Me has a default hardware profile that uses every device on your system. If you access System Properties in Control Panel (or right-click on My Computer and click Properties), then click the Hardware Profiles tab, you see the Original Configuration in the window, as shown in Figure 6-9.

If you want to create a new hardware profile, click the Copy button. This copies the default hardware profile that uses all devices, and you can make changes to it as you want. When you click the Copy button, a dialog box appears prompting you to give the new profile a name. Enter a name and click OK. The new hardware profile now appears in the list.

Configuring the Hardware Profile

Once you have created the new hardware profile, you'll need to decide its configuration. First, reboot your computer. You'll see a menu appear where you can select either the original profile or the profile you just created. Select the new one in the list and click OK. Once Windows Me boots, you can then use Device Manager to disable any devices you do not want used under this new profile. From that point on, those devices will not be available in the profile, but your original profile configuration will not be changed.

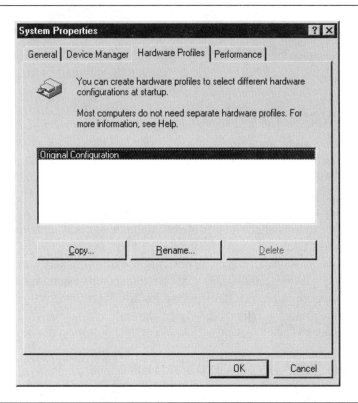

FIGURE 6-9   Your computer has an original hardware configuration profile

Deleting a Hardware Profile

If you decide that you no longer want to use a hardware profile you created, you can easily delete it from your computer by accessing the Hardware Profile tab, selecting the profile you no longer want, and clicking the Delete button.

Hardware Troubleshooting Tips

I wish I could tell you that you will never have hardware problems with Windows Me. Many of you will escape hardware difficulties, but I'm afraid some of you will have problems (I have had problems as well). Fortunately, hardware problems do not have to be too difficult to solve if you take appropriate actions. Here's a list of my best troubleshooting tips regarding Windows Me hardware:

- Relax. If a problem occurs or you can't get a device installed, work through the problem calmly and slowly. A hardware problem or failure will not cause your computer to disintegrate, so work slowly and carefully.

- If you are trying to install a new device, verify that the device is Plug and Play and that it is supported by Windows Me. If you are not sure if the device is supported by Windows Me, visit **www.microsoft.com/hcl** to see if the device is listed.

- Check the device to make certain it is attached to the correct port or installed in your computer correctly. Reread the installation instructions, and don't forget to power down and unplug your computer!

- Check your Windows Me installation CD-ROM. When the auto-screen appears, click Documentation. You will find a bunch of Readme files. These are text files that contain information about known problems or hardware incompatibilities. Check out these files to see if your device is listed and a solution is provided.

- Use Windows Help to access the Hardware Troubleshooter. This feature can often help you solve problems with a particular device (see Chapter 18).

- If a device is installed but not working or not working properly, check the General and Resources tabs of the device's properties sheets in Device Manager. These tabs may tell you what is wrong with the device.

- If a hardware device is installed and not working well, the odds are very good that a driver problem exists. Check the manufacturer's Web site for an updated driver.

- If you cannot get the device to work properly, call the manufacturer for technical support. Often, users are hesitant to seek telephone help, but these services are provided for you to help you solve problems. Take advantage of them!

- If you are still having problems, call Microsoft technical support. You should have a telephone support number and related information with the documentation that came with Windows Me. Again, don't hesitate to get help from Microsoft if you need it.

TIP *Depending on your product and status, your call to Microsoft may be free, or it may cost you up to $35.*

Chapter 7

Using Printers, Scanners, and Digital Cameras

How To...

■ Install a Printer

■ Manage Printers

■ Mange the Print Queue

■ Install Scanners and Digital Cameras

■ Use and Manage Digital Cameras

When the personal computer first came onto the scene, many people speculated that the PC would save a lot of paper. After all, with data stored electronically and viewable on your computer screen, who would need hard copies? As we all know, these speculations were inaccurate. Even with the vast abilities personal computers have, printing remains an important part of computing. Additionally, with the development and availability of scanners and digital cameras (not to mention the Internet), Windows operating systems have become more multimedia-oriented. In this chapter, you will learn all about using printers, scanners, and digital cameras with Windows Me.

Checking Out the Printers Folder

Like its predecessors, Windows Me contains a Printers folder that stores information about any printers connected to your computer and enables you to set up new printers. Previously located in My Computer, your Windows Me Printers folder is now located in Control Panel. If you open the Printers folder, you see a simple interface that gives you an icon for any existing printers set up on your computer, shown in Figure 7-1. You also see a wizard that helps you set up new printers.

Installing a New Printer

You can use the Add Printer wizard in the Printers folder to help you install a new printer on your computer. Before tackling the wizard, however, you have to do a little work away from your keyboard. First, make certain that your printer is compatible with Windows Me. If you are thinking of buying a new printer, read the label carefully. The printer should explicitly say that it is compatible with Windows Me.

FIGURE 7-1   Use the Printers folder to manage and configure printers

> TIP *The odds are very good that if a printer is compatible with Windows 98, it will work just fine under Windows Me. The only potential problem could be an incompatible driver. Check out Chapter 6 for more information about device drivers.*

Before starting the wizard, you need to unpack, set up, and attach your printer's cable to the correct port on your computer. You will probably be using a parallel port on the back of your computer; your computer may even have a picture of a printer next to the port where you should connect it. You may also be using a USB printer, in which case you connect the printer USB cable to the USB port or hub.

> TIP *It's important to break out the printer manufacturer's instruction booklet and take a few minutes to read through it. The instruction booklet will tell you exactly how to attach your printer to the computer and how you should proceed with setup.*

Some printers are shipped with their own setup program on a CD-ROM. Just read the instructions and make sure you know what you are supposed to do to get the printer correctly installed on your computer.

Once the printer is attached to your computer and you have read the printer documentation, you may need to use the Add Printer Wizard to get the printer installed, depending on the instructions that came with your printer. The Add Printer Wizard is very easy to use. Make sure your printer is attached to your computer correctly and that it is turned on. Then, just follow these easy steps:

1. In the Printers folder, double-click the Add Printer Wizard.

2. Click Next on the Welcome screen.

3. The next window gives you two radio buttons, and you can select either a local printer or a network printer. A local printer means the printer is attached to your computer, which it probably is. If you are on a network and you want to use a printer attached to another computer, then click the Network option. Make your selection and click Next. (If you are installing a network printer, skip to step 8.)

4. If you selected local printer, a window appears where you can select the make and model of your printer, as shown in Figure 7-2. If you have an

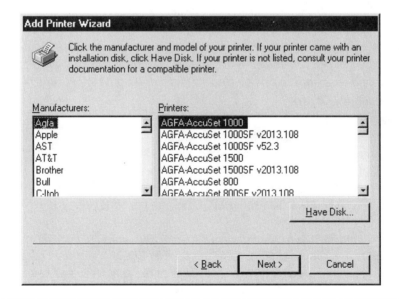

FIGURE 7-2   Select the make and model or click Have Disk

installation disk or CD-ROM, you can also click the Have Disk button to complete the installation from the disk or CD-ROM (check your printer documentation to see what you should do). Make your selection and click Next.

5. Select the port your printer is attached to. Under most circumstances, your printer will be attached to the printer port, LPT1. You also see a Configure Port button. Depending on which port you use, you may have additional port options. See your printer documentation for more information. Click Next.

6. In the Name window, give your printer a friendly name. You also have the option of telling Windows-based programs to print to this printer. Click Yes if you want to use this option or No if you don't. Click Next.

7. The next window asks if you want to print a test page. Choose Yes or No, then click Finish.

8. If you chose to install a network printer in step 2, a window appears so you can enter the network path (UNC) to the printer or queue name, as shown in Figure 7-3. If you are not sure, just click the Browse button to locate the network printer you want to use. Also, if you have MS-DOS–based

7

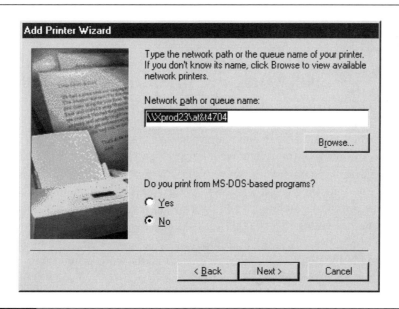

FIGURE 7-3   Enter the network path or queue name of the network printer

programs that you need to print from, click the Yes button in the bottom of the window. Make your selections and click Next.

9. Set up locations for the network printer. Enter a friendly name for the printer and click the Yes radio button if you want your Windows programs to use this printer as the default printer. Click Finish.

Configuring Your Printer

Once you install a printer, a printer icon appears in the Printers folder representing the printer. You can use this printer icon to access the printer's Properties window so that you can configure a number of different options for your printer. Some of these options are a bit confusing, so the following sections explain each of them to you. To access the printer's properties, just right-click its icon in the Printers folder, then click Properties. You see a Printer Properties window with several tabs.

General

The General tab gives you the name of your printer and contains two basic options. First, you can choose to use a separator page between documents, if your printer supports the use of separator pages. A separator page is simply a blank page that is inserted between several print jobs. This option is typically used in an

Network Permissions and Access

It is important to note that if you want to use a network, your Windows Me computer must be configured to use a network and share resources on a network. You can learn how to set up your computer for network service in Chapter 11. Also, the person who owns a network printer can allow you to use the printer or not, depending on what permissions they assign. Just because you see a printer on your network does not mean that you have permission to use it. When in doubt, ask a network administrator. If you are trying to connect to a printer in a home network, make sure the shared network printer is set up, functioning, and available.

office environment to make finding print jobs easier once they are printed. Also, you have the option to print a test page. Just click the Print Test Page button to use this feature. Once you click the button, a window appears asking you if the test page was printed correctly. If it was not, click No and the Windows Help files open to help you solve the problem.

Details

The Details tab gives you information about how the printer is connected to your computer, as shown in Figure 7-4. These are not details about print jobs. You have several different configuration options on this page, most of which are not needed unless you are making changes to the printer or you are having problems printing.

As you can see, there are several different options on this tab.

7

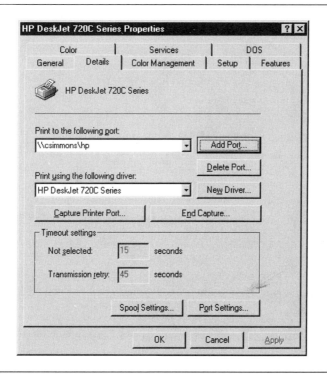

FIGURE 7-4   Use the Details tab to make connection configuration changes

Adding or Deleting a Port

Windows Me uses ports to communicate with printers and other devices that are attached to your computer. In order to communicate with a printer, Windows Me has to know which port the printer is attached to. This may be a local port on your computer, such as LPT1 or a USB port. A port can also be a network location that holds a shared network printer. In Figure 7-4, you can see that my printer is actually a shared printer on a different computer.

You set up the port when a printer is installed—but what happens if you need to change the port later? For example, what if you move the printer to a different port on your computer or the network port changes? No problem: just make that change on this page by adding a printer port. This way, you don't have to completely reinstall the printer software.

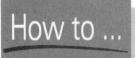

It is important to remember that you do not need to change printer ports unless you have physically moved your printer to a different port on your computer or the network path to a particular network printer has changed.

How to ... Add a New Printer Port

Follow these steps to add a new printer port:

1. On the Details tab, click the Add Port button.

2. In the Add Port window, shown in Figure 7-5, select either Network Port or Other Port. If you choose Network, enter the network path to the printer or click Browse to find the printer. If you click Other, select Local Port and click OK.

3. Depending on the option you select, you may be prompted to enter a port name. Enter a name and click OK.

4. The new port appears in the port dialog box on the Details tab.

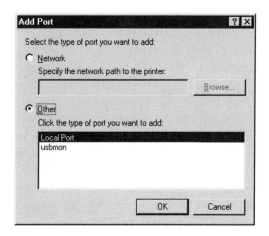

FIGURE 7-5   Select a different port

7

You can remove ports that your computer no longer needs to use to access a printer in the same manner. Just click the Delete Port button and remove the port you do not want to use.

Changing Printer Drivers

From time to time, your printer manufacturer may produce a new driver for your printer. The new driver may increase performance or solve compatibility problems with a new version of Windows. If you need to update the printer driver, you can do so by clicking the New Driver button on this tab. This action opens a portion of the Update Driver Wizard that can help you install the new printer driver. See Chapter 6 for more information about device drivers.

Capturing a Printer Port

You can use the Details tab to capture a printer port. This means that a particular port is assigned to a printer and the printer can only use that particular port. For example, if I want to use a network printer, I can use the capture option to ensure that all documents are sent to that particular port. To capture the port, just click the Capture Printer Port button, select a port number, and enter a network path (if necessary). You can click the Reconnect At Logon check box to make sure your computer always reconnects to a network printer.

In the same manner, you can end a port capture by clicking the End Capture button. Select the capture you want to remove in the list and click OK.

Spool Settings

Windows printing uses a spooling feature. This simply means that print jobs are stored on your hard disk while the computer waits for the printer to be ready. For example, let's say you print ten Word documents. It may take several minutes to print the documents, and while one document is printing, the others wait in the spool until it is their turn. Why? The answer is simple. Spooling moves the documents to the hard disk so you get control over your application without waiting. Without the spool, your application will be tied up until the print job finishes. With the spool, you can return to work or play and not have to wait for the file to be printed.

You can adjust how the spool in Windows Me operates by clicking the Spool Settings button on the Details tab. This action opens a Spool Settings window, as shown in Figure 7-6.

The following list tell you what these settings mean and which ones you should use:

- Spool Print Jobs—This option is enabled by default and tells your printer to spool print jobs to your hard disk. You should leave this setting enabled.

- Start Printing After Last Page Is Spooled—This option holds the print job until the application spools all of the pages. This frees up your application more quickly, but it delays printing longer.

- Start Printing After First Page Is Spooled—This option (enabled by default) starts the print job when the first page is spooled. This option starts

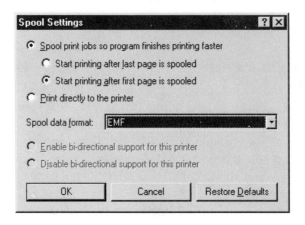

FIGURE 7-6   Use the Spool Settings window to alter how your printer spool operates

the printing more quickly, but it may take longer to free up your application. Most users prefer this setting.

■ Print Directly To Printer—This option does not spool print jobs, it sends them directly to the printer. This setting will cause your application to have to wait until the document finishes printing before you can work on other tasks. In other words, this setting does not use the spool. I do not recommend this setting because you'll end up waiting for jobs to print before you can continue to work or play.

■ Spool Data Format—You have the options of EMF or RAW. EMF is used by default, and this is all you need. EMF and RAW settings simply tell Windows Me how to store print jobs on your disk. You don't need to change anything here unless you're directed to do so by your printer documentation.

■ Bi-directional Printing—Depending on your printer, your computer and printer may communicate with each other during a printing session. You don't need to do anything with these radio button options unless your printer documentation tells you to do so.

Port Settings

The Port Settings button on the Details tab normally contains an option or two, depending on the port your computer is using. The default settings are all you need, and you do not need to configure anything with this option unless directed to do so by your printer documentation.

Sharing

The Sharing tab is much like the Sharing tab for Folder Properties. You can use this tab to share your printer so that others users on your network can use your printer. On the Sharing tab, shown in Figure 7-7, just click the Shared As button and give the printer a friendly name. You can also insert a comment if desired, and you can assign a password if you want to require users on your network to input a password to access the printer.

TIP   *As I noted earlier, network printer sharing involves setting up additional networking components, which you can learn about in Chapter 11. In Windows Me, you can only control printer access through the use of a password. Other Windows operating systems, such as NT and 2000, can finely control printer usage based on individual users and permissions.*

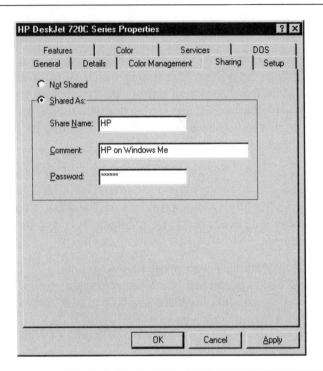

Use the Sharing tab to share your printer

Other Tabs

Depending on your printer, you will probably see several other tabs available in Printer Properties. You can use these tabs to manage color, page orientation, font usage, and other print quality settings. These tabs are specific to your brand and model of printer, so you'll need to explore your printer documentation to learn about the options available to you on these tabs.

Managing Print Jobs

Once your printer is set up and configured the way you want, you can print all kinds of documents and files—almost anything you like. As you print documents, a small printer icon will appear in your System Tray. This icon represents the Print Queue, which is where the documents in your print spool wait to be printed. You can right-click this icon and manage the Print Queue as you need by clicking Properties. This action opens the Print Queue window, as shown in Figure 7-8.

HP DeskJet 720C Series				
Printer Document View Help				
Document Name	Status	Owner	Progress	Started At
file://C:\My%20Documents\Wel...	Printing	csimmons	0 of 2 pages	11:46:28 AM 8/2/2000
	Spooling	csimmons	0 bytes	11:46:31 AM 8/2/2000
file://C:\My%20Documents\Wel...	Paused	csimmons	2 page(s)	11:46:41 AM 8/2/2000
file://C:\My%20Documents\Wel...		csimmons	2 page(s)	11:46:55 AM 8/2/2000
4 jobs in queue				

FIGURE 7-8   Use the Print Queue window to manage print documents

As you can see in Figure 7-8, there are several documents waiting to be printed. You can take several actions by using the menus to manage documents that are in the Print Queue. From the Printer menu, you can do the following:

- Pause Printing—This action stops all printing.

- Use Printer Offline—This action enables you to send jobs to the Print Queue, but they are not printed until you are ready.

- Purge Print Documents—If you accidentally print a bunch of documents, you don't have to waste your paper and ink. Just use the Purge Print Documents option to dump everything out of the Print Queue.

From the Document menu, you can do the following:

- Select a print job in the list and click Pause to stop printing.

- Select a print job in the list and click Cancel to cancel it.

Troubleshooting Common Printer Problems

Windows Me includes better printer support than previous versions of Windows, and troubleshooting does not have to be a major chore. Keep in mind that you should also consult your printer documentation when you experience a problem because there may be issues specific to your printer you need to solve. The following sections tell you about some of the most common printer problems and their solutions.

 *If you are having printing problems, you can also use the Windows Troubleshooter tool to help you resolve the issue. See Chapter 18 for details.*

Printed Text Is Garbled

You have a document you want to print. It is nice and neat on the screen, but when you print the document, the text comes out garbled. This is a common problem that is typically caused by one of two things. First, the document that you are trying to print may be damaged or corrupt. You can test this by printing a different document. If the text still appears garbled, the most likely cause of the problem is your printer driver. Your printer driver is not compatible, the wrong driver is installed, or the driver has become corrupt. Use the Details tab of the printer's Properties window to reinstall the driver.

The Printer Does Not Work

If your printer does not seem to work, make sure the printer is turned on and that it is attached to the correct port on the back of your computer. If it is, you may need to reinstall the driver and reboot Windows Me. Sometimes internal problems can prevent a printer from working properly, and a simple reboot can bring the printer back online. If these actions do not solve the problem, consult your printer documentation. You may have a printer hardware problem.

Printing Is Very Slow

If printing to a local printer is very slow, you may be running low on hard disk space. Remember that your printer uses part of your hard disk space to spool documents for background printing. You should have at least 10MB of free hard disk space available.

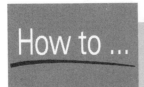 **Check Your Hard Disk Space**

You can easily check the amount of free disk space on your computer by double-clicking My Computer, right-clicking the hard disk icon, and clicking Properties. Consult the General tab. You will see a pie graph showing how much hard disk space is used and how much is free.

If you have enough free disk space, check your spool settings on the Printer Properties Details tab to make sure spooling is enabled. Also, try defragmenting your hard disk. For more information about defragmentation, see Chapter 16.

A Certain Document Will Not Print

If you have a certain document that will not print, try to print a different document from within the same application. If you can print another document from within the same application, the problematic document is most likely corrupt. If printing is sporadic with the application or several applications, turn the printer off, wait ten seconds, and turn it back on. This may resolve the problems (you may try rebooting as well).

Print Quality Is Poor

If your files will print but the print quality is poor, there may be changes you need to make to printer-specific tabs within the printer's Properties pages. Consult your printer documentation for help.

7

Using Scanners and Digital Cameras with Windows Me

During the past few years, the use of scanners and digital cameras has exploded. We all like to use electronic pictures that we can print, e-mail to friends and family, or just store on the computer's hard drive instead of in an album under the couch. Because of these devices' popularity, Windows Me includes a Scanners And Cameras folder in Control Panel that looks much like the Printers folder. With this folder, you can install and manage scanners and cameras.

Installing Scanners and Cameras

Installing a scanner or digital camera is a lot like installing a printer. First, always carefully consult the documentation and instructions that came with the scanner or digital camera for setup and management instructions. Some models have their own installation disk or CD-ROM. Also, make sure any scanner or camera you purchase is compatible with Windows Me.

In many cases, Windows can automatically detect your scanner or camera, but if it does not, you can use the Add Device Wizard in the Scanners And Cameras folder in Control Panel to install a new scanner or camera. Like the Add Printer

Wizard, the Add Device Wizard is easy to use. Just connect the scanner or camera to your computer, turn it on, and follow these easy steps:

1. Double-click the Add Device Wizard in the Scanners And Cameras folder in Control Panel.

2. Click Next on the Welcome screen.

3. Select the make and model of your camera or scanner, or click the Have Disk button to install it from a floppy disk or CD-ROM. Make your selection and click Next.

4. Select a port for the device (refer to your scanner or camera's documentation) and click Next.

5. Give the device a friendly name and click Next.

Once you have your scanner and camera installed on Windows Me, icons for them will appear in the Scanners And Cameras Folder, as shown in Figure 7-9.

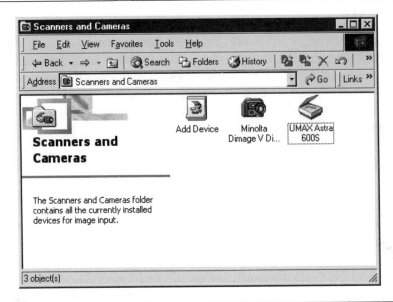

FIGURE 7-9   Installed devices appear in the Scanners And Cameras Folder

Using the Content Wizard

If you right-click a scanner or camera icon in the Scanners And Cameras Folder, you see a Use Wizard option. This feature opens the Content Wizard, which guides you through the process of using the scanner or camera to input digital images into your computer. Depending on the device, the wizard will vary. However, the wizard is very easy to use and self-explanatory, and I recommend using it if you are new to scanners and digital cameras.

 Once you install a scanner or digital camera, this wizard, called the Scanner And Camera Wizard, also appears in your Accessories menu.

Managing Scanner and Camera Properties

7

You can right-click a scanner or camera icon in the Scanners And Cameras Folder in Control Panel and click Properties to access the device's Properties window. As you might guess, much as with printers, the contents of this window depend on the type of device and the make and model. Various options are available to you. For example, you can have a camera or scanner always save files to a certain folder, and depending on your device, you can manage color settings here. Check your scanner or digital camera documentation for information about configuring these Properties pages.

Chapter 8

Creating and Managing Internet and Dial-Up Connections

How To...

- Configure Your Modem
- Set up Dialing Rules and Options
- Create Internet and Dial-Up Connections
- Edit Dial-Up Connections

It wasn't too many years ago that the Internet was an anomaly of sorts—something weird computer geeks did on the weekends and nothing more. Most of us never thought the Internet would become so pervasive. Now I wonder how we ever survived without it! If you are like me, you use the Internet every day for all kinds of work and play—it has become and will continue to be an integrated part of our lives.

Windows Me makes Internet access and surfing easy, not to mention dial-up access to private networks. In this chapter, you'll learn how to create and configure connections to the Internet so you can access the Internet on your Windows Me computer. You'll also learn about dial-up networking connections to private networks.

About Internet Connections

Before we jump into the business of creating and managing Internet connections, let's make sure you're up to speed on those connections. An Internet connection allows your computer to access the Internet. You can send e-mail, look at Web pages, download information, or do virtually anything with your Internet connection. An Internet connection is achieved through an Internet Service Provider (ISP). You pay the ISP a fee (usually monthly, but there are annual or semi-annual plans as well) to access the Internet. The Internet itself is free, but you must pay an ISP for the access.

Think of the Internet as a busy freeway. In order to get on the freeway, you must drive onto an access ramp so your car can enter the traffic. The Internet is the same. In order to access the busy "information highway," you must have an on-ramp so your computer can get "into the traffic." The ISP is your on-ramp. All the information you send and receive over the Internet comes through server computers at your ISP before it reaches your computer.

The most common type of Internet access today is a dial-up account. This means your computer uses a modem, which uses your phone line, to dial an access number, just as you would a telephone call. Once the ISP answers the call, your computer sends user name and password information so your computer can be authenticated by the ISP. You can then use the Internet through the ISP. 56Kbps modems are currently the most common for dial-up access.

However, the Internet now contains rich multimedia and all kinds of surfing experiences. Although a great addition, multimedia and the cool Web pages of today are much larger in size than they once were, and 56Kbps modems are quite slow. Because of this, many people are turning to broadband "always-on" Internet access. ISDN, DSL, cable, and even satellite access are now available from major ISPs. These solutions leave your computer always connected to the Internet, they do not use your phone line at all, and they offer speeds many times faster than a 56Kbps modem.

Configuring Your Modem

As I mentioned in the previous section, the most common type of Internet access is a dial-up account, which uses a modem in your computer. Unless you have paid for DSL, ISDN, or some other broadband service (and the hardware to connect to your computer), you will access the Internet via your modem.

8

What about Smalltown, U.S.A.?

I know a thing or two about living in a small town, believe me. Perhaps you have read about ISDN, DSL, or cable Internet access. Perhaps you made a few calls, only to have some salesperson say, "Sorry, those services are not available in your area." While it is true that these broadband solutions are great, they are simply not available everywhere, at least not yet. The good news is these broadband solutions are the way of the future, so you may have to bide your time until they become available.

Another solution to consider is Internet satellite access. Much like DirecTV, these services use a small satellite dish attached to your house to access the Internet through a satellite. The results are very fast access from any location (in the continental United States only, at the moment). Visit **www.direcpc.com** or **www.gilat2home.com** to learn more.

Configuring modems has been a painful experience for Internet users in the past. I remember staying up late at night and pulling my hair out trying to get a modem to work. Although modems can still be complicated, we're a long way from those days, and setting up your modem in Windows Me should be no problem.

Before getting into the details, I do want to mention that dial-up connections tend to be problematic for computer users because there are two different components to work with. You have to configure the actual connection (which we will do in an upcoming section), and you have to configure your modem, which the connection uses. Successful Internet access requires the configuration of both of these. The following sections show you how to configure your computer's modem.

Installing a Modem

Your computer probably already has a modem installed—after all, modems are a standard piece of hardware these days. You may have purchased a different modem from the one that's currently installed, and that's fine too. Windows Me should be able to automatically detect and install a Plug-and-Play modem, so modem installation works just like any other piece of hardware. Check out Chapter 6 for more information about installing devices.

Configuring Modem Properties

In order to make modem configuration easier, a modem icon is included in Control Panel. If you double-click the icon, you see a Properties window with General and Diagnostics tabs. The following sections show you what you can configure on each of these (and why you would want to). *fig 8.1*

General Tab

Today's modems do a good job of setting themselves up. You don't have to worry about inputting a lot of information to make the modem work, but you may want to adjust some of the settings to meet your needs. The General tab, shown in Figure 8-1, provides a simple interface that lists the modem(s) installed on your computer and provides you with a few buttons.

First, you see Add and Remove buttons. If you click the Add button, the New Modem Wizard appears, which searches for additional modems attached to your computer. If the wizard finds one, it automatically installs it. If not, you can select it from a list. This is the same type of installation wizard you see when installing various other hardware devices (see Chapter 6). If you select a modem in the list and click Remove, the modem's software is uninstalled from your computer.

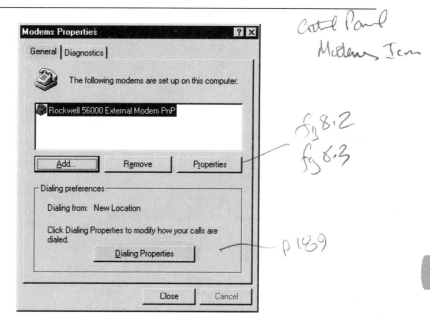

(handwritten notes: Ctrl Panel / Modems Icon; fig 8.2; fig 8.3; p 189)

FIGURE 8-1   The General tab is used to configure your modem

Under most circumstances, you don't need to use either of these buttons, unless you just love modems and want to use two or three of them on your computer.

Next, you see a Properties button. Select the desired modem in the list (if there is more than one), then click the Properties button to see specific properties. There are two tabs: General and Connection. The General tab, shown in Figure 8-2, tells you which port the modem is attached to, gives you a speaker slider bar option, and gives you a maximum speed setting. The only thing you need to change here is the modem's speaker volume. You can turn it down low or turn it very high if you want to get a headache from all the aggravating connection noise. You don't need to change the maximum speed setting or use the Only Connect At This Speed check box unless you're instructed to do so by your ISP in order to resolve connection problems.

On the Connection tab, shown in Figure 8-3, there are a few different options to manage how the modem makes and manages a connection to the Internet. There are two major parts to this tab: Connection Preferences and Call Preferences.

(handwritten: fig 8.2) First, the Connection Preferences section provides some connection values your modem uses to connect with an ISP. These are set up automatically when you install a modem, and you should not change any of these settings unless instructed to do so by your ISP.

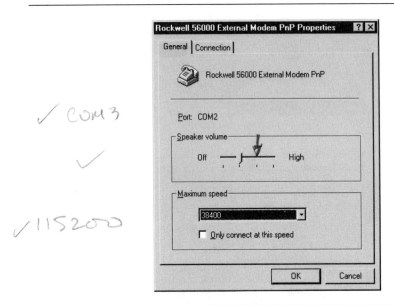

FIGURE 8-2   The Modem Properties General tab allows you to adjust speaker volume and modem speed

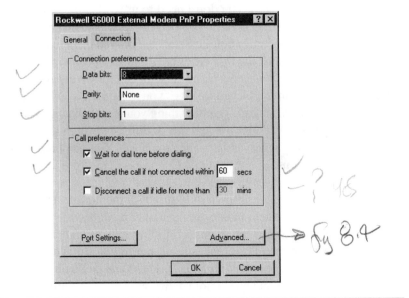

FIGURE 8-3   Use the Connection tab to adjust the modem's management of Internet connections

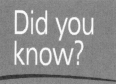

Modem Speeds

So, you're using a 56Kbps modem—you should get 56Kbps, right? Wrong. First of all, due to regulations, the highest speed you are likely to get with a 56Kbps modem is about 53Kbps. Even then, the speed must be matched with your ISP's modem, and telephone line conditions can bring the speed even lower. If you have used the Internet before, you may wonder why you get different connection speeds at different times. Both local, ISP, and Internet traffic all affect modem speed. You can use the Maximum Speed option on the Modem Properties General tab to set a minimum connection speed, but this may prevent you from getting a connection if your ISP's modem can't handle it. For example, let's say that you want a minimum speed of 38Kbps, so you use the drop-down menu, select 38 Kbps, and click the Only Connect At This Speed check box. That's all well and good, but what if the ISP modem you connect with isn't doing 38 Kbps at the moment? You get disconnected. So, use these settings with care. Speed is important, but getting there at all is nice too.

8

 Incorrectly changing the Connection Preferences settings may result in connection failure or difficulty.

Fig 8.3

The second section, Call Preferences, contains three check box options you can use, depending on how you want the modem to handle the connection:

- ■ Wait For Dial Tone Before Dialing—This option, which is typically enabled, tells your modem to listen for a dial tone before dialing the access number. If your modem does not recognize your phone's dial tone, you can clear this check to try and resolve the problem.

- ■ Cancel Call If Not Connected Within *x* Seconds—This option, which is typically enabled with a 60-second setting, tells your modem to disconnect if the connection is not established within the specified time period. This prevents your modem from trying to establish a single connection for an indefinite period of time. The 60-second setting is a good one—if the connection is not established within one minute, there is probably some error, and your modem needs to try again.

■ Disconnect A Call If Idle For More Than x Minutes—This setting enables your computer to automatically disconnect a call if the connection is idle for a specified period of time. For example, let's say you're surfing and you decide to take a quick trip to the store. You forget to disconnect from the Internet. This setting will automatically disconnect you after a period of inactivity. This is a good setting to use (it is not enabled by default), but don't set the inactivity period too low or you'll get disconnected if you stop to ponder a Web page for a few minutes.

At the bottom of the Connection tab, you also see a button called Port Settings. The options found under Port Settings are automatically configured by your modem; you do not need to change them unless you are directed to do so by your ISP.

 *Changing settings on the Port Settings window can stop your modem from functioning properly.*

Finally, you also see an Advanced button. If you click this button, you see a single Advanced Connection Settings window, as shown in Figure 8-4.

These settings are very important for your modem's connection to your ISP. You normally do not need to make changes here unless directed to do so by your ISP, so leave this tab alone unless you have a specific reason to change any of

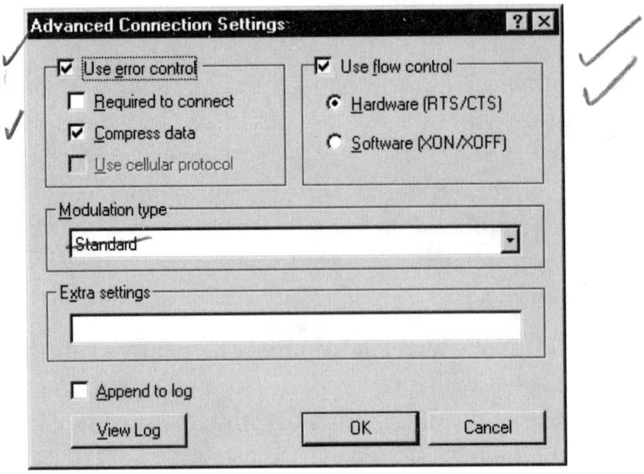

![Advanced Connection Settings window showing checkboxes for Use error control (with Required to connect, Compress data, Use cellular protocol) and Use flow control (with Hardware RTS/CTS selected, Software XON/XOFF), a Modulation type dropdown set to Standard, an Extra settings field, an Append to log checkbox, and View Log, OK, and Cancel buttons]

FIGURE 8-4   The Advanced Connection Settings window contains specific modem connection settings

these settings. If you are having problems with your connection to the ISP, you can call the ISP's help line for specific instructions. Often, a tech will want to take a look at this window for potential problems or to specify additional settings. As with many of your modem settings, incorrectly changing these will stop your modem from connecting with your ISP.   *P 185*

Finally, we're back to the Modem Properties General tab. Your last button on this tab is the Dialing Properties button. If you click this button, a single window opens where you can configure the way your modem dials out to the Internet, as shown in Figure 8-5. This tab is important, and it's easy to configure.

In a nutshell, all this tab does is configure the way your modem should dial up to your ISP. Sounds simple enough, but there are a lot of potential needs people may have when dialing from a certain place. This tab enables you configure the dialing process to meet your needs.

At the top of the window, you see the I Am Dialing From drop-down menu. You also see the New and Remove buttons. This option enables you to create

8

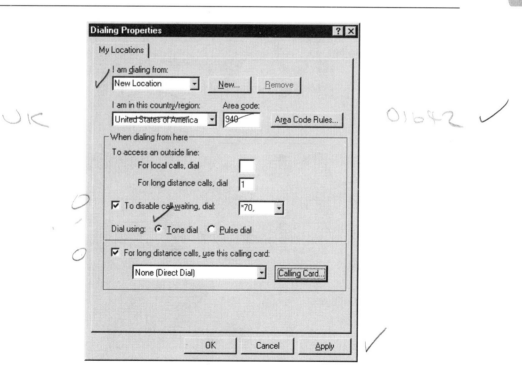

UK   *01642* ✓

Use Dialing Properties to manage the way your modem dials phone numbers different dial-out configurations. For example, let's say I have a laptop and I work from a home office. However, from time to time, I have to travel to another state for business. I can configure one location for home and one for when I am on the road. This lets my modem use different dialing rules, depending on my needs.

You also see drop-down menus to choose the country and area code you are dialing from, and you see an Area Code Rules button.

When you press the Area Code Rules button, a window appears, shown in Figure 8-6, where you can configure your modem to work with various area codes.

Because some area codes require a 1 to be dialed first for long distance and some do not, you can use this window to configure area code dialing. For example, as you can see in Figure 8-6, I need the modem to dial a 1 in front of this area code, but 972 and 940 are local area codes that do not need a 1. Just use the New and Remove buttons to enter numbers in the appropriate box as needed.

The remainder of the Dialing Properties tab contains several check box setting options. For example, you can disable call waiting, dial an outside line, and configure your computer to use a calling card for long distance calls. If you want to use the latter option, click the Calling Card button and enter your card information.

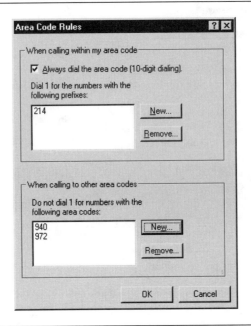

FIGURE 8-6 Use the Area Code Rules window to manage how your modem should dial area codes

Diagnostics Tab

The second tab of the Modem Properties sheet is the Diagnostics tab. This tab tells you what port the modem is attached to. You can click the Driver button to find out more information about the driver the modem is using. If you click More Info, a diagnostics test is run on the modem to determine if it is working properly.

About Telephony

If you look in Control Panel, you see an icon called Telephony. If you open the icon, you see the same interface as Dialing Rules in the previous section. Telephony is used to get global dialing rules settings for computers that have several telephone or modem-enabled devices. Under most circumstances, you do not need to use the Telephony options, and if you are accessing the Internet via a single modem, you do not need to configure anything here.

8

Creating Connections to the Internet

Once you are sure your modem in installed and you have configured any connection and dialing rules you need, you can create your Internet connection. Remember, your Internet connection uses your modem to dial a connection, and your modem uses the modem settings to manage the call. Think of these two items as a duet—two pieces that work together to accomplish one goal.

Fortunately, creating connections to the Internet is rather easy, due to the Internet Connection Wizard included in Windows Me. If an Internet connection has never been established on your computer, just double-click Internet Explorer on your Desktop, or click the Internet Explorer icon on your Taskbar. This automatically launches the Internet Connection Wizard. The wizard can also be found in Accessories in the Communications menu.

Once you start the wizard, it walks you through a series of steps collecting information from you in order to create a connection. First, you see a Welcome screen, shown in Figure 8-7, which allows you to select from three options:

- Sign Up For A New Internet Account—If you select this radio button and click Next, you are prompted to let the wizard dial a toll-free Microsoft referral number. Information about ISPs for your area is downloaded to your computer. You can then select one and continue with the registration process by connecting to the ISP of your choice.

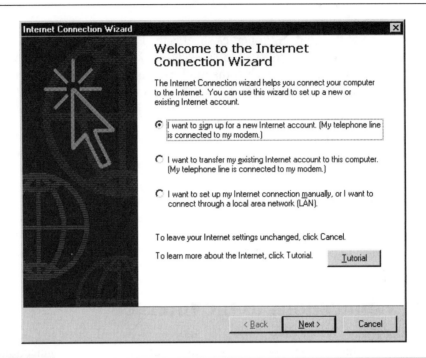

FIGURE 8-7 Use the Internet Connection Wizard to help you create an Internet Connection

Before signing up with an ISP this way, you may want to do a little homework. There are probably local ISPs in your area that offer better rates than national companies. As with any purchase, shop around a little before you make a final decision.

■ Transfer An Existing Account To This Computer—The Internet Connection Wizard provides a way for you to transfer your existing Internet connection to your new computer. This option works well if your current ISP is registered with Microsoft—if it's not, the option doesn't work. If you want to set up an existing Internet account, you can also use the Next option.

■ Set Up The Internet Connection Manually—This option walks you through several wizard screens on which you enter information about your ISP, such as access phone numbers, user name, password, mail server name, and so forth. This information is provided with your ISP access account, so refer to that documentation.

Several ISPs provide you with software that you install on your computer. This software adds utilities and functionality to your computer for that particular ISP and configures your computer to access the ISP. Check out your ISP documentation for details and instructions.

If you want to learn a little more about the Internet before configuring a connection, just click the Tutorial button on the Welcome screen of the Internet Connection Wizard. The tutorial is not too exciting, but it does provide you with useful information.

Creating Connections Using the Dial-Up Networking Folder

In Control Panel, you'll find a Dial-Up Networking folder. This folder looks similar to the Printers folder. There is a wizard to help you create dial-up connections and you see an icon for any connections that currently exist, as shown in Figure 8-8.

So far, we have explored connections in terms of the Internet. You can use the Internet Connection Wizard to create an Internet connection to an ISP, but why does Microsoft include yet another wizard here? The Internet Connection Wizard

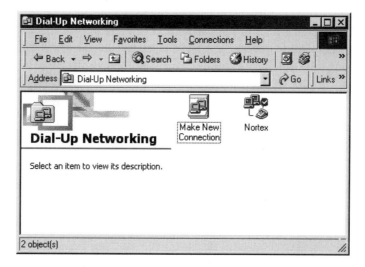

FIGURE 8-8   The Dial-Up Networking folder contains existing connections and a New Connection Wizard

is used only for Internet connections. While it is true that you can use the Make New Connection wizard for an Internet connection, you can also use this wizard to create other dial-up connections. For example, let's say you work for a small company. Instead of using expensive networking technology for remote users, the company may implement dial-up accounts where you can dial-up to a private server and get information from the network. Regardless, the Make New Connection Wizard is very simple and straightforward. If you need to create an additional dial-up connection, just double-click the wizard to start it. Answer the questions, and once you are finished, a new connection icon will appear in the Dial-Up Networking folder.

Editing a Dial-Up Connection

As I mentioned, all dial-up connections you create within Windows Me are stored in your Dial-Up Networking folder in Control Panel. You can open this folder, right-click on a connection of your choice, click Properties and make changes to the connection as needed. This is a great feature that prevents you from having to recreate connections when something changes. There are several tabs on the Properties window, and the following sections tell you about each of them.

General

The General tab, shown in Figure 8-9, allows you to change the phone number the connection uses to your ISP. Since phone numbers can frequently change, access this tab to make adjustments as necessary. You can also use this tab to tell the connection to use the dialing rules you have configured for your modem. To make configuration changes directly to your modem, click the Configure button. This opens the Modem Properties window we explored in the first half of this chapter.

Networking

The Networking tab contains several check box options that determine how your connection communicates with your ISP or dial-up server. The primary options involve the use of various protocols, and you do not need to make any changes on this tab unless instructed to do so by your ISP or a dial-up server administrator.

 *Incorrectly making changes to the settings on this tab will cause your connection to fail.*

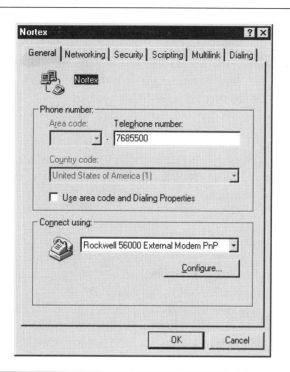

FIGURE 8-9   Use the General tab to make dial-up access and modem configuration changes

What Are Protocols?

Just like humans, computers must use the same language when communicating with each other. Without a common language, computers would not be able to understand each other. A networking protocol is a communications rule of behavior—it tells computers how to communicate with other computers that use the same protocol. The protocol of choice is Transmission Control Protocol/Internet Protocol (TCP/IP). TCP/IP is the most widely used protocol today. In fact, all computers that use the Internet and send and receive e-mail use TCP/IP.

Security

The Security tab contains your user name, password, and other security information your connection uses to authenticate with the ISP or dial-up server. You should refer to your ISP documentation or dial-up server authentication information before making any changes on this tab.

Scripting

Some older dial-up servers and ISPs use logon scripts in order to authenticate your computer. These are rare these days, so the likelihood of you ever needing this tab is quite small. Follow instructions from your ISP or dial-up server administrator if you do.

Multilink

Windows Me supports the use of multiple modems for a multilink connection. Multilink solutions use several modems on the server's side and several modems on the client's side to create faster transmission speeds. This technology is seldom used. If it is used, it requires both client and server configuration. This isn't anything you are likely to use with an ISP, so you don't need to do anything on this tab.

Dialing

The last tab is the Dialing tab. On this tab, shown in Figure 8-10, you can make some basic changes to the way your particular connection is dialed. Remember that you can configure dialing options for your modem. This tab enables you to override certain modem settings so that your connection operates in a certain way. This is particularly useful if you have several different connections you use.

The settings on this tab are self-explanatory. You can determine if this connection should be your default connection, determine the redial time if you get a busy signal, enable idle disconnect when the connection is not needed, and other similar settings. You can change these to meet your needs.

Some of you may have heard about Windows Me's ability to share an Internet connection so that other PCs in your home or office can use the shared connection. You can learn all about this configuration option in Chapter 11.

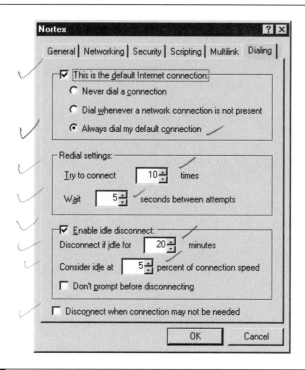

FIGURE 8-10   Use the Dialing tab to enforce dialing restrictions and options

About Broadband Connectivity

As I mentioned earlier in this chapter, you may have other broadband options available to you, such as DSL, ISDN, cable, and so forth, depending on where you live and how much money you want to spend. These broadband solutions are truly the wave of the future, but that future has not quite arrived just yet. At any rate, Windows Me does include an ISDN Configuration Wizard in Accessories in the Communications menu. You need ISDN hardware attached to your computer to use this wizard. If you are using a broadband solution, consult your documentation for information about how to set up your connection. Since broadband solutions do not use a dial-up connection to the Internet (the Internet is "always on"), you'll need to use your provider's documentation to make any necessary configuration changes.

Chapter 9

Surfing the Web with Internet Explorer

How To...

- Use Internet Explorer
- Configure and Use MSN Messenger
- Customize Internet Explorer
- Use the Web Publishing Wizard

Windows Me is designed to be a "Web machine." This means that Windows Me comes to you with everything you need to access and surf the Internet and make use of all the Internet has to offer. In the past, the Internet was quite static—Web pages contained mostly text and some formatting. Today, the Internet is a rich land of multimedia experiences and interactive Web pages. In order to do everything on the Web, your Web browser and multimedia player have to be able to use and understand Web content. Windows Me provides all of this for you, and in this chapter, you learn how to use the Web browser portion of Windows Me—Internet Explorer.

A Quick Glance at Internet Technology

Microsoft Internet Explorer is a Web *browser*. A browser is simply a program your computer uses to access and view Web pages and content. At its core, the Web is made up of HyperText Markup Language (HTML) documents. HTML is a kind of programming language your browser reads to draw and create the nifty Web pages you see. HTML documents are transferred from place to place using the HyperText Transfer Protocol (HTTP). HTTP is a communications protocol that is a part of the Transmission Control Protocol/Internet Protocol (TCP/IP) suite of protocols. These common protocols and programming languages are universally used on the Internet. Now, do you really need to know anything about HTML, HTTP, or TCP/IP to use the Internet? Not at all, which is good news! But, it may help you to know that just as you need Microsoft Word to read a Word document, you need a Web browser to access and read Web pages. Microsoft Internet Explorer is built right into the Windows Me operating system. You can find the Internet Explorer icon (a blue *e*) on your desktop or taskbar. Internet Explorer is integrated with the Windows Me operating system and you cannot uninstall it from your system, which leads us to various debates and lawsuits, as you can read about in the following "Did You Know" box.

Browser Wars

What's the big deal with Microsoft and the Department of Justice? It all started when Netscape and other companies believed that Microsoft was being unfair because Internet Explorer was tied together with the Windows 98 operating system. This, in effect, gave Microsoft an "unfair advantage" in the browser wars between Netscape Navigator and Internet Explorer. This is the controversy that caused all of the lawsuits and DOJ decisions. What does it mean for you? As this hits the press, Microsoft is continuing with business as usual, so Internet Explorer is integrated with Windows Me. This does not at all mean that you cannot use Netscape Navigator. In fact, if you bought Windows Me on a new computer, the computer vendor may have already put Netscape Navigator on the computer for you (see your documentation). If not, you can download Netscape Navigator from **www.netscape.com** and use the browser instead of Internet Explorer if you like—the choice is yours. However, since Internet Explorer is a built-in part of Windows Me, this chapter only covers Internet Explorer usage and configuration. You might ask, "Which browser is best?" That depends on who you ask, but from my point of view, they are both good browsers, and both essentially do the same thing and work the same way.

9

Checking out the Internet Explorer Interface

You can start Internet Explorer by double-clicking on the Internet Explorer icon on your desktop or by clicking on the same icon on your taskbar. This action opens the Web browser and, if you have a dial-up connection to the Internet, probably launches the connection automatically. If you have not configured a connection for your computer, the Internet Connection Wizard appears instead of Internet Explorer. See Chapter 8 to learn how to configure an Internet connection.

One thing you'll notice right away about Internet Explorer is that it looks a lot like any other folder on your computer if you have Web view enabled on your folders (see Chapter 3). This is by design. Microsoft has made Windows Me more integrated with the Internet so that your computer can look and feel more like a Web page. The Internet Explorer browser, like your Web folders, contains several menus across the top, toolbars, and a primary interface area, as shown in Figure 9-1.

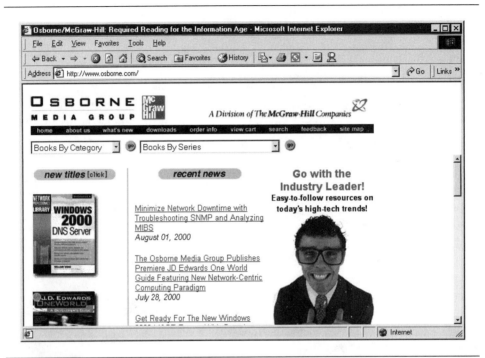

FIGURE 9-1   Internet Explorer enables you to access and view Web pages

At the top of the Internet Explorer window, you see several common menu options, such as File, Edit, View, Favorites, Tools, and Help. These menus are virtually the same as folder menus that you learned about in Chapter 3. However, there are a few differences that are specific to Internet Explorer. The following list summarizes these menu functions and points out major features:

- File—This menu contains typical options, such as Open, Save, Save As, Print, and related file menu options. There is also a Send feature that enables you to send a Web page to a friend via e-mail, send a link to a Web page via e-mail, or create a desktop shortcut to a Web page.

- Edit—The Edit menu contains your typical cut, paste, and copy functions.

- View—The View menu enables you to control how your page is viewed by selecting different font sizes. You can also use this menu to change Internet Explorer's toolbars as desired.

■ Favorites—The Favorites menu contains a few folders of generic favorites and "channels" that Microsoft configures for you. You'll use this menu to add favorites that you want to keep. For example, let's say you find a Web page you really like. You don't have to remember where the Web page is located on the Internet—Favorites can do it for you. Just click Add To Favorites to save the Web page to your Favorites list. The next time you want to visit the page, just click the Favorites menu and click the page title you want to visit.

> **TIP**
> *If you have a lot of favorite items, click Organize Favorites to group them into different favorites folders. This helps keep your favorites organized and easy to locate.*

■ Tools—The Tools menu allows you to send and receive e-mail using Outlook Express (see Chapter 10), synchronize with other Web folders, configure the MSN messenger service (which I'll address in a moment), and access Internet Options, which is the place where you configure Internet Explorer (which I'll also address in this chapter).

■ Help—This option opens the Windows Me help files for Internet Explorer.

Directly below the menus, you see the primary Internet Explorer toolbar. The options you see are fairly intuitive, but the following list tells you about each one:

■ Back—This button returns you to the previous Web page you visited. Think of each Web page as a page in a book. You can move back to previous Web pages using this button.

■ Forward—In the same manner, you can move forward to other Web pages you have visited using this button.

> **NOTE**
> *The Back and Forward buttons apply to your current surfing session. If the Forward button is grayed out, you haven't moved back any pages, so you are not able to more forward. Again, think of your surfing as thumbing through the pages of a book.*

■ Stop—Is a page not downloading correctly or taking too long or have you just changed your mind about wanting to view it? Just click Stop to stop the download process.

9

■ Refresh—Some Web page content changes frequently. Use Refresh to make sure you are looking at the latest version.

■ Home—This button returns you to your desired home page (see the Configuring Internet Explorer through Internet Options section for details).

■ Search—This action opens a search window hosted by the Microsoft Network (MSN). You can then perform a Web search for a topic of your choice.

■ Favorites—This button opens your favorites list in a different window.

■ History—Want to know what Web pages the kids have been visiting? Just click History to view a list of previously visited Web pages. But be aware that you can edit the History by right-clicking a listing and clicking Delete, which your Internet-savvy children probably already know how to do.

TIP *The History list is a good way to find a Web page that you have visited but forgotten the address of.*

■ Send Mail—This option opens an Outlook Express mail message. See Chapter 10 to learn more about Outlook Express.

■ Print—This option prints the current Web page.

■ Edit—You can play around with editing a Web page and changing its content by clicking this button.

■ Discuss—If you want to use discussion and newsgroups, you can click this button to set up a preferred discussion server.

■ MSN Messenger—This option enables you to send and receive instant messages to other users.

■ Address—You can enter the Web address of a site you want to visit in this text box. For example, to visit Microsoft, just type Microsoft.com here and press ENTER. Although all Web addresses require the http://www portion of the address, Internet Explorer will automatically enter this part of the address, or Uniform Resource Locator (URL), in for you. If you want to see a recent list of addresses you have visited, just click the down arrow at the end of the drop-down menu to see a list.

- Go To—You can press this arrow button after you enter a Web address in the Address dialog box. As I said, you can also just press ENTER to go to the Web page, which is probably a lot easier.

- Links—This list, or drop-down menu, depending on your configuration, gives you a set of predefined links, which you can change if you like. The Links bar gives you an easy way to access your favorite pages, just by pointing and clicking. To manage the existing links on the Link bar, just right-click the Web page icon (you can also delete it this way). Do you want to add your own links? Just enter the URL in the Address line, then drag the Web page icon from the Address to your Links bar.

MSN Messenger Service

I have mentioned a couple of times that MSN Messenger service is now available in the Internet Explorer browser. This is a newer feature of Internet Explorer, so I'll spend a moment telling you about it. First off, MSN (the Microsoft Network) is both an Internet search engine and an Internet Service Provider (ISP). You can visit **msn.com** and read news, information, and search the Web. You can also sign up with MSN and, for a monthly fee, MSN will be your ISP—your on-ramp to the Internet.

MSN and Windows Me

You'll see MSN pop up from time to time and in various places in Windows Me—including the Windows Me help files. It seems that Microsoft is using Windows Me to help advertise MSN—after all, there are a lot of Windows Me customers out there who are potential MSN customers. You'll definitely get the feeling that Microsoft would like you to be an MSN customer, but you don't have to use Microsoft's ISP to make the best use of the Windows Me Internet. (I'm sure this tactic is going to aggravate many of the other ISPs out there who may again start screaming "unfair business practices!")

MSN Messenger Service is included in Windows Me, and you do not have to be an MSN ISP customer to use the service. In a nutshell, this service allows you to directly communicate with other MSN Messenger service participants. It is a quick and easy way to bypass your typical static e-mail. You can talk back and forth instantly and even use voice over the Internet instead of text. You can send files and pictures to others using this service, and MSN Messenger Service users can even use the service via Web-enabled telephones. Overall, it's a cool service that you'll want to check out.

Setting Up MSN Messenger Service

To set up MSN Messenger Service, just click the MSN icon on your Internet Explorer toolbar, then follow these easy steps:

1. When you click the MSN Messenger icon, the Welcome screen appears, shown in Figure 9-2. You can click the Click For More Information button to read more about MSN Messenger, or just click Next to continue.

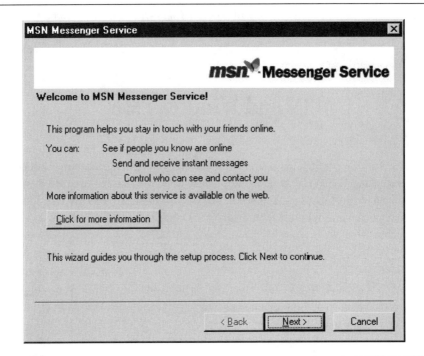

FIGURE 9-2   MSN Messenger Welcome screen

2. You need a Microsoft Passport to use this service. The Passport is free. If you already have a free Hotmail account, just use your account name and password. If you don't, click the Get A Passport button. This opens another Internet Explorer window in which you complete an application page to get a passport. Follow the instructions that appear and, once you have a passport, continue with MSN Messenger setup.

3. Enter your Passport name and password, then click Next.

4. Click Finish.

MSN Messenger sets up on your computer and the MSN Messenger Service appears, as shown in Figure 9-3. You may be prompted to download the latest

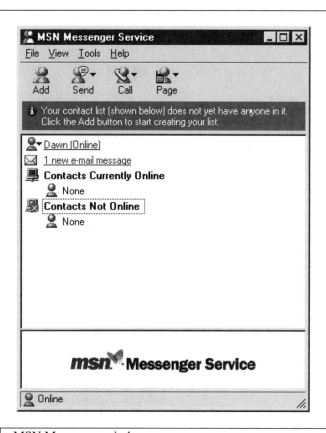

FIGURE 9-3   MSN Messenger window

version of MSN Messenger, and you should choose to do so in order to take advantage of the latest features.

Using MSN Messenger Service

As you can see in Figure 9-3, the MSN Messenger Service window is an easy, scaled down window option with a few buttons. You can use the window to add new contacts with either an MSN or Hotmail account or you can set up a Microsoft Passport to send and receive messages. The window tells you which of your contacts are currently online and which are not. Messages are automatically displayed in the window as you receive them. This feature lets you talk back and forth instantly. You can also place a phone call or call a pager number from the MSN Messenger window. As you can see, using MSN Messenger is very

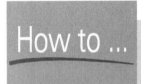 **Change Your MSN Messenger Profile**

Let's say some things change in your life and you need to update your MSN Messenger profile, or you just want to change what other MSN Messenger users can view about you. It's easy to change your profile, and here's how:

1. In MSN Messenger, click the Tools menu, then click Options.

2. On the Personal tab, click the Edit Profile button.

3. This action opens an Internet Explorer window that takes you to your account on the Microsoft Passport site.

4. Examine the information in your account and change it directly on the Web page as desired.

easy—just play around with it, get some of your friends signed up and online, and see how you like it!

| TIP | *If you are using your computer with MSN Messenger turned on and you need to step away for a moment, you can let your friends know you are away from your computer. Just click File, point to My Status, and a list of options appear, such as "out to lunch, be right back, on the phone." Your MSN Messenger friends will see your status and know you are unavailable at the moment!* |

Configuring Internet Explorer through Internet Options

You can make changes to the way Internet Explorer behaves so that the application meets your specific needs. You have a variety of useful options, and I'll guide you through them so you can decide which ones are the best for you. You can configure Internet Explorer through Internet Options, which is in your Tools menu. There are six different configuration tabs in Internet Options, and the following sections show you what you can do on each tab.

General Tab

The General tab, shown in Figure 9-4, contains three major categories: Home Page, Temporary Internet Files, and History.

The Home Page section simply allows you to choose the Internet site that Internet Explorer will connect to as a default site. Whenever you open Internet Explorer, it will always connect to this site first. If you want to change the site, just type a new site in the dialog box. If you don't want to use a home page, just click the Use Blank button.

The Temporary Internet Files section allows you to determine how temporary Internet pages are stored. When you surf the Web, your computer stores pages that you visit in a temporary folder. This speeds up your access to those pages when you revisit them. You can change the default options by clicking the Settings

9

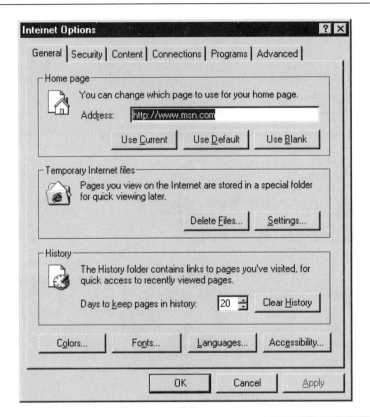

FIGURE 9-4 The General tab contains Home Page, Temporary Internet Files, and History settings

button. This opens a Settings window, shown in Figure 9-5, where you can adjust how Internet Explorer uses the temporary pages.

By default, Internet Explorer automatically checks for new material. This setting ensures you that you are looking at the most current version of the Web page, and I recommend you leave this setting as the default. You can also adjust the amount of disk space that is used for temporary Internet files (the default is 128MB). You can increase this setting if you like, but 128MB is quite a bit of storage just for temporary Internet files, and this is probably all the space you need.

You can also use the buttons at the bottom of the Settings window to view your temporary Internet files and objects and move the temp folder to a different location on your computer (which doesn't help anything, so its best to just leave it alone).

FIGURE 9-5   Use this window to change the default temporary Internet page settings

Finally, there is a History section. Remember that History lists the sites that have been visited by Internet Explorer. By default, Internet Explorer keeps a history listing for 20 days—in other words, every site that has been visited in the last 20 days will appear. You can change the period of time a history is kept depending on your individual needs; you can also click the Clear History button to clean out current history items.

At the bottom of the General tab, there are buttons labeled Colors, Fonts, Languages, and Accessibility. These options enable you to change the way Internet Explorer looks and displays Web pages. These options are self-explanatory, so check them out if you want to make appearance changes.

Security Tab

The Security tab allows you to configure how Internet Explorer handles Internet or Intranet sites, as shown in Figure 9-6. A typical home user does not need to make any configuration changes on this tab. By default, the Internet option (shown in Figure 9-6) is set to Medium. This setting gives you all of the browser

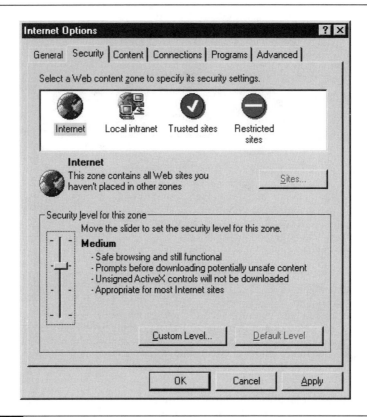

FIGURE 9-6   Use the Security tab to manage the way Internet Explore handles browsing security

functionality but prompts you before downloading questionable content. You can change this behavior by moving the slider bar to different settings. Each slider bar movement gives an explanation of how the browser behaves. Typically, however, the Medium setting is best.

You can also use the Trusted Sites or Restricted Sites option, if you desire. These options enable you to list sites that you know are safe or sites that you know are questionable. This, in turn, affects how your browser acts when handling these sites.

Content Tab

The Content tab allows you to configure how Internet Explorer manages different kinds of content from the Internet as well as information about you. There are three sections on this tab: Content Advisor, Certificates, and Personal Information, as shown in Figure 9-7.

The Content Advisor section allows you to manage how (and if) Internet Explorer handles different kinds of potentially offensive Web content. If you click the Enable button, you see a Content Advisor window, as shown in Figure 9-8.

You see different categories of potentially offensive material. You can use the slider bar to adjust the level of offensive content that users are able to view. This feature is great if you have children who use the Internet on your computer. You can enable this feature to try and prevent accidental access to offensive Web content.

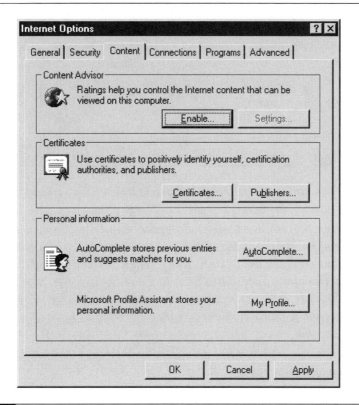

9

FIGURE 9-7 Use the Content tab to manage the way Internet Explorer handles Web content

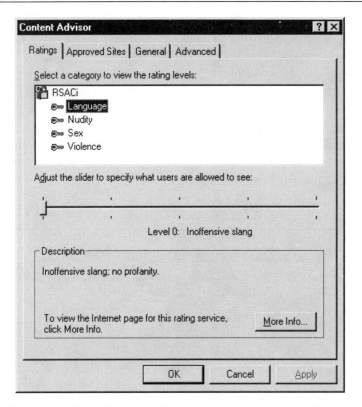

FIGURE 9-8 Use the Content Advisor to control offensive Web content

CAUTION *These settings are not foolproof. Internet Explorer examines the requested Web site for keywords that provide clues about offensive content. Internet Explorer can also use a site's rating system to determine if it is safe. As you might guess, a lot of this is up to the individual site, so don't think that your kids are safe just because you enable these settings. You still need to monitor them, and you might consider investing in some other third-party software that can also help manage access to offensive Web sites.*

Once you make some settings decisions, click Apply, and Windows Me will prompt you to enter a password. This prevents other users of your computer from changing the content settings. Also note that you can access the other Content Advisor tabs to create a list of approved sites, and you can make some basic changes on the General and Advanced tabs. Normally, however, you don't need to use these tabs; if you do, you'll find them self-explanatory.

The second part of the Content tab is Certificates. In some organizations, Internet Explorer is configured to use various digital certificates in order to verify certain Web site authenticity. Home users do not use certificate options, so you don't need to configure anything here, although there may be circumstances where you want to use a digital certificate to communicate with a highly secure Web site. If this is the case, you will need to follow that Web site's instructions about obtaining and using a digital certificate.

Finally, you can use the Personal Information section of the Content tab to change or turn off AutoComplete. Internet Explorer tries to learn what Web sites and information you enter into Web pages. If Internet Explorer recognizes what you are typing, it will try to complete it for you. You may find this helpful or aggravating, depending on your point of view. At any rate, you can click the AutoComplete button to change the behavior. This button opens another window with some simple check box options you can consider. Also, there is a My Profile button; click this to change personal information about yourself that Internet Explorer keeps.

9

Connections Tab

The Connections tab, shown in Figure 9-9, lists any Internet connections you have configured on your computer. You normally do not need to configure anything on this tab because you configure these options when you create a dial-up connection (see Chapter 8). However, you can use this tab to specifically tell Internet Explorer what connection to use if your computer has multiple connections. If you are on a network where your computer accesses another network computer to reach the Internet (a proxy server), you may need to perform some configuration here. Refer to your network administrator for specific setting information.

Programs Tab

The Programs tab, shown in Figure 9-10, allows you to pick which Windows Me programs perform which Web functions. For example, by default, Internet Explorer uses Outlook Express for Internet mail (in other words, if you are visiting a Web page and click a Send E-mail link, Internet Explorer opens an Outlook Express mail message). However, you may want to use a different mail client that you have installed on your computer. You can use the Programs tab to change the applications that Internet Explorer uses for HTML editor, e-mail, newsgroups, Internet call, calendar, and contacts list. If you plan on using both Internet Explorer and Outlook Express, you won't need to change any of these settings.

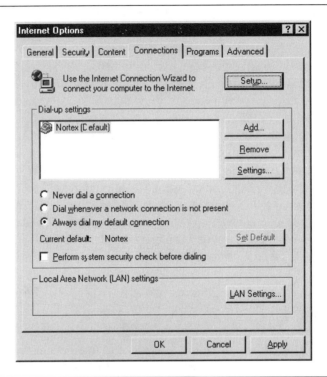

FIGURE 9-9   You can manage connections from this tab

Network Connections to the Internet

Most business networks do not maintain individual connections for each network computer. Instead, the network computers access the Internet through a proxy server. This proxy connects to the Internet and retrieves information for the client computers. In most cases, the proxy server contains additional security and content settings. These network environments may also use a *firewall*, which can either be hardware or software that ensures (hopefully) that no Internet interlopers gain access to the private network from the Internet. As you can see, Internet access can be quite an issue for network administrators.

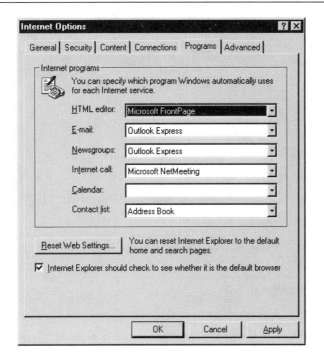

FIGURE 9-10   Use the Programs tab to change the default applications that Internet Explorer uses

Advanced Tab

The Advanced Tab contains a bunch of check box options for a variety of processes. For example, you can change some browsing behavior, multimedia settings, printing settings, and so forth, just by checking or unchecking different options, as shown in Figure 9-11.

The real question, of course, is what do you need to change? In reality, under most circumstances, nothing. Do not start making changes on this tab unless you have a specific goal in mind. For example, Internet Explorer does not print background colors and images on Web pages in an attempt not to burn up your color ink cartridge on unnecessary graphics. However, if you want Internet Explorer to print them anyway, you can click the Print Background Colors And Images check box under Printing. The key is to identify a goal you want to accomplish, then see if you can enable or disable that option on the Advanced tab. The most common settings are already configured for you.

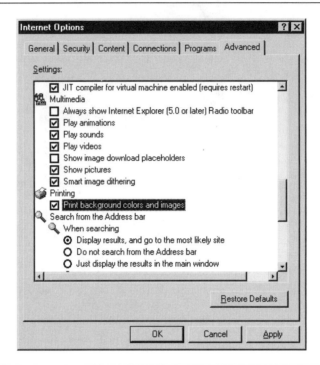

FIGURE 9-11   Use the check boxes on this tab to make configuration changes

If you choose to ignore your wise author's advice and change a bunch of these settings, you can click the Restore Defaults button to put everything back to the original settings.

Using the Web Publishing Wizard

Along with Internet Explorer, Windows Me includes a related tool called the Web Publishing Wizard, which you can find in Accessories under Internet Tools. Often, ISPs give their customers a certain amount of server Web space. This means that you have a block of space on their server's hard drive where you can post Web pages and pictures. Friends and family can then access the Web address and view your files on the Internet. The Web Publishing Wizard can help you set up your Web space.

Another example of when to use the Web Publishing Wizard is an intranet Web server. If you have a small company that uses an intranet and you want to send files and folders to an address on that server, you can use the Web Publishing Wizard to accomplish this task.

Basically, all the Web Publishing Wizard does is gather information about what files you want to publish and the Web server you want to publish them to. The Web Publishing Wizard then takes this information, connects to the Web server, authenticates with it, then transfers the files you indicated should be transferred to the Web server. This makes the process easier for you. In order to use the Web Publishing Wizard, you'll need information from your ISP or intranet server on how to access the Web server so you can transfer your files to it. Once you have this information, just start the Web Publishing Wizard, enter the information as requested, and let Windows Me handle the rest for you.

9

Chapter 10

Using E-mail with Outlook Express

How To...

- ■ Set Up Outlook Express
- ■ Send and Receive E-mail
- ■ Configure Interface Views
- ■ Create and Manage Message Rules
- ■ Customize Outlook Express
- ■ Use the Address Book

Electronic mail, or e-mail, has become so commonplace, it's easy to forget that it has only been widely used for the past few years. Today, millions of people send e-mail messages both for work and play every day. In order to send and receive e-mail messages, your computer must use an "e-mail client," which is software that sends, receives, and manages e-mail. In Windows Me, that software is Outlook Express. Like Internet Explorer, Outlook Express is built right into your Windows Me operating system. In this chapter, I'll show you how to set up and use Outlook Express so you can be a part of the e-mail revolution!

A Quick Glance at E-mail Technology

Primarily, e-mail is sent over the Internet to a specific person or group of people, although businesses and organizations also send e-mail over their local networks. Like everything else on the Internet, e-mail uses TCP/IP, the default protocol used for Internet communications. Typically, e-mail uses Simple Mail Transfer Protocol (SMTP) to move mail from one place to another.

An e-mail address is made up of a user name and a domain name, such as *myname@mydomain.com*. When you send an e-mail to someone, e-mail servers first examine the mydomain.com portion of the address to find a mydomain.com server. Once this server is located, the mail is sent to the server, which recognizes mydomain.com as its own domain. It then examines the user name to see if there is a user by that name. If myname is in fact a user, the mail is held on the server until it is downloaded. If not, it is sent back to the sender with a "user unknown" message. In many respects, e-mail is just like regular mail: your address is inspected by the main post office to route a letter to your local post office, and then your name is inspected by your local post office to make sure it gets to your personal mailbox.

Of course, e-mail is a lot faster. You can send a message to any e-mail address anywhere in the world and it normally arrives in less than a few minutes. Also, you can send any kind of electronic file as an attachment—pictures, documents, video, applications, you name it.

Setting Up Outlook Express

When you install Windows Me, Outlook Express is installed by default, and the Outlook Express icon is displayed on your taskbar—it looks like a letter with blue arrows wrapped around it. To use Outlook Express, however, you will need to set up your mail account so Outlook Express will know how to connect to a mail server to send and receive e-mail. This information is available from your ISP.

You probably received printed instructions about setting up your computer for a connection to the Internet from your ISP (see Chapter 8). Once you have made this connection, you then use your documentation to set up Outlook Express. As with Internet Explorer, I would like to note here that you do not have to use Outlook Express in order to send and receive e-mail with Windows Me. You can use Netscape, Eudora, or some other mail client. However, this chapter only focuses on Outlook Express because it is included with your operating system.

To start the setup process, just click the Outlook Express icon on your taskbar. Outlook Express opens, and the Internet Connection Wizard will appear. The Internet Connection Wizard will guide you through a series of steps, collecting information about you and your ISP. You'll need to think of a user name and password and have e-mail server information from your ISP that is typically provided in documentation you receive when you sign-up with the ISP. Get this information ready, then follow these easy steps to complete the wizard and set up your e-mail account with Outlook Express:

10

TIP   *If the Internet Connection Wizard does not start when you open Outlook Express, click the Tools menu, then click Accounts. Click the Mail tab, then click Add, then click Mail. This will start the Internet Connection Wizard.*

1. Enter your display name. This is the name that you want other e-mail users to see when you send mail. Typically, you should use your real name here and not something that can't be recognized, such as "Biker Dad" or "Sweet Cakes."

2. In the Internet E-mail Address screen, shown in Figure 10-1, you can choose to use an existing account or you can set up a free Web-based e-mail account on the Internet with Hotmail, which is a part of MSN. If you are using an ISP, you are probably going to select the first radio button. If your ISP does not give you an e-mail account, choose the second option. If you click the second option, the Internet Connection Wizard finishes and you are taken to the Hotmail site to register. If you want to use an existing account, enter your e-mail address in the provided dialog box and click Next.

Hotmail is not the only free Web-based e-mail that is available. Yahoo.com, Netscape.com, Go.com, and many others also offer free e-mail accounts.

3. In the E-mail Server Names screen, you'll need to enter your e-mail server information, as shown in Figure 10-2. Almost all e-mail servers use POP3 (Post Office Protocol) to manage e-mail messages. Outlook Express needs to know if your server is a POP3 server or a different kind of server, such as IMAP or HTTP. Check your ISP documentation and fill in the appropriate type of server. Then, in the next text boxes, enter the incoming mail server name and outgoing mail server name. Typically, both of these

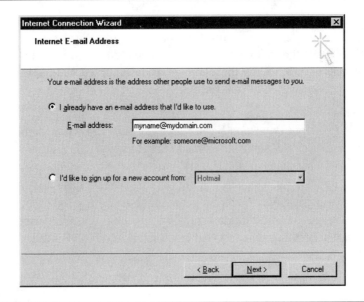

FIGURE 10-1   Select an existing or Web-based e-mail account

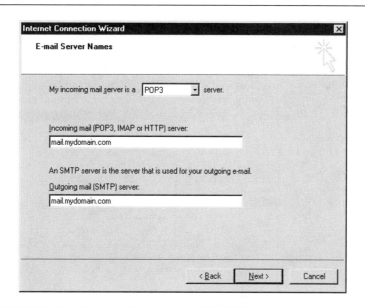

FIGURE 10-2   Select the type of mail server and enter the mail server name

names will be in the form of *mail.mydomain.com*. You'll need to check your ISP documentation to know for sure. Enter the correct information, then click Next.

4. In the Logon and Password window, enter your logon name and your password. Check your ISP documentation to make certain you are entering the correct information, and remember that passwords are case sensitive. Also, you should not check the secure password authentication check box at the bottom of the window unless your ISP documentation explicitly tells you to do so.

5. Click Finish to complete the Internet Connection Wizard.

Checking Out the Outlook Express Interface

Outlook Express provides an easy to read and easy to use interface with which you can quickly view mail messages. By default, Outlook Express uses four major panes to separate different mail components. These four panes, or views, make using e-mail easy, but you can customize this interface as well (I will show you how to do this later in this chapter). Figure 10-3 gives you a look at the default Outlook Express interface.

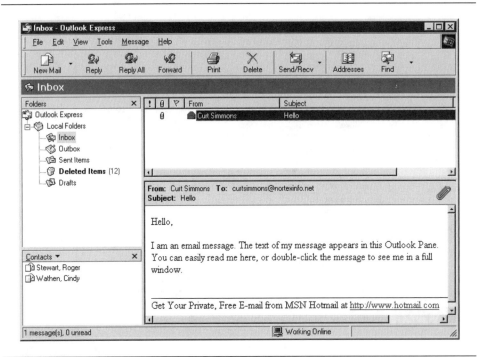

FIGURE 10-3   The Outlook Express interface is made up of menus and panes

First let's take a look at your menu options. At the top of Outlook Express window, you see common menus, such as File, Edit, View, Tools, etc. The standard options appear on these menus, such as open, save, cut, and paste, but there are also quite a few Outlook Express specifics. The following list highlights the most important features:

- **File**—You use this menu to perform standard open and save functions, but you can also create additional mail folders in which you can store mail. In addition, you can import and export mail settings, messages, and address books to and from other e-mail programs. You can also use this File menu to establish different identities. This way, two different people can send and receive mail using a single Outlook Express program. All of these options are easy and self-explanatory.

- **Edit**—You use this menu to delete e-mail, copy and move e-mail between folders, mark e-mail messages in various ways, and perform other standard editing features.

- View—You use this menu to change how current messages are viewed as well as the entire Outlook Express interface. See the "Changing Outlook Express Views" section later in this chapter for more information.

- Tools—This menu allows you to send and receive e-mail, configure message rules, and customize Outlook Express. All of these items are explored in more detail later in this chapter.

- Message—This menu contains typical message functions, most of which you can perform using a toolbar button. You can, however, use this menu to "watch" messages or discussions. You can use Outlook Express to connect to newsgroups where you can flag messages so you can watch the message and all its replies. This is a great way to organize and keep track of information that is useful to you. Check out the Outlook Express Help files to learn more about message watching.

- Help—Use this menu to get help from the Outlook Express help files or the Microsoft Web site.

Below the menu options appears the standard Outlook Express toolbar. You'll use this toolbar quite a bit when working with Outlook Express. It includes the following standard buttons:

10

- New Mail—Click this button to start a new mail message.

- Reply—Select a message and click this button to reply to a message.

- Reply All—Select a message and click this button to reply to all the people that the message was originally sent to.

- Forward—Select a message and click this button to forward the message to someone else.

- Print—Select a message and click this button to print the message.

- Delete—Select a message and click this button to delete it.

- Send/Receive—Click this button to send or receive messages.

- Addresses—Click this button to open the Address Book.

- Find—Click this button to find specific messages. You can search by sender, message subject, or keywords.

The final portion of the Outlook Express interface is the four primary panes, which are as follows:

- **Folders**—The top left pane shows your Outlook Express folder structure. You can easily move between your inbox, outbox, sent items, deleted items, as well as additional folders that you can create using the file menu.

- **Contacts**—The bottom left pane shows your contacts. Contacts are people you have sent e-mail to. Outlook Express keeps up with your contacts and their e-mail addresses by maintaining this list for you.

- **New Mail**—The top right pane contains a message list. These are messages that you have received but not deleted.

- **Preview**—The bottom right pane contains the text of the selected message. This is an easy "preview" view of the message so you can read through your messages without actually opening them.

Sending and Receiving E-mail

Once you have an account set up, you can send and receive e-mail. Sending and receiving e-mail is very easy, and the following sections show you how to do it.

Sending an E-mail

To send a new e-mail message, just click the New Mail button on your toolbar. A new mail message appears, shown in Figure 10-4. To send a new mail message, type the recipient's e-mail address in the To box, type any additional e-mail addresses in the Cc box if you want other individuals copied, enter a subject, type your message in the provided message box, and then click the Send button on the toolbar—it's that easy!

TIP   *When you enter a subject, be as descriptive as possible. E-mail users often get many e-mails in a given day. Descriptive subjects help identify important messages. Also, if you message is very important, you can attach a High Priority notification with it. Just click Message | Set Priority | High.*

FIGURE 10-4   Use this easy interface to create new mail messages

Message Editing

Outlook Express supports advanced message-editing features. As you are typing your new message, notice that you have bold, italic, bullet lists, and other button features on the message toolbar. You can also cut, copy, and paste message text as well. You can use the Format menu to use different color styles in your message and even use a background picture or graphic. You can also check your message for spelling errors by clicking the Tools menu, then clicking Spelling. All of these features are really nice, but do be aware that not all mail clients can receive these formatting features, except, of course, Outlook Express. Even though you style your text and add a background, some of your recipients may only see plain text.

When you're finished with your message, just click the Send button. You can now type another message if you would like. If you are currently connected to the Internet, the message is immediately sent. If you are not currently connected to the Internet, click the Send/Recv button on your Outlook Express toolbar. This launches an Internet dial-up connection so the message can be sent.

Attaching a File to an E-mail

If you want to send an e-mail with an attachment, which is just a file of some kind, you can easily do so. Just click the New Mail button on your Outlook Express toolbar, then follow these steps:

1. Enter the recipient's e-mail address, a Cc address if desired, a subject, and type a message to the recipient.

2. To attach a file, click the Insert menu and click either File Attachment or Picture. Or just click the paper clip icon on your taskbar.

3. A browse window appears. Browse to the location of the file, then select it.

4. Click the Attach button. The file now appears in your New Message window as an attachment, shown in Figure 10-5.

FIGURE 10-5   Attach a file to your message with the Insert menu

SHORTCUT
Want to know an easier way to attach a file to message? Just shrink your message window so you can see your desktop, then locate the file you want to include. Drag the file into the message portion of the window. It will appear in the Attachment line.

TIP
Before sending an attachment, you should consider putting the attachment(s) in a new folder and compressing the folder. This makes your transmission time shorter. To learn more about folder compression, see Chapter 4.

Receiving Messages

When you are ready to check for messages, just open Outlook Express and click the Send/Recv button on your toolbar. This launches an Internet connection if you are not already connected so mail can be downloaded to your computer. New messages appear in the New Message pane. If you click each message, you can read its text in the Preview pane. You can also double-click a message and read it in its own message window. Once you have received and read your messages, you can delete them or drag them to a desired folder for safekeeping.

10

TIP
A great feature of Outlook Express is that deleted messages aren't really deleted—they are just moved to the Deleted Items folder. You can click this folder and find a message that has been previously deleted and reread it. You can also right-click the Deleted Items folder and click Empty "Deleted Items" Folder to permanently delete the items, but I don't recommend you do this. Invariably, you will need to refer to a mail item you thought you no longer needed.

Receiving Attachments

Any attachments that are sent to you are automatically downloaded with the mail message. Messages that have attachments have a small paper clip displayed beside them in the New Message pane. In the preview pane, you see a larger paperclip on the right side of the window. If you click the paper click, a pop-up menu appears where you can either open the attachment or save it to your computer (such as in the My Documents folder or on your desktop), as shown in Figure 10-6.

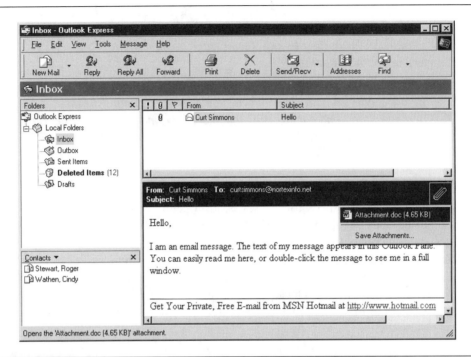

FIGURE 10-6   Click the paperclip button to get an e-mail attachment

Did you know?

Setting the Record Straight about E-mail and Viruses

There's a lot of talk and confusion about computer viruses and e-mail—and rightfully so. Computers do get viruses from e-mail. However, it is important to note that you cannot get a computer virus from the text of an e-mail. For example, let's say you download your mail, you select a message, and its contents appear in the Preview pane. Let's say you even open the message and read it. You cannot get a computer virus this way. Computer viruses always come in the form of some kind of attachment. Opening an attachment can give your computer a virus. Virus attachments normally contain some kind of executable code that launches on your computer and does all kind of annoying and nasty things. In short, don't open attachments from someone you don't know. Also, watch for the .exe. or .vbs extensions on attachments (such as *attachmentname.exe* or *attachmentname.vbs*). These are executable files and are more likely to contain viruses than other attachments, such as a picture file. There are also "macro" viruses that can hide within word processing documents, such as a Microsoft Word document. All major brands of antivirus software include an e-mail scan feature that can check your e-mail attachments for viruses before you open them. This software is very inexpensive and a great investment.

Changing Outlook Express Views

As we have discussed, Outlook Express has a four-pane option that I think is great. However, you may not think it's so great and want to change it. That's fine and easy to do as well. To change the appearance of the Outlook Express interface, just click the View menu and click Layout. A single layout window appears, as shown in Figure 10-7.

10

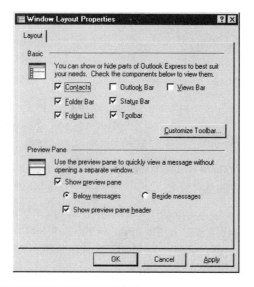

FIGURE 10-7   Use the Layout window to change the interface appearance

As you can see, you have two sections: basic and preview pane. You can select or clear the various check boxes to use or not use the different panes. Try different settings to find the one that you like best. Also, if you click Customize Toolbar, you can add other toolbar icon features, which are discussed in more detail in Chapter 4.

Aside from using the Layout feature, you can also customize the current view, which allows you to determine which messages are displayed and which are hidden. You can use different views by clicking View | Current View and selecting an option from the submenu. As with an appearance configuration, you may need to play around with the settings to find the ones that are right for you.

Creating Message Rules

Message rules let you control how various messages are handled by Outlook Express. Message rules are most helpful to people that receive a lot of e-mail or who receive a lot of "spam," or junk e-mail. You can set up rules to help you manage messages so that Outlook Express can automatically delete certain messages or move certain messages to other folders.

Rules are easy to create, but be careful of overdoing it. Too many rules usually become more confusing than helpful, so plan carefully before you create a bunch of e-mail rules. Make sure you have a specific reason for a rule or specific problem you want the rule to solve.

Creating a New Rule

To create a new rule, just follow these easy steps:

1. In Outlook Express, click Tools | Message Rules | Mail.

2. The New Mail Rule window appears, as shown in Figure 10-8. In the top portion of the window, select a condition for your rule. Scroll through the list and click the check box next to the desired condition.

3. In the second portion of the window, select an action for your condition. Scroll through the list and click the check box next to the desired action.

4. Depending on your selection, you may need to enter a rule description or perform some editing. If a link appears (blue, underlined wording), click on it to enter the additional information that is needed for the rule.

5. In the bottom of the window, give the rule a friendly name, then click OK.

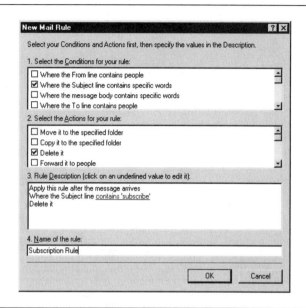

FIGURE 10-8   Use the New Mail Rule window to create new mail rules

Managing Message Rules

Once you create message rules, you can manage them from the same Mail Rules interface. Just click Tools | Message Rules | Mail. A window appears listing your current rules. You can use the provided buttons to create new rules, delete existing rules, edit existing rules, and perform related management features. This interface is very easy to use and self-explanatory.

Blocking Senders

Let's say you meet Chatty Cathy in a chat room and you make the mistake of giving Chatty Cathy your personal e-mail address. Now Chatty Cathy writes to you everyday and sends you piles of junk mail. You decide you really don't like Chatty Cathy and you don't want any more mail from her. What to do? No problem. You can block Chatty Cathy so that your computer automatically moves Chatty Cathy's mail to the Deleted Items folder without informing you of the mail.

To use the Block Senders option, just click Tools | Message Rules | Block Senders List. A simple window appears. Click the Add button and enter the e-mail address of the sender you want to block and click OK. The sender appears in the Blocked Senders list, shown in Figure 10-9. You can modify this list at any time.

FIGURE 10-9   Use the Block Senders List to automatically move a sender's e-mail to the Deleted Items folder

Managing Your Accounts

When you first begin using Outlook Express, you set up an account so that your computer can send and receive e-mail from your ISP. Over time, that account information may change or you may need to add other accounts. You can make changes to your accounts by clicking Tools | Accounts. This action opens a window where you can view your current mail account, news account, or even directory service account. Use the provided buttons to create a new account, edit an existing one, and perform other related account management tasks. Before making changes to an account or creating a new one, remember that you will need information from your ISP on the correct user name, password, and e-mail server information.

Customizing Outlook Express

Outlook Express contains quite a few customization options that you can access by clicking Tools | Options. There are several tabs, but the good news is that each tab is rather easy to use. Most simply give you a list of check box options to choose from. The next list gives you an overview of what you can do on each tab. Remember, one of the best ways to find the settings that work for you is to experiment with them—you can always change them later if you don't like them.

■ General—This tab contains information about the way your computer receives messages. The default options are all you need on most of this tab. If you want Outlook Express to automatically check for messages by launching a dial-up connection at specified intervals, you can select the option on this tab and enter the amount of time you want between checks (such as 30 minutes or so).

■ Read—This tab contains settings for messages you have received. You can choose to view messages in various colors and fonts.

■ Receipts—Some messages you receive (or send) can request a receipt, which is return e-mail notification that the message was read. Use this tab to enable this feature and determine how it should be used.

■ Send—This tab contains basic settings for sending messages. Almost all options are enabled by default, and you should probably keep these options enabled for the best functionality.

■ Compose—Use this tab to select font and business card settings and attach stationery to your e-mail messages. Remember that not all mail clients can read these style features.

■ Signatures—You can automatically add a signature, such as your name and phone number, to all new messages you type. Use this tab to enter the signature text.

■ Spelling—Use this tab to enable automatic spelling and spell settings.

■ Security—If you use encrypted mail with digital certificates (and you probably don't), you use this tab to enable the option.

■ Connection—This tab contains information about your dial-up connection. One item of interest here is that you can tell Outlook Express to automatically hang up the dial-up connection once mail has been sent and received. If you use the General tab to automatically dial a connection to get mail, you should use this option on the Connection tab so those dial-out sessions will be automatically terminated (unless you want your computer tying up the phone line all day).

■ Maintenance—This tab contains options for Outlook Express to handle deleted items. The default settings are all you need here.

10

Using the Address Book

A great feature of Outlook Express is the Address Book. You can use the Address Book to store e-mail addresses as well as postal address, phone numbers, and all kinds of other information. The Address Book is fully searchable and easy to use.

You can access the Address Book by clicking on the Addresses icon on the Outlook Express taskbar. The Address Book provides you with a simple interface listing your contacts or groups, as shown in Figure 10-10.

Adding a Contact

You can easily add a contact to the Address Book by clicking the New button on the toolbar and clicking Contact. A Properties window appears, as shown in Figure 10-11, in which you can enter the contact's information. Notice there are several tabs where you can enter all kinds of information. You only need to complete the tabs you want, and you can enter very little or a lot of information about each contact as desired. When you have entered all of the desired information, just click OK. The new contact will be added to your contacts list.

You can use the same New feature to create a group. You can use the group feature to group your contacts as needed. Many users create a Distribution List of people to whom they send fun e-mail. When you want to send the group a message, just enter the group name on the To line of your new mail message and everyone in the group will receive the e-mail. If you e-mail a lot of people, this feature can make your life much easier.

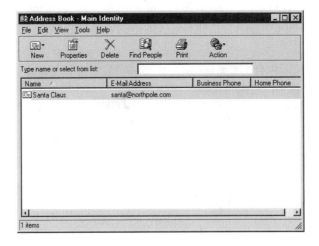

FIGURE 10-10   Use the Address Book to keep track of people

Porky Pig Properties

Name | Home | Business | Personal | Other | NetMeeting | Digital IC's

Enter name and e-mail information about this contact here.

First: Porky Middle: [ ] Last: Pig

Title: [ ] Display: Porky Pig Nickname: [ ]

E-Mail Addresses: porkypig@cartoons.com [Add]

[Edit]
[Remove]
[Set as Default]

☐ Send E-Mail using plain text only.

[OK] [Cancel]

FIGURE 10-11 Enter the desired information for the contact and click OK

10

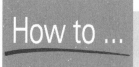

How to ... Add Members to a Group

Once you have created a new group, you can easily add and remove members at any time. Just follow these steps:

1. Locate the group in your Address List.

2. Double-click the group icon to open the group.

3. Click the New Contact button, enter the contact's name and e-mail address, and click the Add button.

4. Repeat Step 3 to add more contacts to the group.

5. You can remove any contact in the group by right-clicking on the contact in the contacts window and clicking Delete.

6. Click OK when you're done.

Managing Addresses

As you can see, you can easily manage your Address Book by using the buttons on the toolbar. You can add new contacts or groups at any time, delete contacts or groups, launch a mail message from the Address Book, find contacts, and print the list. If you need to change a contact's information, just select the contact in the list and click Properties. You can then make changes as needed. All of these features are quick and easy.

Chapter 11

Networking with Windows Me

How To...

- Get Ready to Create a Home Network

- Plan Your Network

- Create Your Network

- Use Internet Connection Sharing

- Use My Network Places

- Use a Direct Cable Connection

Computer networks have been in use for years, even before any of us ever had a home PC. Computer networking has changed a lot during that time—it has become more important and, in many ways, it is easier than ever before. Only in the past year or so, however, has home networking become so important. It used to be that users had no need for a home network because the typical home had only one PC. All of that is changing today as the number of homes with two or more PCs is quickly growing. Do you need to share a printer? How about an Internet connection? Do you need to share files and applications? You can do all of this and more with home networking. Windows Me is designed to be a home networking machine. Never before has home networking been so easy, and in this chapter, you learn how to set up a home network using Windows Me.

Windows Networking Basics

Before you jump into home networking, you need to know a few basics about what it takes to create a home network. Networks require both hardware and software in order for your computer to communicate with another computer. First, each computer on the network has to be equipped with a network adapter card. Like a sound or a video card, a network adapter card is an internal card that fits into an expansion slot on your computer. The network adapter card allows information to flow to and from your computer. In the past, a special cable, usually an RJ45 cable (which looks like a large telephone cable), connected to the network adapter card. The cables from all of the computers connected through a device called a *hub*, which is a small piece of hardware with a bunch of ports. The hub routed information to and from computers so that the information traveled to the right one.

Now, if all that sounds a little overwhelming, don't worry. You can still use standard networking cabling and hubs if you want (I do), and they're not terribly expensive. However, with the growth of home networking, a number of solutions are available in which cabling and a hub are not needed. For example, you can purchase network adapter cards that plug into your phone jacks, and the computers will use the existing phone wiring in your house to communicate with each other at no expense or interruption to you. Some versions also use power outlets and even wireless technology so your PCs and peripherals can communicate with each other. The key is to shop around and find a solution (and dollar amount) that works best for you.

Many new computers come equipped with a standard network adapter card when you purchase them. Check your computer documentation to find out.

Besides the hardware, your Windows Me software must also be configured for networking. This includes turning on Microsoft file and printer sharing and configuring the TCP/IP protocol so that computers can understand each other. Fortunately, Windows Me helps set up these components with the new Home Networking Wizard (which we'll explore later in this chapter), so this is not a painful process.

11

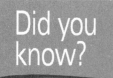

Configuring TCP/IP

TCP/IP is an advanced topic that gives even network administrators severe headaches from time to time. Fortunately, Windows operating systems have evolved to help humans deal with TCP/IP. In a TCP/IP network, each computer must have a unique IP address, which is a series of numbers, such as 131.107.2.200. In order for computers to communicate, you must configure each computer with an appropriate IP address in the same IP class as the other computers. (Actually, this is just a brief overview and it's even more complicated than this!) Windows Me, like Windows 98, can give itself a private IP address in an appropriate range reserved for small networks. Windows Me does all the work and you don't have to do anything, which is really nice!

Getting Ready for Home Networking

So, you want a home network. Before trying to configure your Windows Me computer, you have a few tasks to complete to make sure your home networking experience will be a positive one. I've arranged these tasks into a quick and easy step-by-step format, but make sure you perform these steps before moving to the next section in this chapter.

1. If you have one Windows Me computer, it needs to be the primary computer. For example, if you are using Windows Me and another computer uses Windows 95 or 98, Windows Me will be the primary computer on your network (sorry, using Windows 3.x is not supported). Shared peripherals, such as a printer or scanner should be connected to the Windows Me computer, and if you want to share one Internet connection, it should on the Windows Me computer (this is especially true if you are using a broadband solution, such as DSL). Of course, if you have multiple peripherals, other computers can share those, but just remember that Windows Me will be your primary, or *server*, machine for your home network.

2. Make a list of all the hardware you will need. Inspect your computers to determine if you have available expansion slots or if any computers already have a network adapter card. You'll need to determine what kind of network you want (typical wiring, phone wire, etc.). You can learn more about these different kinds of networks on the Web or from your local computer store. Keep in mind that some solutions provider faster network transfer speeds. Always go for the fastest solution you can afford. Also, many home networking hardware components are sold as a single kit with a single instruction list. These kits are great solutions, and they make certain you have everything you need. Check out your favorite computer store for details.

TIP   *Your computer has different kinds of expansion slots. The most commonly used slots for a network adapter card are PCI and ISA (although you can use USB in some cases). More than likely, you will have available PCI slots, so you'll want to buy a PCI network adapter. Consult your computer documentation for more information.*

3. Once you determine which type of network you will use, buy the required hardware pieces and install them. Follow the manufacturer's guidelines during the installation process.

 Your computer must be powered down and unplugged from its outlet before installing a network adapter. See Chapter 6 for more information about managing hardware.

4. Check to make sure your computers and peripherals are connected together correctly, as well as your Internet connection. The Windows Me help files contain several diagrams of different configurations so you can check your own against their samples. Access the help files and search under "Using Home Networking" for more information.

About Internet Connection Sharing (ICS)

ICS, first introduced with Windows 98SE, allows you to have one computer connected to the Internet and to have all other computers on the network share that Internet connection. This feature is specifically designed for home networks or small office networks with ten or fewer computers. Why is ICS so helpful? With ICS, you only need one Internet connection and one piece of hardware—each computer does not need a modem or broadband hardware, such as ISDN or DSL connections. Through sharing, you save money and aggravation because you don't have to configure each computer to use the Internet.

While you are designing your home network, you need to decide if you want to use ICS. On a practical note, ICS is designed for use with broadband Internet access (ISDN, DSL, cable, satellite, etc.). Although you can use ICS with a 56K modem, your modem will operate very slowly if several people are trying to use the Internet connection at the same time. This is because a 56K modem does not have enough bandwidth to perform at a desirable speed for more than one computer. However, if users on your network do not access the Internet at the same time, the 56K modem shared connection will be fine.

When you use ICS, your Windows Me computer becomes the ICS *host.* All other computers on your network, called ICS *clients,* access the host to get information from the Internet. All Internet communications flow over your home network to the host computer, then to the Internet and vice versa. Using this setup,

11

your host computer has a connection to the Internet and a connection to your home network. The client computers need only a network adapter so they can connect to the host (again, versions of Windows earlier than 95 need not apply). As far as the Internet is concerned, it only appears as though one computer is accessing the Internet.

CAUTION *Now, let me contradict what I just said. It appears that only one computer is connected; however, in terms of logging onto various services, you may have a problem. For example, AOL versions earlier than 6.0 do not allow concurrent connections of the same account, so each computer on your home network will have to log on to AOL with a different account in order for multiple computers to use AOL. Also, some versions of AOL are incompatible with ICS, so you'll need to do a little checking if you use AOL. Also note that some ISPs may charge you an additional fee for using ICS where multiple computers are accessing their servers. It's unlikely, but check with your ISP to be sure.*

Using the Home Networking Wizard

Once all of your hardware and computers are connected to each other, you can run the Home Networking Wizard, which will set up home networking on your computers. The following steps walk you through the Home Networking Wizard:

NOTE *Depending on the kind of home network you chose to install (such as typical cable, phone line, etc.) you may have a custom setup CD, especially if you purchased a home networking kit. Refer to the kit's documentation about setup, but if you have a custom CD for the kit you purchased, use the kit's setup program instead of the Home Networking Wizard.*

1. Turn on all computers on your home network so they are all booted and operational.

2. On your Windows Me computer, click Start | Programs | Accessories | Communications | Home Networking Wizard.

3. Read the information on the Welcome screen and click Next.

4. The Internet Connection window appears. If you want to use ICS on your network, you can enable it here. Click Yes, This Computer Uses The Following if you want to use ICS, and then click the appropriate radio

button that defines how the computer connects to the Internet, as shown in Figure 11-1. If you don't want to use ICS, click the No, This Computer Does Not Use The Internet radio button. After you make your selections, click Next.

TIP *If ICS doesn't appear within your wizard, then you need to install Internet Connection Sharing. Open Add/Remove Programs in Control Panel, click the Windows Setup tab, then select Communications and click the Details button. Then, select the Internet Connection Sharing check box and click OK to complete the installation.*

5. If you chose to use ICS, a window appears asking you if you want other users on your network to use the connection on this computer. Click either Yes or No. If you click Yes, the drop-down menu should list the network adapter card installed on your computer. This is how other computers will contact your computer for Internet access. Make your selection and click Next

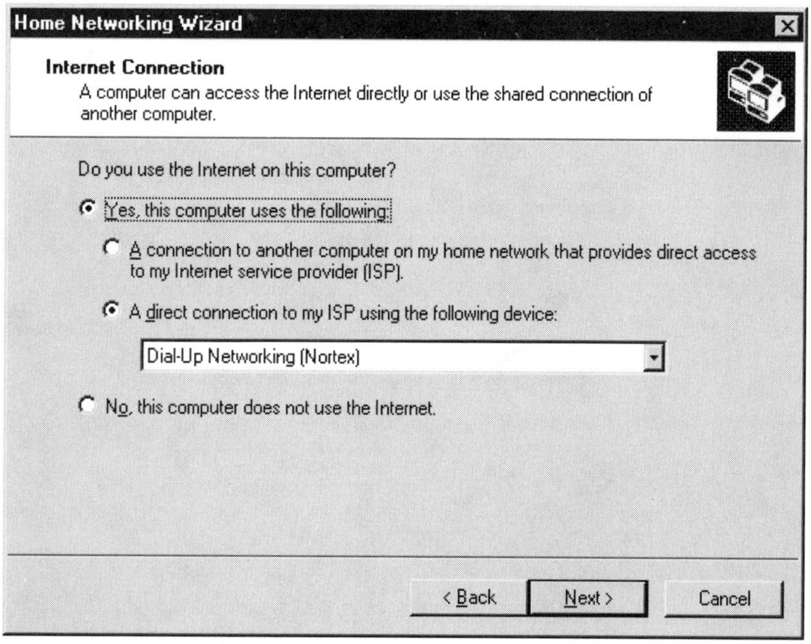

FIGURE 11-1 Select the appropriate radio button to use ICS or not

6. The next window asks you to decide on a computer name and a workgroup name, as shown in Figure 11-2. Each computer on a Windows network must have a unique name so that the computers can talk to each other. Give the computer a friendly name that you and other family members or coworkers can remember. Also, the default name for your home network is MSHOME, but you can change it to a different name by clicking the Use This Workgroup Name radio button and entering a new name.

You can use letters and numbers in your home network name, but you cannot use keyboard symbols, such as !, @, #, $, etc. Keep the name recognizable and friendly.

7. The Share Files And Printers screen appears, as shown in Figure 11-3. Once your computers are networked together, you can share your printer with other computers on your network and virtually any files you want (or programs or whatever). This window gives you the option to share My Documents and all folders within My Documents. If you want to share My

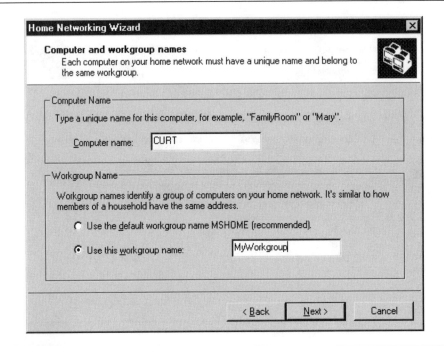

FIGURE 11-2   Use a friendly computer and workgroup name

Documents, just click the check box. If you want to assign a password to the share so that only certain people in your home or small office can use My Documents, click Password and enter the desired password. If you don't want to use a password, don't click the Password button. In the bottom of the window, any printers attached to your computer are listed. You can choose to share the printer(s) by clicking the check box next to them. Make your selections and click Next.

NOTE
If you choose not to use a password for My Documents, you'll get a message telling that you should use one. You can ignore it—just click OK, then click Next again to continue with the wizard.

TIP
You can share other folders individually, not just My Documents. Basically, any folder on your computer can be shared. It's quick and easy, and Chapter 4 shows you how.

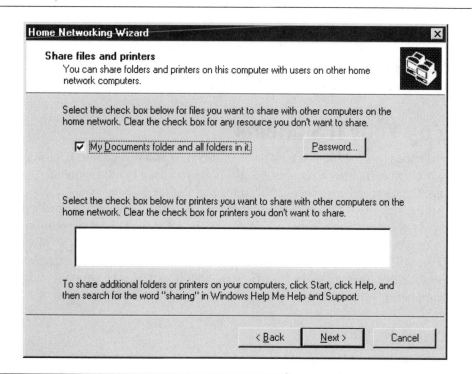

FIGURE 11-3 Use this window to share My Documents and your printer(s)

8. The Home Networking Setup Disk window appears. If you have Windows 95 or 98 computers on your network, you'll need to make this setup disk in order to run the Home Networking Wizard on those older computers. If all of your computers are Windows Me computers, then you don't need the disk. Make your selection and click Next.

 Each computer on your network must be configured to use networking. The disk creation option creates a disk so you can run the Home Networking Wizard on Windows 95 or 98 computers.

9. If you clicked Yes to the disk option, insert a formatted floppy disk into your floppy disk drive. If there is any data on the floppy, it will be destroyed, so watch out! When the disk is ready, click Next.

10. The Home Networking Setup Disk is created. Click Finish to complete the wizard. The Home Networking Wizard configures your computer for home networking and then prompts you to reboot. Remove the floppy disk from the computer and reboot Windows Me.

11. Once Windows Me has rebooted, you'll need to perform these steps on the other computers on your network. Use the Home Networking Wizard in Accessories on Windows Me computers, and use the disk you created to run setup on Windows 95 or 98 computers.

Setting up Your ICS Clients

If you decided to use ICS, you now have an ICS host and ICS client(s). In order for your client computers to access the ICS host, you need to tell Internet Explorer, Outlook Express, and any other applications that use the Internet how to access the Internet through the ICS host. Without this configuration, your applications will think your computer has a direct connection to the Internet. This configuration is easy, and this section shows you how to make the change with Internet Explorer and Outlook Express. If you are using other browsers, e-mail clients, or applications, consult their documentation for specific steps (but it will be very similar to what you learn here).

Internet Explorer

To configure Internet Explorer to access the Internet through the ICS host, just follow these easy steps:

1. Open Internet Explorer. If you get an error message about connecting to the Internet, just click OK.

2. Click Tools | Internet Options. Click the Connections tab.

3. On the Connections tab, select any existing dial-up connections in the window, and click Remove.

4. Because you have configured your computer for ICS with a host computer with the Home Networking Wizard, your computer should use the default LAN setting to find the shared connection.

If you have problems with client computers connecting to the ICS host, there is an ICS Troubleshooter in your Windows Me help files. See Chapter 18 for details.

Outlook Express

You do not need to perform any additional configuration in Outlook Express if you configured Internet Explorer to access the Internet through the ICS host. Outlook Express uses the connection settings Internet Explorer uses.

Using My Network Places

My Network Places is an icon on your desktop that you can use to browse your network. This means you can see all of the computers on your network and you can see what resources each computer shares. You can also right-click My Network Places on your desktop and click Properties to see the specific network configuration. For a home network configured with the Home Networking Wizard, you don't need to make any changes here since Windows Me configured these options for you. In fact, making changes on the My Network Places properties sheet may stop your computer from functioning on your network, so be careful!

When you open My Network Places, you see a few different items; you may see several, depending on your network. As you can see in Figure 11-4, I have connections to several network folders that I use and even a folder on the Internet.

You can open Entire Network to see all of the computers on your network. You can double-click a computer icon to view the resources available. Any resources you access also show up in this folder for easy future access, and the Home Networking Wizard is also available from this location.

11

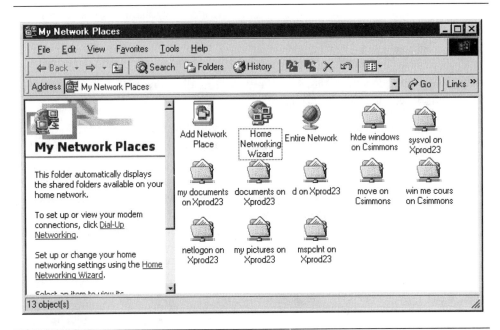

FIGURE 11-4   Use My Network Places to manage network resources

One item here you may find very useful is the Add Network Place Wizard. This wizard lets you easily add a folder to My Network Places for a network resource so that you can easily access the resource by opening My Network Places. To add a network place, just follow these easy steps:

1. Double-click the Add Network Place icon in Control Panel.

2. In the Welcome screen of the Add Network Place Wizard, shown in Figure 11-5, enter the location of the network place. This can be a network location (*computername\sharename*), a Web address, or an ftp address. You can also use the Browse button to browse for the desired resource. Enter your selection and click Next.

3. The Add Network Place Wizard accesses the desired network resource and prompts you to enter a user name/password or whatever information is required to access the resource (if any).

4. The wizard completes the network place. Click Finish, and the new network place appears in My Network Places. From now on, you can directly access the resource from this location.

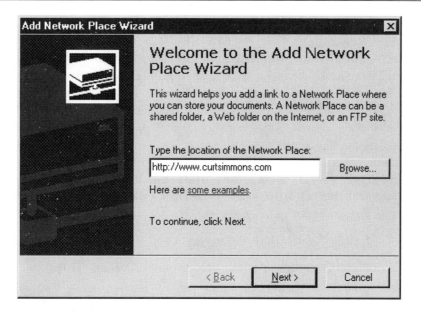

FIGURE 11-5   Enter the location of the desired network resource

11

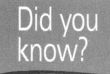

Network Icon in Control Panel

If you right-click My Network Places and click Properties, you see Network Services Properties sheets. These are the same Network Properties that you see if you double-click the icon in Control Panel. You can configure network services using these tabs, and if Windows Me is used on a larger network, a network administrator will configure TCP/IP information here. Also, on a network with servers, Windows Me can be configured to log on to a particular server or Windows domain. On a home network, you do not need to change or configure any information here because Windows Me takes care of the configuration for you.

Creating a Direct Cable Connection

Consider this scenario: Let's say you have a PC at home and a laptop computer at work. From time to time, you want to transfer files from the laptop to the PC, but you do not want the trouble and expense of setting up a home network just for these file transfers. You could e-mail the files to yourself and download them from home, but the files are multimedia files and you only have a 56K modem—downloading would make you old before your time. Now what?

This solution to this problem is quite easy: you can use a direct cable connection between the two computers to move the files. Windows Me makes this option very easy. To create a direct cable connection in Windows Me, you need a serial or parallel cable that you can use to connect the two computers together (a printer cable usually works great). Once you have your cable ready, just follow these easy steps:

1. Click Start | Programs | Accessories | Communications | Direct Cable Connection.

2. In the window that appears, as shown in Figure 11-6, decide if your computer will be the host or guest. In a cable connection, one computer is the host and one is the guest. It doesn't really matter which, so just click the Host radio button for your main computer and the second computer can be the guest. Click Next.

3. Select the port in the list (either serial or parallel), as shown in Figure 11-7, then plug the cable into the port on your computer. When the cable is plugged in, click Next.

NOTE   *You must use the same port on both the host and guest. In other words, you can't use a parallel port on one and serial port on the other.*

4. If you want to set a password, click the Use Password Protection check box, then click the Password button to enter the password. Click Finish.

The host computer is now set up. Now, go to the guest computer and repeat these same steps, but select the guest option on the first page. Once this is done, you can move files between the computers through the connection.

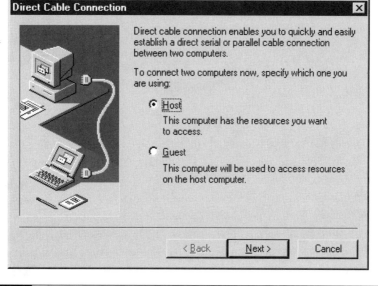

FIGURE 11-6   Choose either Host or Guest

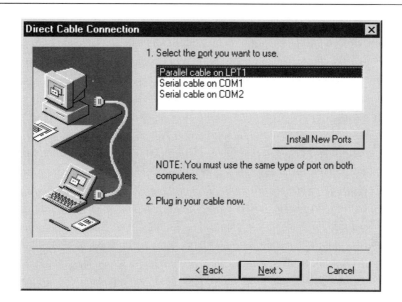

FIGURE 11-7   Select the port you want to use, then plug the cable into the port

11

Chapter 12

Using Additional Windows Me Internet and Networking Tools

How To...

- Set Up and Use Microsoft NetMeeting

- Enable Virtual Private Networking

- Use the Phone Dialer

- Use HyperTerminal

As I have mentioned a few times during this section of the book, networking has changed a lot over the past few years. Once restricted to corporations with thick wallets, networking was something only large businesses could afford. When the Internet came on the scene, networking began to change because people all over the world could communicate with one another on the largest network in the world. Since that time, the technologies developed to support and make the most of the Internet have exploded. Aside from Internet Explorer and Outlook Express (along with ICS), Windows Me includes a few other tools to help you use the Internet and dial-up networking to its greatest potential. You can learn about those tools in this chapter.

Having Fun with NetMeeting

NetMeeting is a tool that enables you to hold virtual, private meetings, or informal "get-togethers" over the Internet. Provided you have fast Internet access, it is a great way to spend time with family and friends or even to conduct business. In fact, many companies today use NetMeeting for virtual meetings and classes.

With NetMeeting, you can send voice, text, video, and all kinds of data. You can teach a class, and with the proper equipment, network the class over the Internet. Students on the other end can ask questions and be directly involved with the class, just as if they were actually in the classroom. With a little organization, you can even have family visits. As you'll see, NetMeeting is a very cool tool that has many useful features—the possibilities are endless.

What You Need to Use NetMeeting

NetMeeting is included with Windows Me, but to use all of its features, you need:

■ Fast bandwidth—Sadly, NetMeeting will not work well with a 56K modem. You can use NetMeeting with a 56K modem, but many of its features will be too slow.

■ Sound card and speakers—To hear voice transmissions, your computer must have a sound card and speakers installed.

■ Video camera—Your computer needs a video camera installed to send video.

Setting Up NetMeeting

To set up NetMeeting, click Start | Programs | Accessories | Communications | NetMeeting. The NetMeeting Wizard appears to help you set up NetMeeting. The following steps walk you through this process:

1. The NetMeeting Wizard welcome screen appears. Read this screen, then click Next.

2. In the next screen, shown in Figure 12-1, enter information about yourself. Note that your first and last name and e-mail address are required. Click Next when you're done.

3. In the next screen, you can choose whether to log on to a directory service, which is the Microsoft Internet Directory. This option lists your name and contact information in the directory so that other people can get in contact with you. If you don't want to meet new people using NetMeeting, choose the Do Not List check box option. After you make your selection, click Next.

4. In the next screen, select the radio button that best describes your Internet connection (modem, DSL, LAN, etc.). Click Next.

5. The next screen asks if you want a shortcut on your desktop and taskbar. Clear the check boxes if you don't want to use these. Click Next.

6. NetMeeting will now test your speakers. Close any open programs that are using your sound card, turn on your speakers, and then click Next.

7. In the Audio Tuning test screen, click the Test button to hear a test sound. If the sound is not loud enough, turn up your speakers or sound control using the slider bar. Click Next when the sound is loud enough.

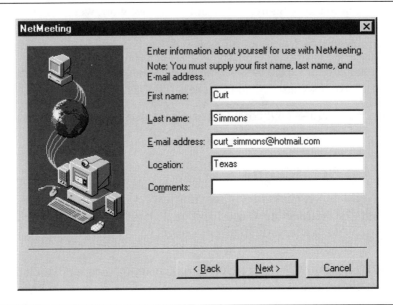

FIGURE 12-1   Enter information about yourself

8. A microphone test screen appears. If you want to use a microphone so others can hear you speak, use the microphone and read the paragraph on the page, then click Next. The next screen tells you if your voice was heard.

9. Click Finish. The NetMeeting interface appears, as shown in Figure 12-2.

Once NetMeeting is set up, you can see that the interface is quite simple and that NetMeeting simply combines a number of different Internet tools into one interface. Using this interface, you can place Internet calls so you can connect with another NetMeeting participant, chat, host a chat or meeting, transfer files, share applications, and send and receive live video and sound. Note that there are buttons to use each of these features in the NetMeeting window.

Placing a NetMeeting Call

Placing a NetMeeting call is similar to using a telephone. Click Call | New Call to place a call, or just click the Telephone icon on the NetMeeting interface. In the Place A Call window that appears, enter the e-mail address, computer name,

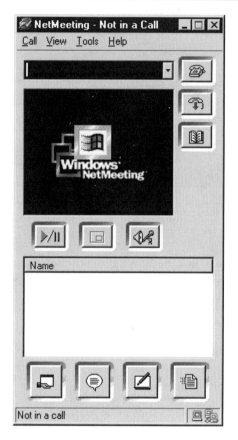

FIGURE 12-2   The NetMeeting Interface

telephone number, or IP address of the other NetMeeting participant you want to call, as shown in Figure 12-3.

Once you have established a connection with another NetMeeting user, you can then begin to use NetMeeting's features with the other person. You can do the following:

■ Send and receive live video using a video camera—Press the Start Video button on the NetMeeting interface to start recording.

■ Send and receive live sound—Press the Sound/Microphone button to begin sending and receiving voice transmissions.

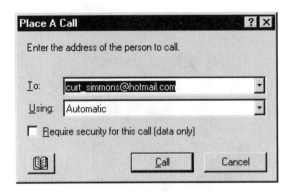

FIGURE 12-3   Use the Place A Call window to place a call

- Share programs—Click the Share Program button. In this window you can determine which programs or files on your computer you want to share.

- Chat—Chat lets you communicate with other NetMeeting callers in real time. Just open the chat window and type your message.

- Whiteboard—The Whiteboard looks and works just like Paint. You can draw sketches on the Whiteboard, and NetMeeting recipients will see the drawings on their Whiteboard.

- Send Files—You can send files of any kind to your NetMeeting recipient. Just click the Send Files button and determine which file on your computer you want to send.

These tools are very easy to use and have a simple interface. The best way to master them is simply to play with the tools during a call. A typical computer user can master all of these tools in half an hour of experimenting.

Setting Up Remote Desktop Sharing

Remote Desktop Sharing is a very cool feature of NetMeeting. With Remote Desktop Sharing turned on, you can call your computer from a different computer and manage your computer from the remote location. This feature is helpful if you are going to be away and want to be able to access your computer at home. To set up remote desktop sharing, follow these easy steps:

1. In NetMeeting, click Tools | Remote Desktop Sharing.

2. Click Next on the Welcome screen.

3. Enter and confirm a password you want to use when contacting your computer. You should use a complex password made up of both letters and numbers. The password must be at least seven characters long. Click Next.

4. The next window asks if you want to use a password-protected screen saver. When you access your computer from a remote location, Windows Me can lock your computer with the screen saver password option so that no one at your home or office can use the computer while you are accessing it from the remote location. This setting is highly recommended. Click the Yes button and click Next.

5. The Screen Saver tab of Display properties appears. Enable the screen saver and provide a password here. Close the window.

6. Click Finish.

When you close NetMeeting, right-click the NetMeeting icon in your System Tray and click Activate Remote Desktop Sharing. Your computer is now ready to be accessed remotely.

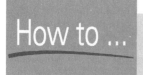

How to ... Enable Your Computer to Receive Calls

If you want Windows Me to be able to receive calls, you need to install a small component called Dial-Up Server. This component allows your Windows Me computer to receive calls. All you need to do is install the component from Windows Setup. Double-click Add/Remove Programs in Control Panel, click the Windows Setup tab, then click Communications | Details. Click the check box next to Dial-Up Server and click OK to install the component. You will need to reboot your computer.

Keep in mind, however, that enabling your computer to receive calls can be a potential security risk because unauthorized persons may access your computer. This is a situation where you have to weigh your needs and the risks involved.

Configuring NetMeeting Options

As in most Windows programs, you can click Tools | Options in NetMeeting to configure a number of important items. There are four tabs available to you, which are described in the following sections.

General

The General tab, shown in Figure 12-4, contains the information you configured during NetMeeting setup. You can change any of the information on this tab as needed. Also, if you click Bandwidth Settings, you can select a different connectivity option, such as DSL, modem, etc. The Advanced Calling button opens a window where you can enable a gatekeeper. In some networks, a single line can be used to access the Internet; this is called a gatekeeper. In this instance, your computer needs to send and receive data through the gatekeeper. If you are in an environment that uses a gatekeeper, you can configure the option on this window.

Security

The Security tab allows you to specify how your computer handles incoming calls and outgoing calls. You can also to choose to use digital certificate for call authentication.

Audio and Video

The Audio and Video tabs let you make changes and tweak the performance of audio and video transmissions. These tabs are easy to use and are self-explanatory.

Virtual Private Networking

Virtual Private Networking (VPN) has been around for a few years, but it has recently become more popular. As a home user, you are probably not going to use a VPN, but it is possible—especially if you are a part of a small office—that you may find VPN quite helpful.

VPN enables Windows Me to create a private networking session using a public network (see the next "Did You Know" sidebar for more information on how VPN works). For example, let's say you work for a company based in Seattle. You travel to Atlanta for a conference. While you are in Atlanta, you want to access your company's network over the Internet. To ensure privacy, you can use a VPN connection. Another use for VPN is if your company has an intranet and you need to send very private files to another employee. You can create VPN over the intranet for the file transfer.

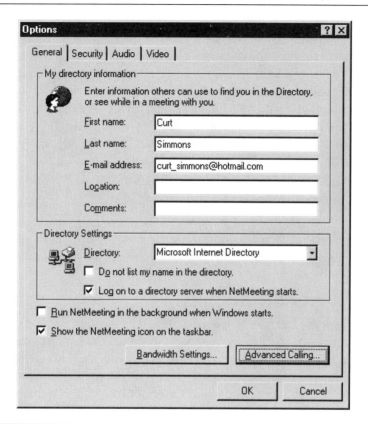

FIGURE 12-4 Use the General tab to make standard changes to your NetMeeting configuration

TIP   *Your private network must support VPN in order for it to work. Also, if your network uses an ISP to access the Internet, it must support VPN as well.*

Installing VPN Support

Depending on your Windows Me computer's configuration, you may need to install support for VPN. To install the VPN support, just open Add/Remove Programs in Control, click the Windows Setup tab, then select Communications and click Details. Click the check box next to Virtual Private Networking and click OK. Windows Me installs the component; you'll need to reboot your computer after it's installed.

Some Scary VPN Details

VPN uses a protocol called Point-to-Point Tunneling Protocol (PPTP). To send private communications over the Internet to and from a corporate network, PPTP hides the data you are sending inside of a PPTP "packet." A PPTP packet looks and acts like all of the traffic on the Internet, but it hides the real network data inside. Think of a PPTP packet as a Christmas present. The wrappings and paper hide what is inside the box. The PPTP packet allows the data to traverse the Internet unharmed. When it reaches the private network, the PPTP "cover" is stripped away, revealing the real data hidden inside. Because of PPTP, both your private network and your ISP must support VPN for it to work.

Using VPN over the Internet

To use VPN over the Internet, you need a dial-up connection to the Internet and a dial-up connection to your private network. Open the Dial-Up Networking folder in Control Panel to create these connections. When you are ready to use VPN, open the Dial-Up Networking folder and start your Internet connection. When the connection is established, start your private network connection.

Using VPN to Connect to a Corporate Network

To use VPN to connect to a corporate network, you need to create a dial-up connection that uses the VPN adapter. In the Dial-up Networking folder, double-click the Make New Connection Wizard. On the first screen, in the Select A Device list, select Microsoft VPN Adapter. Complete the wizard as instructed. You can then use this connection to complete VPN.

Using the Phone Dialer

Phone Dialer is a very simple utility found in the Communications folder in Accessories. In a nutshell, the phone dialer gives you a telephone interface so you can make calls to other computers using your modem or other telephony devices. As you can see in Figure 12-5, the phone dialer looks just like a telephone. Use the phone dialer to set up speed dial options and other related dialing information.

Using HyperTerminal

HyperTerminal is an older utility included in Windows Me that allows you to directly dial another computer and trade files with that computer. You may be thinking, "Wait a minute! Isn't that what Dial-Up Networking connections are for?" Quite true. The difference here is that you can only use Dial-Up Networking

FIGURE 12-5   Phone Dialer gives you a simple telephone interface

12

connections to connect to other Windows computers. You use HyperTerminal to connect and trade files with computers that are not running Windows. You can also use HyperTerminal to connect to computer bulletin boards and similar services.

In most cases, the Internet has replaced HyperTerminal since you can e-mail files to users on the Internet, regardless of what computer platform they are using. Still, HyperTerminal is useful to a number of people.

Essentially, HyperTerminal allows you to make connections to other computers. Open HyperTerminal from the Communications menu in Accessories; a window appears in which you can enter the name of the new connection and select a representative icon for it, as shown in Figure 12-6.

You then enter the phone number and configure dialing rules, much the same way you would for a typical dial-up connection. Once you enter the information, you can call the remote computer and establish a dial-up session with it. Use the buttons on the toolbar to send and receive files as well as to manage the call.

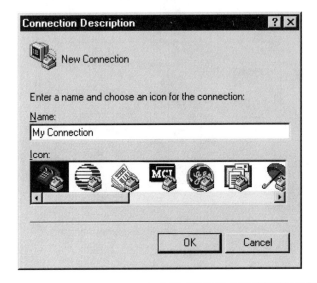

FIGURE 12-6   Enter the name of the connection and select an icon

Chapter 13

Having Fun with Windows Me

How To...

- ■ Play Games on Windows Me
- ■ Use Web TV for Windows
- ■ Use Volume Controls and Sound Recorder

A few times during this book, I've mentioned that Windows Me works and plays better than previous versions of Windows. In many of the previous chapters, I showed you how Windows Me works better, so now let's turn our attention to how Windows Me *plays* better—which may be what you really want to know! Windows Me includes several fun and exciting features that I explore in this and the next two chapters. If you want to learn about the cool things you can do with Windows Me, you have come to the right place.

Windows Me Games

Let's face it. For all the great things a PC can do, one of the most popular things home users do on a PC is play games. Gaming technology has come a very long way in the past few years. With rich PC multimedia support, you can be transported into different worlds, create your own civilizations, race a car—you name it, you can do it in a game and experience awesome graphics and sound while you're doing it. There are three major ways to play games on Windows Me. You can play basic games included with Windows Me, Internet games, or games that you purchase and install yourself. The following sections explore these options.

Games Installed with Windows Me

Unfortunately, operating systems do not give you a bunch of powerful games for free. You have to purchase and install those on your own. However, Windows Me does give you a few basic games you can play to pass the time. These games are Classic Hearts, Classic Solitaire, FreeCell, Minesweeper, Pinball, and Spider Solitaire.

TIP *Some of these games may not appear on your system by default. Go to Add/Remove Programs in Control Panel, then click on the Windows Setup tab. Scroll through the list and select Games. Click the Details button, then click all of the check box options that appear in the list so you can install all of the games (you may need to insert your Windows Me CD-ROM). Click OK, and Windows Me will install them for you.*

If you want to play one of the these games, just click Start | Programs | Games, and a drop-down menu appears from which you can select the game of your choice. As in any Windows program, the game opens in a window that has menu options, such as the Pinball game shown in Figure 13-1.

FIGURE 13-1   Windows Me Pinball

13

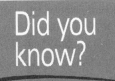

Gaming Options

Each game has a Game menu at the top of the window. Depending on the game you want to play, different options are presented. Some games allow two or more players, some have different settings, such as beginner, intermediate, and advanced, and Pinball even allows you to play the game in full screen mode. Whenever you play a game, be sure to check out the Game menu options so you'll know what is available to you.

Playing Games on the Internet

If you installed all of the game options from Windows Setup (see the previous section), you may have noticed that there are some additional games found in Start | Programs | Games that are for play on the Internet. The included options are Internet Backgammon, Internet Checkers, Internet Hearts, Internet Reversi, and Internet Spades. Accessing these games takes you to the MSN Gaming Zone on the Internet, where you can play against an opponent on the Internet. (If you want to play an Internet game, you'll need an Internet connection, of course.) The game will connect you to **www.zone.com**, where information about your computer and an ID will be sent. No personal information is ever collected from you. Do you want to play? The following steps show you how to do it:

1. Click Start | Programs | Games and select an Internet game of choice. A window opens telling you about the game you can play on zone.com, as shown with Internet Checkers in Figure 13-2.

2. Click the Play button. The game uses your Internet connection to look in zone.com for another player.

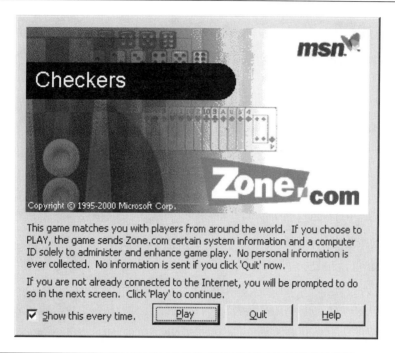

FIGURE 13-2   Click the Play button to continue

3. If a player is found, the game commences, as shown in Figure 13-3. You
   have the option to chat with the other player as well (using a preselected
   list of comments, which prevents someone from calling you names you
   don't like).

So, what happens if you really like playing Internet games but don't want to
play any of the ones available within Windows Me? You can just go to zone.com,
download some software, and start playing all kinds of free games on the Internet

13

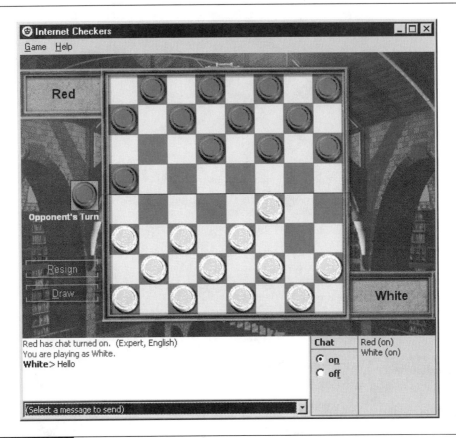

FIGURE 13-3   Checkers on zone.com

with other people. Obviously, there are Internet gaming sites other than
www.zone.com, but since the MSN Internet Gaming Zone is somewhat integrated
with Windows Me, I want to show you what you can do there. Just follow these
steps to start playing other games on zone.com:

1. Open a Web browser, start an Internet connection, enter **www.zone.com** in
   the URL dialog box, and press ENTER.

2. Toward the top of the page, click on the Free Signup button, as shown in
   Figure 13-4.

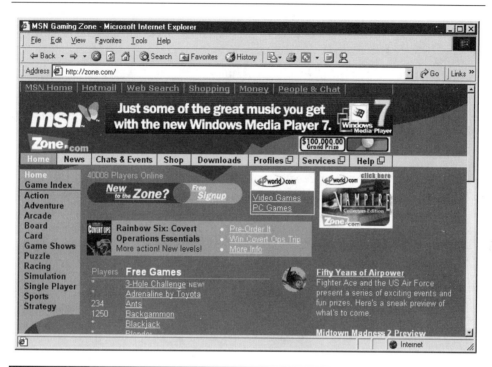

FIGURE 13-4 Click the Free Signup button

3. The next window tells you that you'll need to pick an online ID and password and download a small software package so your computer can play games on the Zone. Click the Start button.

4. Enter a desired Zone name and password. Your name can only have letters, numbers, or underscores (no spaces). Click the Continue button. If the name is already taken, you are prompted to enter a different name.

5. Enter your e-mail address. The e-mail address is only used if Zone needs to contact you—it is not given other users. Enter your address and click Continue.

6. Click the Start Download button to start the software download. This will take a few minutes or less, depending on the speed of your Internet connection.

7. When the download is completed, you see a spade on your screen and a button that says Click Here When You See The Spade. Click the button to continue.

8. You can choose from two different links: to log on and play games or to see a tutorial. Make a selection to continue.

9. If you choose to log on and play games, the Install window appears so final installation of the gaming components on your system can be completed. Click Install.

10. Read the licensing agreement that appears and click Yes. Download continues for another moment or two. A window appears asking if you want a shortcut to the MSN Gaming Zone on your Desktop. Click Yes or No.

11. The Logon dialog box appears. Enter your user name and password and click OK.

12. Depending on your settings, you may get a ZoneFriends dialog box, as shown in Figure 13-5. You should choose Yes to change your setting so that private information about you cannot be viewed on zone.com by other users.

13. A window appears so you can select a level of appearance on zone.com. Click the desired radio button, then click OK.

14. You can now return to zone.com in your browser and select a game that you want to play. Depending on which game you choose, additional

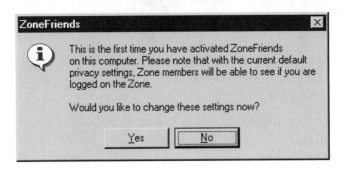

FIGURE 13-5   Click Yes to change your privacy settings

downloads may be necessary. Just follow the instructions as they appear. In Figure 13-6, you can see I'm playing Blender.

 *Although most of the game playing sessions are free, you may have to purchase some games in order to play them on the MSN Gaming Zone.*

Installing and Playing Your Own Games

You can purchase many different kinds of games at your local computer software store or on the Internet. As you might guess, virtually anything you would want is available. The trick is not to get caught up in the excitement until you are sure the

FIGURE 13-6   Blender on zone.com

game is right for your system. As you consider purchasing a game, keep these points in mind:

■ Check the minimum RAM requirements and make sure your computer meets them. A typical game will list the system requirements on the side of the box.

■ A game may require certain graphics and sound capabilities. Make sure your current video and sound cards can support the requirements (such as 3D acceleration or True Color).

■ You may need certain gaming peripherals, such as joysticks and other controllers. Make sure you know what you'll need before buying the game.

With that said, buy the game you want, and read and follow the installation instructions. Most games include one or more CDs that guide you through the installation process. Once you've installed the game, refer to the owner's manual for information about playing the game, game options, and solving problems with that particular game.

About Game Controllers

Due to the popularity of games, Windows Me includes a Game Options icon in Control Panel. If you open the icon, you see a simple interface listing any game controllers you have installed on your system. From this interface, you can access the properties of the game controller and make any configuration changes that are needed and available. Like gaming software, game controllers are different according to type and manufacturer, so always refer to your documentation to learn how to make the most of your game controllers and how to use the Game Options in Control Panel to configure them as needed.

Solving Problems with Games

Naturally, it is impossible for me to offer a solution to every problem you might encounter with a game, particularly those you've installed. If you're having problems with a game, always begin with its documentation. Sometimes there are known issues or common problems the documentation can help you solve. You can also use the Windows Me Troubleshooter to help you solve a problem (see Chapter 18). However, I have listed some of the more common problems and their solutions in the following sections.

A Game Controller Doesn't Work

If you have a joystick or some other kind of game controller that doesn't work or is working erratically, first check the hardware documentation to see if there are any immediate solutions recommended.

Next, check the Game Options icon in Control Panel for the presence of the device. If you don't see it there, Windows Me doesn't think it is installed on the system. Check to make sure the device is plugged in correctly and follow the manufacturer's instructions for installing the device.

If the device works sporadically, you may need to access its properties in Game Options. Click on the Settings tab and click Calibrate to try to resolve the problem. If calibration does not solve the problem, the odds are good that the device driver is incorrect, corrupted, or needs to be updated. Try to reinstall the device driver or obtain an updated one from the manufacturer's Web site.

DirectX Problems

DirectX is a graphics software component used by many games. If you get DirectX error messages, the odds are good that you need to install the latest version of DirectX (found on the Windows Update Web site) or that you are using a version of DirectX that your game does not support. Check your game documentation for more information. If you are using an older video card, you may also experience incompatibility problems with DirectX.

Game Lockup

Lockups are generally caused when a game attempts to use hardware in some way that violates the integrity of the Windows Me operating system. This can cause a hard lock. Press CTRL+ALT+DEL on your keyboard to get control of your system, or you may have to restart it. If this continues to happen with one particular game, there are probably software problems with the game. Consult the game documentation for more information.

Set Display Mode: DDERR_GENERIC

This error message commonly occurs if your video card resolution settings are too high for your video card to handle. You need to lower them to 256 colors on the Settings tab of the Display Properties sheet.

TIP *Tired of playing a game, but you can't seem to make it stop? Just press the ESC key on your keyboard. This is a universal control that almost always halts a game and returns control of the operating system to you.*

Web TV for Windows

Interested in watching a little Web TV? You can use Windows Me to watch local television broadcasts and Web television on your Windows Me computer. You must have a TV tuner card installed on your computer to take full advantage of these features. Some video cards have a TV tuner already built in, so consult your manufacturer's documentation for details.

 *Keep in mind that if you upgraded from Windows 98, some video cards might need updated drivers for the TV Tuner portion to work correctly. Check your manufacturer's Web site for details.*

Installing Web TV for Windows

Web TV for Windows is not installed by default on Windows Me. To install it, open Add/Remove Programs in Control Panel, click the Windows Setup Tab, and select Web TV for Windows in the list. Click OK (you may need to insert your Windows Me CD-ROM). Once Web TV is installed, you will need to reboot your computer, and you may need to reboot it a second time until the configuration is complete.

Using Web TV for Windows

To use Web TV for Windows, click Start | Programs | Accessories | Entertainment | Web TV for Windows. Web TV for Windows launches and will launch an Internet connection if your computer is not already connected. Web TV then asks you to enter your zip and will "start scan" so it can examine the possible local channels that are available in your area. Once found, the rest is rather straightforward—in fact, your Web TV interface looks much like a regular TV with similar controls and the like. You can manage your program stations, save them, and keep track of what you want to watch, just as you would with a *TV Guide* and a remote control.

Using Volume Controls and Sound Recorder

In the Entertainment menu in Accessories, you'll find two simple utilities: Volume Control and Sound Recorder. These are simple to use, but I want to mention a few things about each of them.

Volume Control, shown in Figure 13-7, gives you a window containing different slider controls so you manage the volume of your speakers, microphone, and other Windows sound options.

 *You can access Volume Control by right-clicking on the Volume icon in your System Tray and clicking Properties.*

As you can see in Figure 13-7, the Volume Control window is a simple interface that is easy to use. However, remember that your volume control options may not all be available by default. Click Options | Properties to see a list of volume controls you can add for different devices, as shown in Figure 13-8. Just click the check boxes next to the controls you want to add, then click OK. The rest is self-explanatory!

Sound Recorder gives you a little utility with which to record your voice (or whatever) using a microphone attached to your computer. The controls for Sound Recorder, shown in Figure 13-9, are quite similar to a tape recorder on a stereo.

Just click the Record button to start recording. When you are done, you can save the recording into a file. The menu options give you standard abilities; play

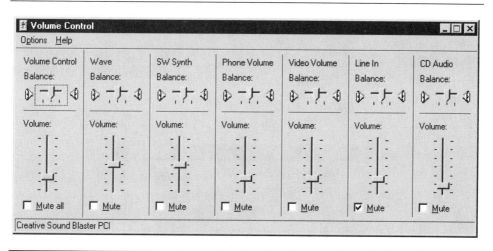

FIGURE 13-7   Use Volume Control to manage multimedia device volumes

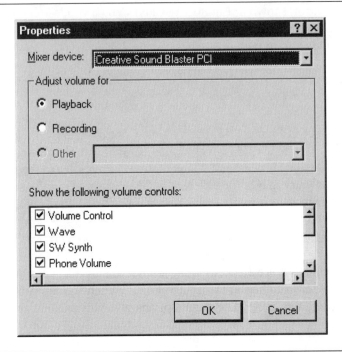

FIGURE 13-8   Use the Volume Control Properties menu to adjust the usage of controls for certain devices

around with these settings to see which ones work best for you. Like Volume Control, Sound Recorder is very easy to use—just spend some time with it and you'll be a recording pro in no time.

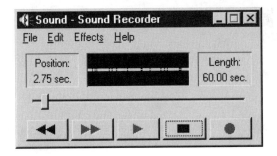

FIGURE 13-9   Sound Recorder can be used to record your voice

Chapter 14

Using Windows Media Player

How To...

- Use Windows Media Player
- Record CD Music
- Create and Manage Playlists
- Manage Your Media Library
- Configure Media Player

Do you like to listen to downloaded music? How about Internet radio? What about videos? We live in a multimedia age, and as I mentioned in other chapters, the Internet has become a "multimedia animal." Windows Me gives you the best-ever Windows Media Player to make the most of your local and Internet media. Although Windows Media Player is not new to Windows, the new Media Player version 7 included in Windows Me is a 150 percent improvement over any previous versions. In fact, I think you're going to love this one, and in this chapter, I'll show you all that the Media Player can do!

Checking out the Windows Media Player Interface

You can access Windows Media Player by going to Start | Programs | Accessories | Entertainment | Windows Media Player. Depending on your system configuration, you may also have a shortcut to Media Player on your desktop or on your taskbar.

Once you open Media Player, you see a default interface. I say default interface because you can completely change the interface using a variety of *skins*, which you will learn about later in this chapter. As you can see in Figure 14-1, the default interface provides you with a primary media area (which is black in the figure because no media is being used), a list of buttons on the left side of the Media Player (called features), and a standard toolbar.

You use Media Player by accessing one of the features on the left side of the Media Player. As you might guess, you have a number of options available with each feature, so let's jump into them!

FIGURE 14-1   The default Windows Media Player interface

Now Playing

Now Playing is your default area of sorts and lists whatever type of media you
are currently playing. Most types of media will automatically launch Windows
Media Player. For example, let's say you want to listen to your favorite CD. All
you need to do is put the CD into the CD-ROM drive. Windows Me scans the
CD, recognizes it as a music CD, launches Window Media Player, and the Media
Player begins playing the CD, which shows up in the Now Playing area, as shown
in Figure 14-2.

14

FIGURE 14-2   Now Playing area with a music CD loaded

What if you decide to watch a home movie you have made with Movie Maker? No problem, the home movie is displayed in the Now Playing window, shown in Figure 14-3. (You can read more about Movie Maker in the next chapter.)

So, what can you change and configure on the Now Playing interface? Since the primary purpose of Now Playing is to provide a quick and easy area where you can see and hear all multimedia, there are no specific configuration options for the media, but you can adjust what is displayed in the Now Playing area and how it is displayed.

First, in the upper right corner of the Media Player, you see three buttons:

■ **Show/Hide Equalizer Settings**—Lets you either show or hide the equalizer settings in the Now Playing window.

FIGURE 14-3   Now Playing area with home video

- Show/Hide Playlist—Shows or hides the playlist in the Now Playing window. For example, if you are listening to a music CD, the songs on the CD are displayed in the Now Playing window if this option is enabled.

- Shuffle—Shuffles your current playlist. This feature is cool if you want to play a music CD and not hear the songs in the same old order.

In addition to the buttons, there is a drop-down menu that you can use to select different media to play.

If you use the buttons to remove the playlist and equalizer features from the playlist, the primary viewing window is simply centered, as shown in Figure 14-4.

Use the standard buttons at the bottom of the Media Player to play the media, stop playing the media, adjust the volume, and use related stereo/video controls. The same controls are in the Play menu at the top of the interface. The little boxes

FIGURE 14-4   You can use the right-corner buttons to change the appearance of the Now Playing area

with an arrow through them shown in the bottom right of the interface allow you to shrink the interface to a compact mode or enlarge it back to full screen mode.

In addition to these options, you can use the View menu to change a number of items concerning the Now Playing area's interface. The following list tells you what options are available to you and what they do:

- Full Mode—The default display. If you switch to Compact mode, use this option to return to Full mode

- Compact Mode—Gives you a smaller interface and takes up less room on your desktop. You have the same options, but some of them appear as drop-down menus. If you are in Full mode, click this option to move to

Compact mode. You'll notice while in Compact mode that the interface changes. This is called a *skin*, which you'll learn more about later in the chapter.

■ Now Playing Tools—This option provides a drop-down menu from which you can choose to:

  ■ Show Playlist—Performs the same way as the Show Playlist button.

  ■ Show Titles—Displays title information about the media (such as the artist, song titles, name of the video, etc.).

  ■ Show Visualizations—For audio media, Windows Media Player can give you visualizations in the Now Playing window. Visualizations are interesting graphics files; I'll address them in more detail later in this list.

  ■ Show Equalizer and Settings—Gives you an equalizer and related video settings on the Now Playing area. You can use these controls to adjust playback quality.

  ■ Show Resize Bars—These bars appear between the different options you elect to show on the Now Playing area and enable you to adjust the size of the components as you desire.

  ■ Visualizations—I mentioned earlier that visualizations give you a graphical view while you are playing audio only media. For example, when you play a CD, the visualization options display interesting graphical patterns that move to beat of the music. If you like this feature, the drop-down menu that appears here allows you select the visualization you want to use.

SHORTCUT *You can also change the visualization directly from the Now Playing area by clicking the arrow buttons under the Graphical Visualization window.*

14

TIP *You can easily manage the visualization available to you by clicking Tools | Options and selecting the Visualizations tab. You'll find a simple interface in which you can add and remove visualization files.*

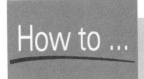

How to ... Do You Want More Visualizations?

Media Player gives you quite a few visualization options when you click View |
Visualizations. However, if you are a visualizations junkie, you can also get
more from the Web, and here's how:

1. In Media Player, click Tools | Download Visualizations.

   This launches an Internet connection and takes you to the Windows
   Media Player site at **http://windowsmedia.com/mediaguide/gallery/
   visualizations.asp**.

2. In the Web browser, inspect the visualizations available, then click the
   one you want to start the download process with.

3. When the File Download dialog box appears, choose Run This Program
   From Its Current Location and click OK.

4. Once the download is completed, installation starts automatically. The
   visualization is installed and now available in Media Player. That's all
   there is to it!

- **File Markers**—When playing video, you can use this option view the
  different markers within the video file. This feature allows you to skip to
  different areas of the video.

- **Statistics**—When playing videos, access this option to view statistics
  about the video transmission quality. The statistics window, shown in
  Figure 14-5, may be particularly helpful when troubleshooting problems
  with streaming media.

- **Full Screen, Refresh, Zoom**—The final options in the View menu provide
  basic viewing capabilities that are self-explanatory.

What Is Streaming Media?

When you download video or music from the Internet or across any other
network, the streaming media feature of Media Player allows you to begin
seeing and hearing the media before it is completely downloaded. The
download stream is held in a buffer and then played to you as it is received.
This feature allows Media Player to return network media to you more quickly
and compensate for transmission delays or problems.

Statistics	☒

Basic   Advanced

┌─ Media ─────────────────────────────┐ ┌─ Connection ──────────────────────┐
Maximum bitrate:	103.0 Kbps		Bandwidth available:	Unknown
Selected bitrate:	103.0 Kbps		Bandwidth in use:	0.0 Kbps
			Protocol:	FILE

┌─ Video ─────────────────────────────┐ ┌─ Packets ─────────────────────────┐
Frames skipped:	0		Received:	178
Frame rate:	0 fps		Recovered:	0
Actual rate:	0.0 fps		Lost:	0

Quality (15s average):   ▓▓▓▓▓▓▓▓▓▓▓▓▓▓   100 %   [Close]

FIGURE 14-5   Use the statistics option to gain helpful information about your
video transmission

14

Media Guide

The next feature in Media Player is the Media Guide, as shown in Figure 14-6. The Media Guide connects to the Internet and provides you information about new media you may wish to view. You can hear pieces of music, view new movie trailers, search for information, and so forth. Essentially, the Media Guide gives you a small Web site directly in Media Player from which you can download items of interest.

CD Audio

The CD Audio feature, shown in Figure 14-7, gives you information about the music CD you are currently listening to. As you can see, the names of the songs, their length, and standard information about the album are displayed.

FIGURE 14-6   Media Guide gives you quick access to various items of interest

In the upper right-hand corner of the interface, you see the Album Details button. You can click this button to get additional information from the Internet about the album. Sometimes this feature gives you additional information, sometimes not, depending on how the album is listed. You may also be able to purchase the CD online from this interface.

The Get Names button takes you into the additional album information downloaded from the Web. This simply gives you the names of the songs, which are typically available within the primary interface anyway.

The Copy Music button may be what you really want to know about. You can copy any music track from a music CD so that the track is stored on your hard drive. This feature has two benefits. First, you can store songs you really like directly on your hard disk so that Media Player can play them without the CD. Also, you can generate your own collection of favorites and create a playlist

FIGURE 14-7   Use the CD Audio feature to manage and save songs on your music CDs

14

(which you learn about later in this chapter). The following sections tell you how to copy and configure copies of songs.

Making a Copy

To make a copy of a song from a CD, just follow these steps:

1. In Media Player, click the CD Audio feature button.

2. In the list of songs, click the check boxes next to the song(s) you do not want to copy so that no checkmark appears. In other words, any songs *with* a checkmark will be copied to your hard disk.

3. Click the Copy Music button. Depending on your configuration, you may be able to hear the song while it is being copied. The feature area shows you the progress of the copy as it occurs.

4. Once the copy is completed, the song is placed in your Media Library, which we explore in an upcoming section.

Configuring CD Audio Options

You can configure how songs are recorded by clicking Tools | Options. Click the CD Audio tab, as shown in Figure 14-8.

Under most circumstances, the default options configured on this tab are all you need, but there may be instances where you want to change them. The following list explains the options found on this tab:

- Digital Playback—This check box tells Windows Media Player to digitally play back music from CDs. Leave this check box selected.

- Use Error Correction—If you have a CD with scratches, click this option. Media Player attempts to correct the problem when playing the CD.

- Copy Music At This Setting—Adjust the slider bar to the level of quality you prefer. Higher quality copies require more disk space; lower quality copies require less. Depending on how much extra disk space you have on your computer, you can choose to use more or less disk space at the expense of quality. A medium setting is typical here.

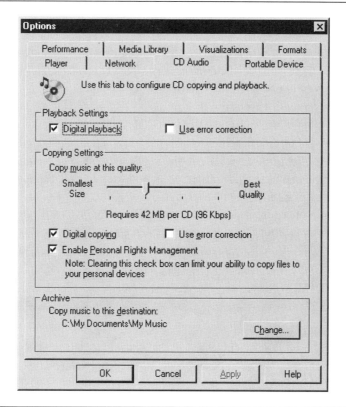

FIGURE 14-8   Use the CD Audio tab to configure how music is copied

> TIP
>
> *Music copies are automatically compressed to help save disk space. This is an internal feature that does not affect playback.*

14

■ Digital Copying—By default, Media Player copies music in digital format, and for quality purposes, you should keep this setting. However, if you are having particular problems, you can clear this check box and try to copy the music in analog format (if your sound card hardware supports it). There is also an Error Correction check box that performs in the same way.

■ Enable Personal Rights Management—Media Player has a personal rights feature that creates a license for you each time you copy a song for personal use. As you might guess, this is a copyright feature designed to help keep people from stealing music. You need to leave this check box enabled—clearing it may reduce some copy and usage options you have (and after all, you want to be in licensing compliance anyway).

■ Copy Music To This Destination—This option allows you to change the location where your music copies are stored. Don't change this unless you have a specific and necessary reason for doing so.

Media Library

The Media Library feature is…well, a library. All of your saved music and video files are stored in the library under different categories so you can easily access them, as shown in Figure 14-9.

In the left side of the interface, you see various categories with plus boxes next to them. Click on a category, and you can see the songs/video in your library for

FIGURE 14-9   The Media Library keeps track of all your multimedia files

that category. For example, when I expand Album, I can select an album and see a list of songs I have copied to my computer from that album in the right window pane. Just double-click on a song to hear it!

So, how can you use the Media Library? The library's purpose is to help you keep track of files, and it's able to detect the type of multimedia you are using and add it to the appropriate location in the library. You can search your library by clicking the Search button at the top of the interface and perform standard add, remove, and delete functions.

> **TIP** *If you delete items, they are stored in the Deleted Items folder until you empty the deleted items folder by right-clicking on it and selecting this option. This helps ensure that you do not accidentally delete a file that you want to keep.*

You can also use Media Library to create a playlist of your favorite tunes or videos. The following sections show you how to use these options.

Adding an Item to the Media Library

To add a new item to the Media Library, just click the Add button on the interface (plus sign). A pop-up menu appears that allows you to add a track that is currently being played, a file, or media found on the Internet. If you want to add a file, a typical Browse window appears so you can locate the file you want to add. If you want to add something from the Web, a window appears in which you can enter the URL to the media item.

> **TIP** *You can easily search your computer, or even your network, for media you want to include. Just click Tools | Search Computer For Media. A dialog box appears so you can perform your search.*

Creating a Playlist

At any given moment, I have about 10 songs that I really love. The problem is that each song is by a different artist on a different CD. Media Player can solve that problem because it lets me copy each of those songs and create a playlist so that each song is played in an order I want directly from my hard drive. Sound interesting? Here's how it works:

1. In Media Library, click the New Playlist button.

2. Enter a name for the new playlist in the dialog box that appears and click OK.

3. In the Media Library, expand the Playlists category to see your new playlist.

 You can also import and export playlists in and out of Media Player. Just click the File menu and use either the import or export option.

Adding Files to a Playlist

Once you have created a playlist, you need to add the items to the playlist. Just follow these steps:

1. In Media Library, find the item you want to add to the playlist and select it in the right pane.

2. Click the Add To Playlist button. A pop-up menu appears so you can determine which playlist to add the file to (if you have more that one playlist).

3. Continue this process until you have all of the files added to your playlist that you want.

Managing and Playing Your Playlist

Once you have your playlist created, you can easily adjust the order of the items on it by selecting an item and using the up and down buttons to move it around in the list, as shown in Figure 14-10. This feature allows you to adjust the order in which the songs are played, and you can come back at any time and adjust the order as desired.

 You can also delete any item in the playlist by right-clicking the item and clicking Delete or clicking the Delete icon on the interface. This action moves the file to the Deleted Items folder. To later restore a deleted item, just open the Deleted Items folder, right-click the file you want to get back, and click Restore.

 *To play your playlist, just select it in the left pane and click the Play button (or right-click it and click Play).*

FIGURE 14-10 Use the up and down arrows to adjust the playlist order

Did you know?

Mixed Playlists

14

You can include any multimedia item currently in your Media Library in a playlist. This means you can mix music, video, radio stations—anything—together into a playlist. In the same manner, you can create a playlist that only contains music or only contains video. The choice is yours—just follow the same playlist creation process, regardless of the kind of media you want to use.

Radio Tuner

The Radio Tuner feature, shown in Figure 14-11, brings Internet Radio to Media Player. With a good Internet connection, you can listen to radio stations all over the world that stream data over the Internet.

As you can see in Figure 14-11, the Radio Tuner has two basic portions of the interface—Presets and Station Finder. The following two sections show you how to use each.

Using Presets

In the Presets section of the interface, you see a drop-down menu where you can select a preset option. Windows Media Player gives you a list of a few popular Internet radio sites to pick from. If you want to reach one of these, just double-click the name in the list to connect to the site. You can create your own preset radio stations by clicking on the Presets drop-down window and choosing My Presets.

FIGURE 14-11   Use Radio Tuner to listen to Internet radio stations

You can create your own preset stations, much like a playlist, so you can easily access radio stations that you like. Use the Edit, Add, and Remove buttons to manage your preset list. To add stations to the preset list, you must locate the station using the Station Finder window, which is explained in the next section.

Using Station Finder

You locate Internet radio stations using the Station Finder window. To find a station, use the Search drop-down menu to find a particular station, or search for a station by category (such as rock, gospel, jazz, etc.). When you find a station you want, just double-click it to connect and listen to it. If you decide you want to add the station to the My Presets list, click the Add button in the Presets section, as shown in Figure 14-12.

FIGURE 14-12   Radio stations you like can be played and added to your My Presets list

Internet radio uses streaming media. The faster your Internet connection, the better results you will get. If you have a really slow connection to the Internet, you'll hear a lot of gaps in the radio play. As with so many things on the Internet today, your best experience will be with a broadband connection (such as DSL).

Portable Devices

The Portable Devices feature, shown in Figure 14-13, provides you with an easy way to copy files from your Media Library to a portable device, such as a Palm PC or even to a remote storage media, such as a Zip or Jaz disk.

As you can see, the interface is very simple. Use the Music On Device drop-down menu to select the device you want to copy to and select the items you want to copy from the Music To Copy menu. Then click the Copy Music button. Your specified items are copied and you can now use them on your portable device.

FIGURE 14-13   Use the Portable Devices feature to copy items to a portable device

Skin Chooser

Media Player includes a number of different *skins,* or interface overlays, which you can apply to Media Player. These skins give Media Player a completely different look, which you may find very appealing or very aggravating, depending on your point of view. For example, you can choose a skin that looks like the inside of someone's head, or one that looks like a heart, as shown in Figure 14-14.

Skins are just for fun. You still have the same functionality in Media Player, regardless of which skin you choose to use. To use a skin, just select the one you want and click the Apply Skin button. Click More Skins to connect to the Media Player Web site where you can download other skins—you'll find several others available on this site.

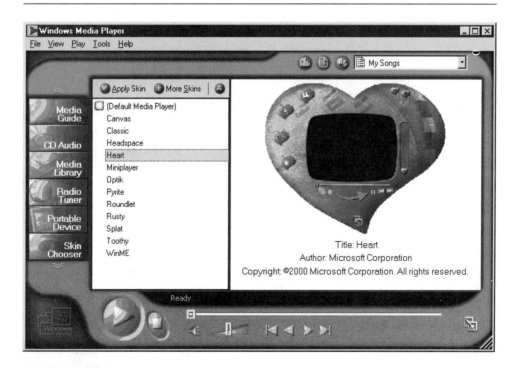

FIGURE 14-14   Skins give Media Player a different appearance

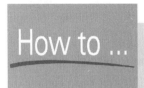 **Download a Skin**

To download a new skin, just follow these easy steps:

1. In the Skin Chooser feature, click the More Skins button.

   Windows Me launches an Internet connection and your Web browser, connecting you to **http://windowsmedia.com/MediaGuide/gallery/skins.asp**.

2. Check out the skins available. When you find one you want to download, click it.

3. Download begins automatically and is installed in Windows Media Player.

Media Player Configuration Options

In addition to all the fun and frills of Media Player, you can click Tools | Options to do a few more things worth mentioning. You see several different tabs with a number of options on each tab. Let me say here that the default options are typically all you need, so this is not an interface where you need to wade around and make configuration changes. However, there may be instances where you need to use these options. The following list tells you what is available on each tab:

- Player—This tab contains a number of basic check boxes. By default, your Media Player checks the Media Player Web site for updates to Media Player on a weekly basis. This setting is all you need. By default, Media Player opens and starts the Media Player Guide. You can change that behavior by clearing the check box on this tab.

- Network—This tab contains protocol usage settings and proxy server enabler settings. You don't need to change anything here unless your computer is on a network that uses a proxy server. And even if you are, unless a network administrator instructs you to make changes, leave this tab alone.

■ CD Audio—This tab is explained in the "CD Audio" section of this chapter.

■ Portable Device—Use this tab to change the copy quality when copying media to a portable device. You can also access the Microsoft Web site to find out more about using portable devices with Media Player.

■ Performance—These settings affect how Media Player uses your Internet connection. You do not need to configure anything here.

■ Media Library—By default, Media Library gives other applications read-only access to the Media Library, and it gives no access to anyone on the Internet. You should leave these settings alone.

■ Visualizations—Use this tab to add and remove visualizations.

■ Formats—This tab lists the file formats Media Player uses. You don't need to change anything on this tab.

As noted, Media Player can automatically check for updates on a weekly basis, but you can disable this feature. However, Media Player is an ever-growing animal, so you'll want to have the latest and greatest. You can easily check for updates by clicking the Help menu and then Check For Player Updates. This action connects you to the Internet and opens an installation options window so you can choose what new features you want to download and install.

14

Chapter 15

Using Windows Movie Maker

How To...

- Import Data into Windows Movie Maker
- Use Windows Movie Maker
- Create and Edit Movies with Windows Movie Maker
- Use Audio with Movies

Windows Movie Maker is one of the coolest new features found in Windows Me. In fact, I'll bet that many of you purchased this book just so you'll know how to do everything with Windows Movie Maker. You have come to the right place. Since Windows Movie Maker is an entirely new feature, I'll tell you all about it and how to use it and point out some pitfalls along the way. So let's get right to it!

Why You Need Windows Movie Maker

If you are like me, you tend to use a lot of videotape. There's everything from Aunt Ruth's birthday party to little Johnny's latest shenanigans. You may also have piles of still photos lying around, and most of them aren't even in an album. Windows Movie Maker is designed to help you both manage and edit your home videos and pictures. You can use Windows Movie Maker to organize the data, edit it, save it, and even share it with others over the Internet. In short, it gives you a way to manage those precious moments electronically and reduce the clutter around your house.

One of the greatest benefits I see to Windows Movie Maker is that you can take an analog video that you taped with a camcorder onto a VHS tape, import the analog video into your computer, and then manage it electronically. So what, you might ask? The great thing about this feature is the *fault tolerance*—once the videos (and even pictures) are stored electronically, you can create multiple copies of them. You can even store your movies on a Zip or Jaz disk and put it in a safe deposit box at your bank. Windows Me gives you the ability to safely and easily make copies of your life captured on film and ensure that nothing happens to those memories in the future.

Another great feature of Movie Maker is editing. In any given video taping session, you are likely to have a lot of dull spots. For example, when you tape a child's birthday party, you have a lot of boring moments while you are waiting for the next present to be opened or the cake to be cut. You can use Windows Movie

Maker to edit out those waiting periods. This makes watching your movies more interesting, entertaining, and shorter. You can even edit together unrelated clips of video. The editing features can also help reduce the amount of storage space you need.

You can have lots of fun with Movie Maker, too. Create your own home movies and edit transitions, voice, background music, and much more in to the movie. Get creative and stretch your brain—as you will see, there are tons of possibilities.

Getting Ready to Use Windows Movie Maker

If you read like I do, you may be tempted to skip over this section and get to the fun stuff, but I encourage you to read this section carefully to avoid a bunch of headaches and sorrow later on. Windows Movie Maker is a great tool, but to make it work, you have to spend a little time inspecting the hardware requirements. The trick, of course, is to get your analog or digital videos and/or pictures inside your computer and to Windows Movie Maker.

First of all, let's consider the basic system requirements you need to run Windows Movie Maker:

- Pentium 300Mhz or equivalent—If you're using Windows Me on an older processor that is limping along, I'm afraid it won't have the power Movie Maker needs to process graphics and sound.

- 64MB of RAM —You need this minimum amount of RAM for Windows Movie Maker to function properly.

- Up to 2GB of storage space—Movie files use a lot of storage space. Make sure your computer has plenty of room to store the movies you create.

- A video card or video capture device.

- A sound card or sound capture device.

 Windows Movie Maker will look for and expect to find both a video and a sound card or other capture device. If it doesn't, you'll receive a message saying that your computer does not meet the Movie Maker requirements.

Now that you know the basic requirements, let's spend a moment talking about getting videos and pictures into your computer. First, if you are using a

15

digital camera or camcorder, you're not going to have any problems at all. Because the media is already digital, you simply connect your camera or camcorder into your computer and follow the manufacturer's instructions for saving the digital content to your hard disk.

For the best performance, your computer needs an IEEE 1394 card so you can import movies from a digital camcorder into your computer; this is especially true if you'll be using any streaming media devices. This type of card provides fast transfer from the camcorder to the computer and is highly recommended by Microsoft. You will need to do a little investigative work to determine if your computer has this card, if your digital camcorder supports it, and if this transfer card is right for you. Check your computer and camcorder documentation for more information.

Windows Movie Maker can recognize all kinds of graphics files, including AVI, MPEG, and basic Web files such as JPEG and GIF. Once the files are loaded and saved onto your hard disk, you can use Windows Movie Maker to import the files and begin working with them.

But what about still pictures or analog videos? What about a song you have written that you want to use as background music in your movie? Once you move

Specifically, Which Files Can be Used?

Want to know exactly which files Windows Movie Maker supports? Here they are:

- MPEG movie files—MPEG, MPG, M1V, MP2, MPA, MPE
- Video files—ASF, AVI, WMV
- Audio files—WAV, SND, AU, AIF, AIFC, AIFF, WMA, MP3
- Pictures—BMP, JPG, JPEG, JPE, JFIF, GIF, DIB

out of the native digital arena, you then must use *capture devices* to move the analog information into your computer where it is converted to digital information and saved.

A capture device refers to a video card that has video and audio input ports and a sound card that has an audio input port. You use these cards to connect your analog camcorder or VCR to the sound and video cards. The cards can then receive the analog data from the camcorder or VCR and convert it to a digital format for use on your computer. In the same manner, your sound card can use data from a different device to record music and voice into a digital format so it can be used on your computer

You may already have a video card and a sound card that support this process. If not, you can purchase new cards at your local computer store. They're not terribly expensive, generally anywhere from $100–$200, but make sure they are compatible with Windows Me. Check the Windows Me Web site (**www.microsoft.com/windowsme**) for constantly updated information about compatible hardware. Also, if you previously owned one of these cards under Windows 98, you may need to download new drivers from the card's manufacturer for it to work correctly with Windows Me. Check out the manufacturer's Web site to see if there is an update.

> TIP
>
> *If you decide to buy a new card, make sure you know what kind of slot is available in your computer for the card—it's usually either PCI or AGP. Refer to your computer's documentation for more information about available ports.*

Once you connect your analog device to the capture device, you can start the video on the analog device and use Windows Movie Maker to view and capture it—in a perfect world, anyway. Unfortunately, depending on your hardware, you may experience problems, and due to the variety of hardware you might pick, it is impossible to solve them all here. However, I can give you a big tip that might save you some headaches. Usually, the capture device will ship with a CD-ROM that contains the card's drivers and a program or two to help you capture video. Use the card's capture program and save the video in a common file format, such as AVI or MPG. You can then import the file into Movie Maker and use it that way (see the next section for information about importing).

15

> TIP
>
> *Check out your capture device's instructions. Most capture devices tell you exactly how to connect the analog device to the card and capture video, and most also provide the cables you'll need to do so.*

 *Many capture devices save video files in their own default format, which may include compression not supported by Windows Me. When you start to save a video using the card's program, make sure you are saving it in a format that is supported by Windows Movie Maker.*

Checking Out the Movie Maker Interface

Before you get started using Movie Maker, you'll need to take a few moments to familiarize yourself with the Movie Maker interface. Fortunately, it follows the typical Windows program interface, so it won't be completely foreign to you. You can find Windows Movie Maker by clicking Start | Programs | Accessories | Windows Movie Maker. The basic interface, shown in Figure 15-1, appears.

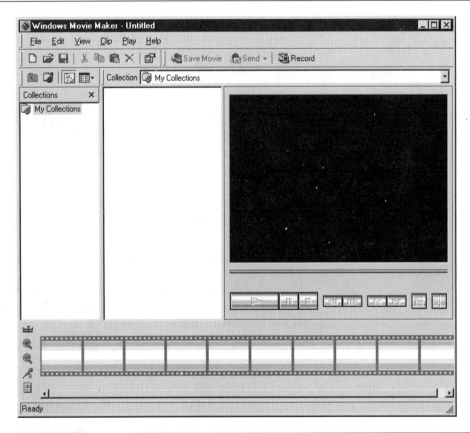

FIGURE 15-1   The Windows Movie Maker interface

There are four major parts of the Windows Movie Maker interface:

■ Toolbars—At the top of the interface, you see the Windows Movie Maker toolbars. The menu options—File, Edit, View, Clip, etc.—contain typical Windows menu features plus those specific to Windows Movie Maker. We'll be using these throughout the chapter. You also see the standard toolbar under the menus with typical toolbar options. Finally, you see a third toolbar called the Collections/Locations toolbar, which is used to manage the video collections you are working on at the moment. Collections are file folders used to hold portions of videos or pictures— a simple way to organize your files.

■ Collections area—The middle left side of the interface is called the Collections area. This area is used to view and manage collections of data and to view clips that you are currently working on. Clips are pieces of videos or pictures; you'll learn about those in a moment.

■ Monitor—The middle right side of the interface is called the Monitor. When you are working with videos or still shots, the picture appears here. You also have standard Start and Stop buttons (along with others) to view video.

■ Workspace—The bottom portion of the interface is called the workspace. You use this area to edit videos and/or combine still shots. You'll learn how to use the workspace later in this chapter.

Recording/Importing Videos

Now that you have taken a look at the interface setup, you are ready to begin recording or importing videos. You record a video if you are streaming it live into your computer. For example, with your digital camcorder, analog camcorder, or other device, such as a DVD player or VCR, you can begin the streaming process, which appears in the Monitor in Windows Movie Maker. To record the video as it appears, just follow these steps:

1. Begin playing the video from the desired device into your computer.

2. Click Start | Programs | Accessories | Windows Movie Maker to open the interface.

3. You see the video appear on the Monitor. Click the Record button on your toolbar. A window appears where you can change the default recording

15

options. Make sure the Create Clips check box is selected, then click the Record button again.

4. The video is recorded by Windows Movie Maker, as shown in Figure 15-2. Notice that clips are being created and appear in the Collections area.

5. When you have finished recording, press the Stop button in the Monitor area.

6. Press the Save button on the toolbar, or click File | Save Project As.

7. The Save As window appears. By default, the project is saved in the My Videos folder found in My Documents. You can select an alternate location if you prefer. The file is saved as a Windows Movie file (.mswmm).

FIGURE 15-2 Windows Movie Maker records the video

Project and Clip Files

A *project* consists of a series of clips that you save together. The project is saved as an MSWMM file (Microsoft Windows Movie Maker). Each clip within the project is saved as a WMV (Windows Movie) file. A clip that contains audio only is saved as a WMA (Windows Media Audio) file.

In addition to recording videos, you can import multimedia files (this includes video, audio, and still pictures). In many cases, you will choose to use the Import feature because you can work with previously saved files. To import a file that has been previously saved, just follow these steps:

1. In Windows Movie Maker, click File | Import.

2. The Select The File To Import window opens, as shown in Figure 15-3. By default, the import feature looks in My Videos for a file to import, so you may have to navigate to another location on your computer if the file is stored elsewhere. Windows Movie Maker looks for all kinds of media files; select the one you want and click Open. Notice there is a Create Clips For Video Files check box. You should leave this check box enabled.

3. The file is imported into Windows Movie Maker. You can now work with it or save it as a project.

> **TIP** *When you import a file, the actual source file that you choose to import is not moved from its current location. Windows Movie Maker imports and uses the data but does not change the location of the existing source file. You are then free to use the source file for other purposes as needed.*

15

Working with Collections and Clips

As previously noted, Collections are folders that contain clips of video/audio data. Collections provide a way for you to organize and save those clips as a project. Whenever you record or import media, Windows Movie Maker creates *clips* by default. It does this to break apart video sequences into manageable chunks.

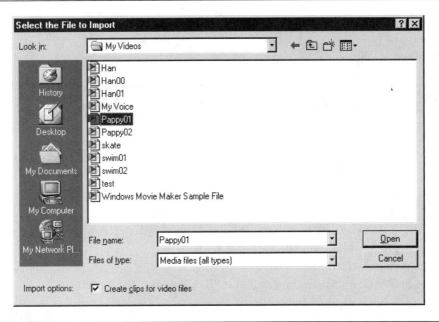

FIGURE 15-3   Use this window to import an existing multimedia file into Windows
Movie Maker

Windows Me examines the video stream and attempts to segment it when the
picture sequence changes. For example, I imported some video of a birthday party.
One portion of the video was of the cake and presents while the next showed the
kids playing outside. Windows Me broke the two sequences into two different
clips that I can manage and use separately. This doesn't always work perfectly,
but it works well enough so that Windows Movie Maker can help you manage
and edit your video easier.

If you right-click on any collection, you can delete the collection (which deletes all
of the clips belonging to that collection), rename it, or import or record more clips into
the collection. Note that you can create collections within collections. Remember,
collections are just folder structures that enable you to organize clips, so do what
works best for you to help you keep your data organized.

You can also right-click any clip and perform cut, paste, and copy functions
(this allows you to move clips from one collection to another), play a clip, or
access a clip's properties. The Properties window, shown in Figure 15-4, allows
you to enter some basic information about the clip.

Use this window to give the clip a title, adjust the clip's creation date, give the
clip a rating (G, PG, R, etc.), and describe the clip. Of course, you don't have to

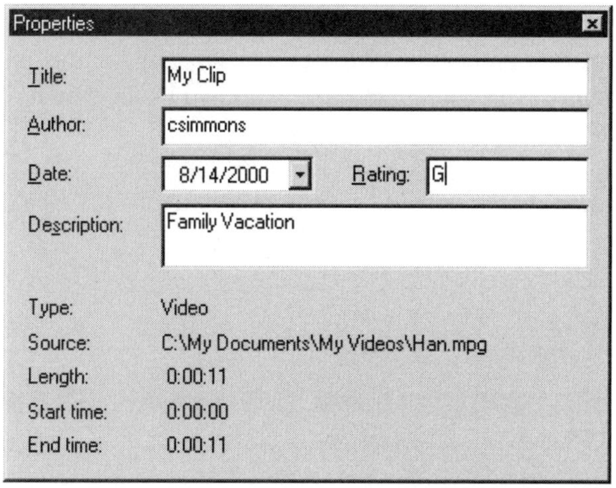

Properties	
Title:	My Clip
Author:	csimmons
Date:	8/14/2000 ▾ Rating: G
Description:	Family Vacation
Type:	Video
Source:	C:\My Documents\My Videos\Han.mpg
Length:	0:00:11
Start time:	0:00:00
End time:	0:00:11

FIGURE 15-4 Access clip properties to enter additional information about the clip

enter any of this information, but it may help you keep clips organized if you are working with many of them.

Making Movies

Now that you know how to record or import data and how to manage collections and clips, it's time to turn our attention to making movies. Using Windows Movie Maker, you can record or import the clips you want to use, organize them into collections, edit them as desired, and save the entire project. You are now ready to begin editing your video/still shot clips. Keep in mind that you can combine videos and still shots into one collection and blend them together as desired. You can also import background music and narrate a movie by recording your voice. The following sections show you how to perform all of these tasks.

Splitting Clips

Windows Movie Maker creates clips for you, but you may need to split those clips into more manageable pieces. You can do this by using the Split command. The following easy steps show you how:

1. In the Collections area, select the clip that you want to split.

2. In the Monitor area, click the Play button.

15

3. When the clip reaches the point where you want to split it, click the Clip menu and click Split. In the Collections area, the clip is split into two pieces. The first part of the clip retains its original name, and the second clip contains the original name followed by (1), as shown in Figure 15-5. You can change the name as desired.

SHORTCUT *You'll find helpful keyboard shortcuts for the Split command and many others on the inside back flap of this book.*

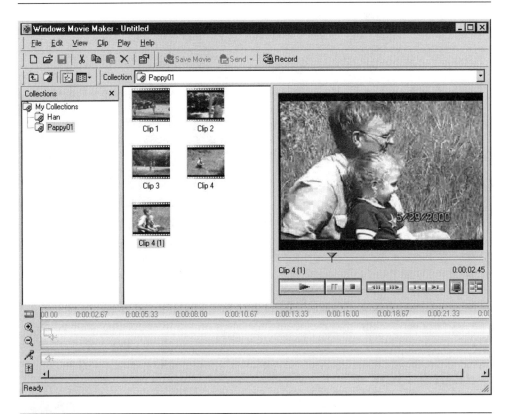

FIGURE 15-5   Split existing clips into more manageable pieces

Combining Clips

Just as you can split a clip so that you have two or more additional clips, you can also combine clips as needed. If you want to combine two or more clips, just follow these steps:

1. In the Collections area, select the clips that you want. Select the first clip, then hold down the SHIFT key on your keyboard and select the remaining clips that you want to combine.

2. Click Clip | Combine. The clips are combined and will be named the first clip's name. The original clips disappear since they are now one clip.

Getting Familiar with the Workspace

■ The workspace area at the bottom of the interface is the area where you edit and assemble movies. In the interface, shown in Figure 15-6, you see a few buttons on the left side of the area that correspond to different areas on the workspace. The areas are as follows: Timeline—Click the Timeline button (it looks like a little piece of film) to make a timeline appear. You'll use the timeline to assemble and edit video clips.

■ Video/Audio area—Use the Zoom In and Zoom Out icons to control this area, where you can place video clips.

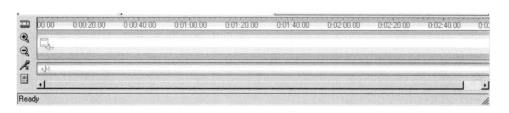

FIGURE 15-6   Use the workspace area to assemble your movie

15

■ Audio Clips Area—Use the Audio button (it looks like a microphone) to work in the Audio Clips area at the bottom of the workspace. You use this area to overlap sound onto a movie.

Creating a Storyboard

In order to create a storyboard or to sequence your clips together, use the workspace. Drag clips onto the workspace area to create the storyboard. You can then edit them as desired for transition purposes. Begin by dragging the first clip in your movie to the Video area of the workspace. Once it's in position, the first frame of the video is displayed with a gray area indicating the rest of the clip. Notice in the timeline that the time of the clip is displayed. This corresponds to the grayed, or blocked out, area in the video frame. By using the timeline, you can connect pieces of clips together while keeping a watch over the time frame of the movie, as shown in Figure 15-7.

The Zoom In and Zoom Out buttons let you see more detail concerning the timeline. While zoomed out, the storyboard is shown to you in increments of ten seconds. You can zoom in and zoom out to see the clips in whatever time measure you want.

Feel free to mix videos and still shots together on the storyboard. By default, imported still shots are given five seconds of time on a storyboard. You can change this default behavior by clicking View | Options. Change the Default Imported Photo Duration value from five seconds to a desired value.

FIGURE 15-7   Drag clips on the workspace area to assemble your movie

 **Create a Title Slide**

You can create title slides or insert other graphics or text slides into your storyboard. It's very easy, and here's how you do it:

1. Create the desired slide using a program such as Paint or Microsoft PowerPoint.

2. Save the file as a graphics file supported by Windows Movie Maker, such as a bitmap or JPEG.

3. In Windows Movie Maker, right-click the collection where you want the slide imported and then click Import.

4. Browse and locate the slide and click Open. The slide is imported and now appears in your Collections area.

5. Drag the slide onto the storyboard to the desired location.

Trimming Clips

As you work with clips in the storyboard, you will notice areas of your video that you want to cut out, or *trim*. These are often dead spots in the video where not

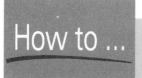 **Preview Clips or Storyboards**

15

As you work with clips and construct a storyboard, you'll want to stop and preview how things are looking so far. Not a problem—to preview a clip, right-click it and click Play. If you want to see an entire storyboard, right-click the storyboard and click Play Entire Storyboard/Timeline. If you don't like right-clicking, you can click the Play menu to get the same options.

much is happening. For example, let's say you have been video taping your dog (OK, it's an example). Your dog does this great trick, but to capture the trick, you end up filming a boring minute or two waiting for the dog to perform. Now you want to lose the boring time when you create the movie. No problem—just trim off the excess.

The Trim feature is very powerful because it gives you a fine level of control over your clips. There are two ways to trim clips, and here's the first:

1. In the workspace, select the clip you want to trim. The first frame of the clip appears in the Monitor.

2. The trimming process *keeps* the portion of videotape from where you start trimming to where you stop trimming, and it discards the rest. That seems a little confusing, but think of a piece of paper. You trim away the pieces you don't want and you keep the primary piece. With the trim feature, you set a beginning and end trim point and everything outside of the area is trimmed away. To begin trimming, press Play in the Monitor area.

3. Watch the clip until it reaches the place where you want to begin trimming. Click Clip | Set Start Trim Point. (Remember, anything previous to this point will be discarded).

4. When the clip reaches the point where you want to stop trimming, click Clip | Set End Trim Point. All video outside of the trim area you just set is cut and discarded.

5. If you don't want to keep the trim points themselves, click Clip | Clear Trim Points.

The second way you can trim clips is by using the timeline. Follow these steps:

1. In the workspace area, select the clip in the storyboard that you want to trim.

2. Above the clip in the timeline, you see inverted triangles on the top edge of the video—one at each end. These triangles are the trim feature. Slide them along the timeline to adjust the location of the trim. As you slide them, the

clip is shown in the Monitor area, frame by frame, so you can tell where to place the beginning and ending trim points.

 *As you can probably guess, the Trim feature is very useful, but it's a little confusing at first. Spend a few moments playing with it and you'll get the hang of it.*

Creating Transitions

Windows Movie Maker provides a default fade transition. This feature places a transition between clips so that the flow from clip to clip is more natural and less choppy.

You can easily create transitions by using the workspace. Follow these steps:

1. In the workspace, make certain that the Timeline view is enabled.

2. Between the two clips you want to make the transition to, select the transition on the right side of the two clips, then drag a portion of the right clip over the left clip, as shown in Figure 15-8. The overlapping area is the transition. From the first clip, the screen will fade into the next clip. You can make the transition as long or short as you like (but it can't exceed the entire length of the clip).

3. Experiment with the transitions by altering the amount of overlap. Remove the transition by moving the clip back to its original position.

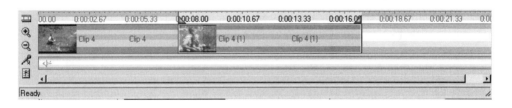

FIGURE 15-8   Drag the right clip over the left clip to create a transition

15

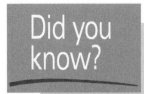

Other Transition Options

As you plan transitions, keep in mind that you can import a variety of graphics file types into your storyboard. This feature allows you to place other kinds of transitional elements in between your clips. For example, you can use PowerPoint to create a slide to insert between your clips, or you can use Paint to create a graphic. You can have the clips transition into these slides as well. Be creative—explore and experiment!

Audio Files and Your Movies

Once you have placed clips on the storyboard and trimmed and transitioned them as desired, you can add audio to your movie. For example, you can add narration, background music, or even background noise. In other words, if it's an audio file, you can add it to your movie.

You may think, "What about the audio on my existing video?" For example, let's say you tape a family reunion. Everyone is talking and laughing, but you want to add soft background music to the movie. Can you add the music without ruining the original audio? Absolutely, and in this section I'll show you how.

Adding Audio to a Movie

There is an audio portion of the storyboard at the very bottom of the workspace area. To record, you should first have your computer microphone or other sound input device that you want to use connected and tested.

 *If you have an existing audio file you want to use, use the Import feature to import the audio file into your existing collection, then drag the audio file to the audio portion of the workspace.*

To record your voice, background music, or other sounds in an audio file, follow these steps:

1. In the workspace area, click the Microphone icon.

2. A window appears listing the sound device that you will use to record the audio, as shown in Figure 15-9. If you have more than one sound device installed on your computer, use the drop-down menu to select a different device as desired. Note the Mute Video Soundtrack option. Click this button if you want to replace the video soundtrack with the soundtrack you are about to record. If you want to keep the existing soundtrack, don't check this. When you are ready, click the Record button.

3. Give the file a name and save it. The file now appears in your Collections area.

Adjusting Audio Levels

Once you add audio to your movie, you can adjust the audio level as needed. This is particularly helpful is you have two streams of audio; for example, a primary audio stream, such as voice, and a secondary audio stream, such as background music. By

FIGURE 15-9   Use this window to record your narration or background

15

default, Movie Maker sets both streams to the same audio level, so you'll need to adjust them for your movie. To adjust audio levels, just follow these steps:

1. In Windows Movie Maker, click Edit | Audio Levels.

2. On the slider bar that appears, move the slider as needed, as shown in Figure 15-10. The video track contains your primary audio and the audio track contains the secondary audio.

Mixing Audio

Feeling creative? You can create sound clips and have them overlap with each other. You do this the same way you create transitions in the workspace. Just drag the audio files to the audio section of the workspace, then drag portions of them together where you want. This way, you can have narration and a funny sound bite or music and some additional narration or sound flowing over the top of it. There are all kinds of possibilities—don't be afraid to experiment!

Saving Movies

When you're all done, you can save your movie project or you can save movies individually. Use the File menu in Movie Maker for both of these options. If you choose either the Save Project or the Save Project As option on the File menu, you

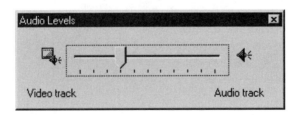

FIGURE 15-10   Use the slider bar to adjust audio track levels

can save the entire project. When you're ready, you can open the project and continue working.

Once your movie is finished, you can then save it as a movie file so that Window Media Player and other media software can read and play the movie. To save the movie, click File | Save Movie. Once you save the movie, you'll be able to view it with Windows Media Player.

Using Your Movies on the Web

As long as your movies are saved in a common audiovisual format (such as AVI or MPEG), you can publish your movies to a Web site or even e-mail them to your friends. However, let me warn you that multimedia files such as movies can be quite large in terms of megabytes, so be wary before you send a movie to someone who accesses the Internet with a modem. You really need a high bandwidth solution, such as DSL or ISDN, before using this option.

To send a movie over e-mail, just click File | Send Movie To. Choose either e-mail or Web server and follow the instructions that appear.

A Word about Copyrights

As you are creating movies, it is important to keep in mind that copyright laws apply. If you are creating any items that will be used on the Internet, you are liable for using information (including music) in your movies that belongs to someone else. For home movies you create for fun, this isn't an issue, but do investigate copyright rules before creating movies that you intend to distribute to other people.

15

Chapter 16

Keeping Windows Me Healthy and Happy

How To...

- Access Disk properties
- Run Disk tools
- Use the DriveSpace utility
- Configure and manage Scheduled Tasks

Windows operating systems have come a long way in the past few years. Your Windows Me computer can do more than ever, both with your help and automatically. A big part of that OS growth is in the area of PC/OS maintenance and problem solving. Windows Me gives you several helpful tools to keep your PC running well and in a healthy operating condition. To make the best use of Windows Me and your PC, you need to know about these tools and options—why they are important and when you should use them. In this chapter, I'll show you how to use these tools and offer some practical tips and advice about them.

Checking Out Disk Properties

As you have learned throughout this book, almost everything in Windows Me has a Properties page—a place where you can get more information. Your hard disks, removable disks, and CD-ROM/DVD drives are no exception. If you open My Computer on your desktop, you'll see an icon for each drive available on your computer: your C drive, a floppy drive, a CD-ROM/DVD drive, and possibly other drives, such as a Zip or Jaz drive. Even Windows CE devices are listed here if they are attached to you computer. If you right-click any of your disks and click Properties, you see a standard Properties page.

There are three tabs: General, Tools, and Sharing, with some maintenance and management features on each one. The following sections examine each of them individually.

 *The tools and options presented in the following sections only apply to writable disks, not read-only CD-ROM or DVD disks.*

General Tab

One of the best things about the General tab is the pie graph, which you can see in Figure 16-1. You can access your drive's General tab at any time and see exactly how much disk space is used and how much disk space is free (available for use). You can get this usage information for any writable disk, including your floppy drive.

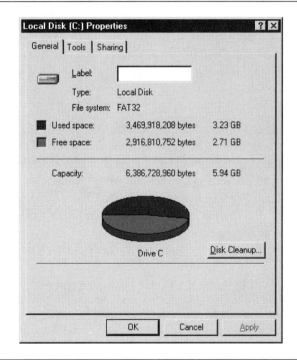

FIGURE 16-1   Disk General tab

16

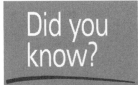

What Is a File System?

On the General tab, you'll see the type of file system Windows Me is using, either FAT16 or FAT32. FAT stands for File Allocation Table. FAT segments your hard drive into logical blocks so that Windows Me can read and write to the drive. Windows Me cannot use a drive that is not formatted or that is formatted with another file system. FAT16, which is used in the early versions of Windows 95, does not support the mammoth hard drives we use today as FAT32 does, so Windows Me always prefers to use FAT32. If Windows Me is installed on a nonformatted drive, it will format the drive with FAT32. If a FAT16 drive is being upgraded to Windows Me, you are given the option to upgrade to FAT32.

Aside from getting quick information, there are only two things you can do on the General tab. First, you can enter a label for the disk. The label isn't anything useful to you, so most people don't put anything here. The other option on the General tab is the Disk Cleanup option, which you will find useful from time to time.

Disk Cleanup is a utility that inspects your hard disk and looks for files that can be safety deleted. By deleting unused or unneeded files, you free up disk space that can be used for other purposes.

To run the Disk Cleanup utility, just follow these steps:

1. On the General Tab, click the Disk Cleanup button.

2. Disk Cleanup scans your disk, then provides you with a window, shown in Figure 16-2, that has two tabs, Disk Cleanup and More Options. The Disk Cleanup tab lists categories of potential items to delete and the amount of disk space you will gain by emptying each one.

3. When you have decided what items/categories you want to delete, click the check boxes next to the categories, then click OK.

4. Click the More Options tab, shown in Figure 16-3, to specify different cleanup options. The three Clean Up buttons on this tab take you to other areas on your computer where you can remove unwanted items, such as Windows Setup and Add/Remove Programs.

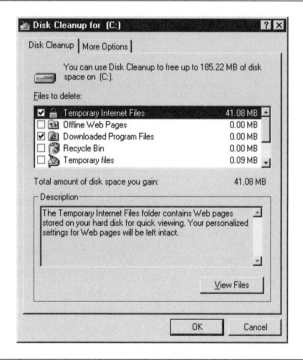

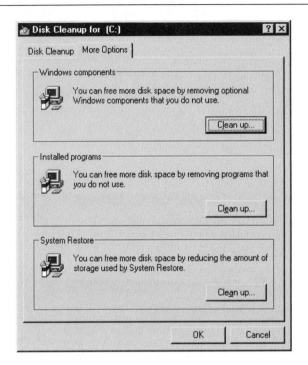

FIGURE 16-3   More Options helps you remove unwanted components and programs

It is important to remember that Disk Cleanup examines only certain areas of your computer, such as temporary files and downloaded Internet items. Disk Cleanup does not inspect every possible category of items that can be deleted—much of that work is left to you. So, how often should you use Disk Cleanup? A typical user should run this utility once every three months to see if there are unused files that can be deleted to free up disk space.

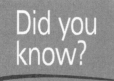

How to Conserve Disk Space

If you have a newer computer, conserving disk space probably isn't a big concern to you—after all, it is not uncommon for a typical computer to ship equipped with a 13GB or higher hard drive. That's a lot of storage space, but if you use Windows Movie Maker and Windows Media Player a lot and hang on to all of your video and multimedia files, you will soon need a lot of disk space. Here are some quick tips to help you conserve disk space on your computer:

- Uninstall programs you do not use. Programs take up a lot of space, and if you aren't playing all ten of those games you installed, then get rid of them. You can always reinstall one if you need it later, but in the mean time, free up that disk space!

- Old personal files can easily be saved to floppy or Zip disks for storage.

- Check Add/Remove Programs from time to time. If you download a lot of utilities from the Internet, you may need to remove unneeded or unwanted ones.

- Use folder compression (see Chapter 4). Compression helps save disk space and doesn't interfere with your work.

Tools Tab

The Tools tab in the Local Disk Properties window gives you two important tools you can use to keep your computer disks happy and working efficiently, as shown in Figure 16-4. The following sections tell you all about these two tools.

16

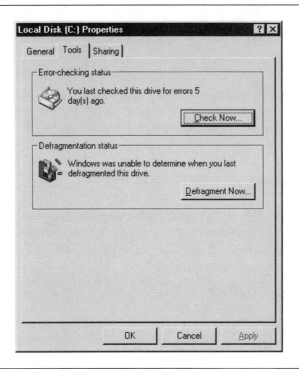

FIGURE 16-4   Tools tab

Error Checking (ScanDisk)

The first tool option you see is Error Checking, otherwise known as ScanDisk. If you click the Check Now button on the Tools tab, the ScanDisk tool is opened so you can check your disk for errors, as shown in Figure 16-5. (You can also locate ScanDisk in Start | Programs | Accessories | System Tools.) ScanDisk has several options.

To use ScanDisk, just click the drive that you want to scan, select either the Standard or Thorough scan radio buttons, and click Start. You should leave the Automatically Fix Errors check box enabled.

If you don't leave the Automatically Fix Errors check box enabled, ScanDisk will prompt you to click OK to fix every error it finds (which can get really annoying).

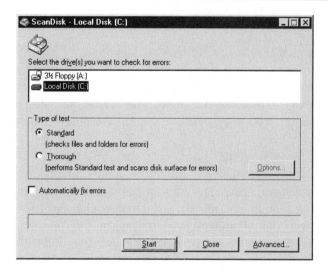

FIGURE 16-5   Use ScanDisk to check your drive for errors

Each test is different. The Standard test only checks your files and your folders for errors. This includes Windows' internal folder structure and links between folders. On a typical computer, this test takes about five minutes. The Thorough test does everything the Standard test does and also scans the surface of your hard disk for errors. This feature enables ScanDisk to find and fix logical errors (files and folders) and physical errors (on the physical disk itself). If you want to use the Thorough test, click the Thorough radio button, and then click Options. This opens a window, shown in Figure 16-6, where you can specify what you want ScanDisk to check. You have the following options:

- System And Data Areas—Checks your entire physical disk for errors.

- System Area Only—Looks for errors only in the System area of your disk. Errors found here usually cannot be fixed by ScanDisk and you will usually be told that you might need a new disk.

- Data Area Only—Looks for errors in the data storage areas of the physical disk. ScanDisk can fix problems found here by moving data out of bad areas and marking the area so that data is no longer stored in the bad area.

16

- ■ Do Not Perform Write Testing—If you click this check box, ScanDisk reads hard disk areas but does not write to them to check for write problems.

- ■ Do Not Repair Bad Sectors In Hidden And System Files—This option tells ScanDisk not to repair bad sectors where hidden files and system files are kept. Remember that to fix bad data sectors, ScanDisk moves files out of the bad sector to problem-free areas. This feature may stop some older programs from working properly if certain hidden files are moved.

Now that you know what the options are, what should you do? First, note that the Standard test is automatically run during reboot after an improper system shut-down. Let's say your computer locks up and you had to turn the power off and then turn it back on. During reboot, ScanDisk checks your file and folder structure. If you use your computer a lot, it doesn't hurt to run the ScanDisk Standard test every few weeks, just to make sure your files and folders are up to par. You do not typically need to run the Thorough test unless you are having problems with your computer. If you are getting a lot of error message or having conflicts or lock ups, you can run the Thorough test to see if ScanDisk finds anything wrong with your hard disk.

A Thorough ScanDisk may take half an hour or longer, depending on the size of the disk being scanned.

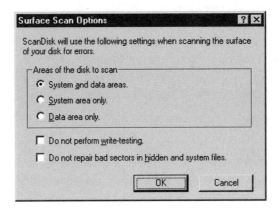

FIGURE 16-6   ScanDisk Thorough test options

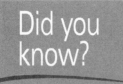

Avoiding Disk Errors

Disk errors are a part of life and not anything to be too concerned about as long as you allow ScanDisk to fix them from time to time. Although a number of different actions and problems can cause disk errors, here are some tips to help you avoid them:

- Always use Start | Shut Down to shut down your computer. This enables Windows to shut down automatically. Avoid shutting down your computer by just turning off the power button (as I tell my four-year-old daughter, "That's a no-no").

- Uninstall programs by using the program's uninstall feature or Add/Remove Programs in Control Panel. Do not delete a program's folder to uninstall it unless there is no other way.

- If you have a lock-up or some other problem that forces a hard reboot, allow ScanDisk to run at reboot to catch and repair new errors.

Disk Defragmenter

Windows Me includes a Disk Defragmenter utility you can access from the Tools tab (or in Start | Programs | Accessories | System Tools). Before you use Disk Defragmenter, I need to tell you a little bit about fragmentation so you'll understand the process.

Fragmentation is a normal part of disk usage, and it occurs at the file system level. Windows Me is not able to use a disk of any kind unless the disk is formatted. Formatting logically divides the disk into sectors and regions, basically making a grid out of the disk so that blocks of data can be stored on the hard disk. In order to create this grid, Windows Me uses a file system (either FAT16 or FAT32). Once the file system is in place, Windows Me can read and write data from the hard disk.

In Windows Me, data is stored on the disk in a contiguous manner. This just means that data is stored "in order." For example, let's say you're working again on that Great American Novel. When you save the document, it is divided into pieces, or blocks of data, and stored in a "row" on the disk. Later, when you make changes to the document, those changes are stored at the end of the row. Over

16

time, as you save, edit, and delete different files, changes to those files are moved to available storage blocks on the disk so that files become *fragmented*. In order words, they are not stored contiguously. When you want to open a file, Windows Me must gather the fragmented pieces together from your hard disk. Since the pieces are in different places, this can take longer than it should. In short, heavily fragmented drives can cause Windows Me to run slower than it should.

The Disk Defragmenter utility takes all of the data on your hard disk and reorganizes it so that it is stored in a contiguous format—or at least close to it. When you start the Disk Defragmenter utility from the Tools menu, the utility automatically begins, as you can see in Figure 16-7.

> **NOTE**   *If you start the Disk Defragmenter from the Accessories | System Tools menu, you are prompted to select the drive you want to defragment before the utility begins working. If you want more information about the process, click the Details button that appears on the utility. This opens a full-screen window that displays a grid of small blocks. The blocks appear in different colors, depending on their fragmentation status. Click the Legend button on this window to see the meaning of each color.*

How often should you defragment your drives? The rule of thumb is to consider how often you use your computer. If you are a typical home user, you should run the defragmenter utility about once every two or three months. If you use your PC all day, every day like I do and you use a lot of files, you should defragment your drives once a month. This will help keep your file system in peak operating order and keep Windows Me happy.

> **TIP**   *Defragmentation may take an hour or longer, depending on the size of disk. Run the utility when you plan to step away from your computer.*

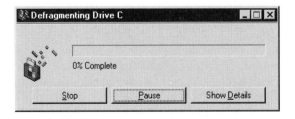

FIGURE 16-7   Disk Defragmenter

NOTE *Disk Defragmenter needs full access to your disk. You cannot have any other programs running while you defragment. Close all programs and close any program icons you see in your System Tray. These programs will interrupt Disk Defragmenter and cause it to start over... and over... and over...*

Sharing Tab

Just as with folders, you can share any drive on your computer so that others on a network can access it. The Sharing tab in the Local Disk Properties window is just like all other Sharing tabs in Windows Me, and you can learn more about network shares in Chapter 11. Under most circumstances, you would not want to give someone else full access to your entire hard drive, but you may want to give someone access to a CD-ROM or Zip drive.

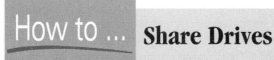 **Share Drives**

Let's say you have a home network. Once of your PC's floppy or CD-ROM drives stops working. What can you do until it's fixed? Easy solution: just share those drives on another computer so the PC can use the shared drive. You can also share Zip or Jaz drives so that any computer on your network can access them. Sharing these drives can save you time and money, and it's very easy to set up. To share a drive, just follow these steps:

1. Right-click the drive you want to share in My Computer, then click Properties.

2. Click the Sharing tab. If there is no Sharing tab, then networking is not set up on your computer. See Chapter 11 for details.

3. Click the Shared As radio button and give the share a recognizable name.

4. Select a share level, either Read-only, Full, or Depends On Password.

5. Enter a password as needed or prompted, and then click OK. A hand icon will now appear under the shared drive.

16

Using the DriveSpace 3 Utility

DriveSpace 3 is a compression technology used to compress the contents on disks so that storage space is conserved. Windows Me does not use DriveSpace 3 for disk compression, but a utility is included to help you manage and decompress drives that are compressed using DriveSpace 3. You'll find the DriveSpace 3 tool available in Start | Programs | Accessories | System Tools. DriveSpace is a simple utility, as shown in Figure 16-8.

 *Depending on your system configuration, DriveSpace may not appear in your System Tools folder. If it doesn't, install it using the Windows Setup tab of Add/Remove Programs.*

To use DriveSpace 3, select the compressed drive that appears in the dialog box (if there are no compressed drives, you don't need to use DriveSpace). Once you have selected the compressed drive you want to manage, you can use the Drive and Advanced menus to manage the disk.

From the Drive menu, you can either format a disk or exit the DriveSpace program. The Format command lets you format (or reformat) a compressed drive. Windows Explorer does not let you format a DriveSpace compressed drive, but this utility gives you that functionality. To use it, just click Format and follow the

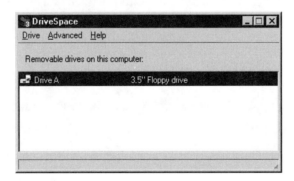

FIGURE 16-8   DriveSpace 3

instructions that appear. The Drive menu also lets you adjust the amount of free space available on a drive; just move the slider bar.

 *If you do not have a DriveSpace compressed drive selected, a message appears telling you to use Windows Explorer to format the drive.*

 *Formatting erases all information on a disk. Make sure you do not format a disk that contains information you want to keep until that information has been removed.*

The Advanced menu gives you a few ways to manage DriveSpace drives. First, you can mount or unmount a compressed drive. Mounting a drive means that Windows Me has access to the drive or recognizes its presence. You typically use the Mount and Unmount commands when you insert a DriveSpace floppy or Zip disk into a disk drive. Permanent DriveSpace drives, such as the computer's hard disk, are mounted automatically by Windows. The Mount command allows DriveSpace to view and use the compressed drive.

You can also use the Advanced menu to delete a compressed drive. When you choose this option, the CVF (compressed volume file) and all data on the disk is deleted, effectively decompressing the drive and removing all data from it. You can now use the disk with normal Windows disk tools because the drive is no longer compressed.

Finally, you can click Settings on the Advanced menu. This opens a single window in which you can adjust the compression method used by DriveSpace, as shown in Figure 16-9. Using these options, you can create more free disk space by increasing compression. You have the following options:

- HiPack Compression—Provides the most free disk space.

- Standard Compression—The default option.

- No Compression, Unless Drive Is At Least *n*% Full—Allows you to specify that the disk is beginning to run out of storage space before DriveSpace compression is used.

- No Compression—Removes any DriveSpace compression used.

16

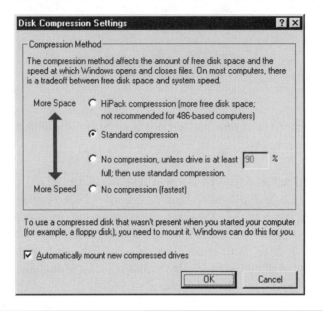

FIGURE 16-9   DriveSpace compression options

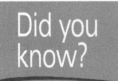

Backward Compatibility

You may wonder why Windows Me includes a DriveSpace utility when Windows Me doesn't support DriveSpace. It's for backward compatibility. Because DriveSpace was used on many earlier computers with Windows 95, Windows Me includes the utility so that users who upgrade to Windows Me from Windows 95 can use the utility to continue to manage compressed drives. Several features are included in Windows Me to ensure backward compatibility for upgraded operating systems and computers.

Higher compression always has a performance cost. Although higher compression saves disk space, Windows Me will require more time to recall and save data to and from a highly compressed drive.

Scheduled Tasks

Remember how I said that you should run Disk Defragmenter, ScanDisk, and Disk Cleanup at regular intervals? What if you don't want to remember to keep up with these housekeeping tasks? The good news is you don't have to. You can use a Windows Me feature called Scheduled Tasks so you can schedule these utilities to run automatically on your computer at certain times and on certain days.

You'll find the Scheduled Tasks in Control Panel, or you can access it by clicking Start | Programs | in Accessories | System Tools. Scheduled Tasks is actually a folder, and when you open it, you see an Add Scheduled Tasks Wizard and two preconfigured scheduled tasks that automatically run on your computer. The first is a PCHealth task that gathers information to use a utility called System Restore. You'll learn all about the fantastic features of System Restore in Chapter 18. Don't do anything to this wizard—it needs to run as configured. The other preconfigured scheduled task automatically runs the Maintenance Wizard on your computer, which you can learn more about in Chapter 17. In short, Windows Me needs these preconfigured tasks, so leave them in the folder.

Add Scheduled Task Wizard

You can use the Add Scheduled Task Wizard to create additional scheduled tasks for your PC. The wizard allows you to select tasks and determine when they should automatically run on your computer. Configuring the scheduled task is easy. Just follow these steps:

1. In the Scheduled Tasks folder, double-click the Add Scheduled Tasks Wizard icon.

2. Click Next on the Welcome screen.

3. In the next window, as shown in Figure 16-10, scroll through the selections and select a task you want to schedule. If the task you want is not available, click the Browse button to locate it on your computer. Click Next when you're done.

16

4. Enter a name for the task (or accept the default) and click a radio button to select how often you want the task to run, such as daily, weekly, monthly, etc. Click Next.

5. In the next window, select the days/times you want the task to run, as shown in Figure 16-11. This window may vary, according to your selection in Step 4. Click Next.

6. In the completion window, click the Finish button. The scheduled task now appears in your Scheduled Tasks folder.

Managing Scheduled Tasks

Once you have created scheduled tasks, the icons for those tasks reside in the Scheduled Tasks folder. If you later decide that you do not need the scheduled task, just right-click its icon in the folder and click Delete. In the same manner, you can choose to manually run the scheduled task at an unscheduled time by right-clicking the icon and clicking Run.

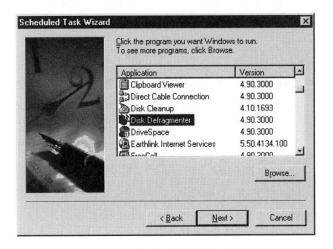

FIGURE 16-10   Select the task you want to schedule

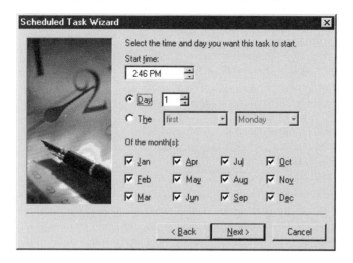

FIGURE 16-11   Select the day and time for the task to run

Another piece of good news is you can access the task's Properties page and change basically anything you configured with the wizard. This is a great feature because your needs may change, and you can just alter the scheduled task without having to delete it and create a new one. To edit a scheduled task, just right-click its icon and click Properties. There are three tabs: Task, Schedule, and Settings. The following sections tell you what you can do on each.

Task Tab

The Task tab, shown in Figure 16-12, lets you change the location of a particular task and the settings for the task.

When a task is scheduled, the Add Scheduled Task Wizard notes the location of the program on your computer. When it is time to run the task, the scheduled task starts the program. However, what happens if that program is later moved to a different folder? Scheduled tasks will not be able to find the program, so it will not run. You can use the Task tab to change the location for the task so that it

16

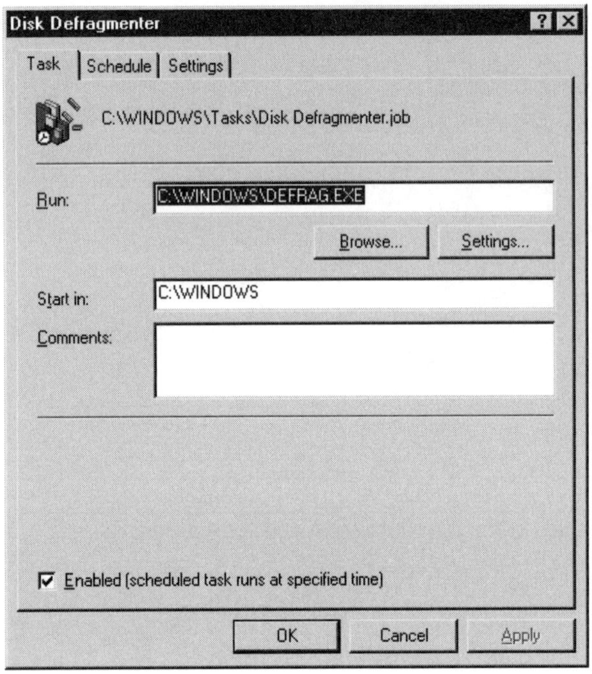

FIGURE 16-12 Task tab

points to the new location of the program on your computer. In most cases, you won't need to do this, but if you are running custom programs, you may need to change the information here if the program is moved.

You can also click the Settings button to access any configurable settings for the program. For example, since I have scheduled Disk Defragmenter, I can click the Settings button and determine which of my computer's hard disks should be checked.

Schedule Tab

The Schedule tab, shown in Figure 16-13, gives you an easy interface with which to change the schedule of the task. Let's say you originally scheduled ScanDisk to run at 8:00 PM once every two weeks. However, you have been using your computer a lot in the evenings and ScanDisk has been interrupting you. No problem—just change the start time to a more convenient one on this tab. As you can see, you can change anything about the task's schedule here.

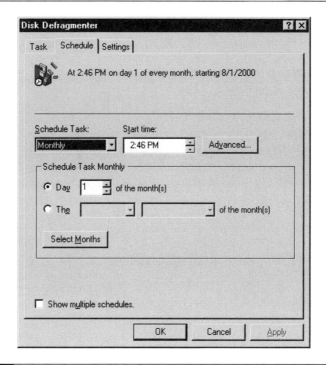

FIGURE 16-13   Schedule tab

16

Settings Tab

The Settings tab gives you several good options. These options are not presented to you when you run the wizard, so you will definitely want to check out this tab (shown in Figure 16-14).

As you can see, the options on this tab are rather self-explanatory, but I do want to mention a couple of things you might consider. Notice that you have the option to stop a task if it has run for a certain period of time. For longer tasks, such as Disk Defragmenter, this can be a good safety check in case another program is interfering with the task and causing it to start over… and over… You get the point. You should not, however, configure this setting too low—24 hours is your best minimum.

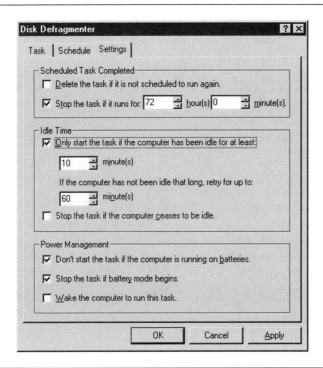

FIGURE 16-14   Use the settings tab to enable additional options

Also, the idle time can be very useful. What if you schedule a task to run at a certain time, but you are using the computer when the task is supposed to run? Without the Idle Time feature enabled on this window, the task runs anyway and may interrupt your work or play. You can use the Idle Time feature so the task will wait until the computer has been idle for a certain number of minutes. If you use your computer a lot, this feature can be very handy!

In the Power Management section, you should leave the two options concerning batteries enabled if you are using a laptop computer. If not, you can clear these settings because they do not apply to a desktop PC.

TIP

You can configure as many scheduled tasks as you like; however, each task should be configured to run at a different time because some programs, such as ScanDisk and Disk Defragmenter, cannot run at the same time. Also, use as many scheduled tasks as you need, but don't over-schedule them. Too many tasks running at close intervals sometimes causes more confusion than necessary and may degrade Windows Me performance.

16

Chapter 17

Monitoring and Optimizing Windows Me

How To...

- Use System Information
- Use System Monitor
- Examine Resource Meter
- Use Net Watcher
- Run the Maintenance Wizard
- Explore performance options

Windows Me includes a number of features that help you monitor what's going on with your computer as well as optimize its performance. Many of these features are designed to give you information to help you make informed decisions about performance problems Windows Me may be experiencing. All of these tools help you keep Windows Me working well and provide you with information you need. In this chapter, I'll explore these options and show you how to use them.

System Information

First introduced in Windows 98, System Information is a powerful tool that provides all kinds of information about your computer system, and it includes some additional tools that can fix problems on your system. The System Information interface is a part of the new Help and Support feature of Windows Me (which you will learn more about in Chapter 18), as you can see in Figure 17-1.

 *You can quickly reach System Information by clicking Start | Run, typing MSINFO32, and clicking OK.*

 *Since the tools in the System Information Tools menu are used to help you solve problems, they are explored in Chapter 18.*

If you take a look at the left pane under System Summary, you see a list of information categories. If you click the plus (+) sign next to each category, you can select specific topics you want to gather information on. It is important to note here that you cannot configure or actually *do* anything with System Information, with the exception of the troubleshooting tools, but the System Information is designed to give

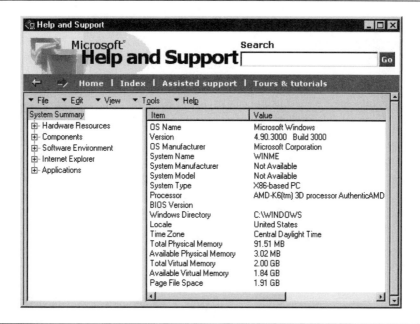

FIGURE 17-1   System Information

you…well, information. Why, you might ask? The answer is simple. The more information you can gather about your computer, the more likely you are to solve problems with your computer. On a more practical note, System Information is very useful to telephone support personnel whom you may need to call in the event of a problem you can't solve.

Of course, it is always best if you can solve your own PC problems, so the next several sections tell you all about the information you can learn in each major category, and I'll point out some tips along the way.

System Summary

When you first open System Information, the default view is the System Summary. This view just gives you an overview, or big picture, of your computer. You see everything from information about the operating system itself to the total amount of RAM installed on your computer. This page is useful to access if you need a quick report about the basics on your computer. You can easily print this page as well.

17

 *As you are looking at different categories, note that clicking View |
Advanced may give you more information, depending on the current
category selected.*

Hardware Resources

The Hardware Resources category of System Information gives you a complete
look at the hardware on your computer. This section is an excellent way to see
exactly what is installed, what's working and what's not, and if there are any
conflicts, as shown in Figure 17-2.

Should there be any conflicts, you'll see warning messages in yellow and
conflict or error messages in red. This helps you quickly identify problems if they
exist. By expanding Hardware Resources in the left pane, you see the following
categories that you can select and view:

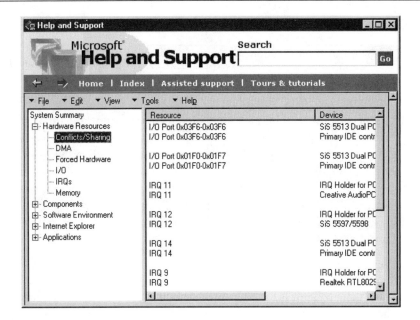

FIGURE 17-2   Hardware Resources in System Information

■ Conflicts/Sharing—Tells you if there are any hardware conflicts between devices. In some cases, hardware devices share certain computer resources, and this section tells you about those as well.

■ DMA (Direct Memory Access)—Tells you what devices have direct access to memory resources.

■ Forced Hardware—If you have problems installing a device and it has been "forced" onto your system using manual settings, the device will be listed here.

■ I/O (Input/Output System)—Gives you a report about input/output operation. Technical support personnel may find this information useful.

■ IRQs (Interrupt Request Lines)—Each device uses an IRQ to access your computer's processor. This option tells you which device is using which IRQ.

■ Memory—Provides a list of memory resource assignment per device.

Components

The Components category provides a list of components installed and used on your system. Some of these include additional information that will appear in the right pane, as shown in Figure 17-3. As a reminder, System Information will display problems in yellow and red lettering so you can easily identify them.

You learn information about the following:

■ Multimedia—Information about your audio and video configuration, including your CD-ROM drive and sound card.

■ Display—Complete information about your display and its operation with your system is provided here.

■ Infrared—If you are using any infrared devices, they are listed here.

■ Input—Information about your keyboard and mouse or other pointing device.

■ Modem—Information about your modem.

■ Network—Information about your network adapters and protocol usage.

■ Ports—Information about ports on your computer, such as serial and parallel.

17

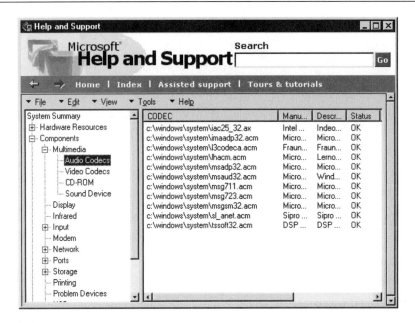

FIGURE 17-3 Components category

- Storage—Information about the drives on your computer.

- Printing—Information about print and print drivers.

- Problem Devices—If any devices are not working correctly, they are listed here. This is a very useful option to quickly find troublesome devices.

- USB (Universal Serial Bus)—USB configuration and devices are listed here.

Software Environment

The Software Environment category, shown in Figure 17-4, gives you information about the software configuration of Windows Me. If there are any problems or errors, they'll appear in red or yellow. This category can be very helpful to technical support personnel who are helping you solve a problem with Windows Me.

You see the following information in this category:

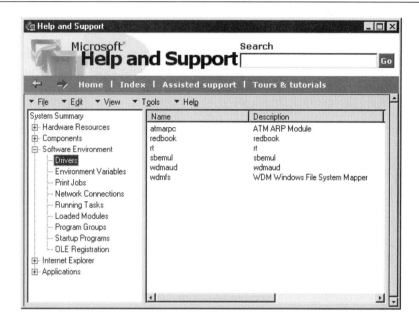

FIGURE 17-4   Software Environment category

■ Drivers—Lists the drivers that manage your computer's software environment.

■ Environment Variables—Lists items such as your TEMP file (which is used for temporary files) and other variables in the software environment.

■ Print Jobs—Gives you the information in your print queue.

■ Network Connections—Lists all network connections currently held by your computer.

■ Running Tasks—Lists all of the tasks on your computer that are currently running.

■ Loaded Modules—Lists all software modules currently loaded.

■ Program Groups—Lists all program groups currently configured on your computer.

17

■ Startup Programs—Lists all programs that are configured to run automatically when your computer starts up.

■ OLE (Object Linking and Embedding) Registration—Windows Me uses OLE so that various system components and programs can communicate with each other. OLE information is listed here.

Internet Explorer

This category provides you information about the configuration of Internet Explorer, as shown in Figure 17-5.

You'll find the following information in this category:

■ Summary—A quick summary of IE's configuration.

■ File Versions—Lists all files and file versions used by IE.

■ Connectivity—A quick review of IE's connectivity configuration. These are the settings you configured in Internet Options in IE.

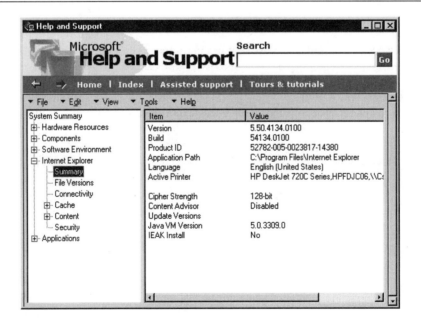

FIGURE 17-5   Internet Explorer category

■ Cache—IE uses a *cache* to store temporary Internet files. Access this option to learn more about the cache size and a list of objects in the cache.

■ Content—Security and content settings.

■ Security—Zone security configuration information.

Applications

Any applications that are installed on your computer are listed here. Click the plus (+) sign next to each one to learn about configuration specific to that application. This is a useful option to find out about problems and conflicts with any installed applications.

Quick Menu Notes

Before ending the System Information section, I do want to point out a few quick menu options that you may find very useful:

■ File—Use this menu to export or print System Information. You can export all of the data to a text file, and you can choose to print all of the information.

■ Edit—Use the search option on this menu to help you find particular information you are looking for.

■ View—Aside from the Advanced option mentioned earlier, you can also use the View menu to see system history and to access System Information on a remote computer on your network.

System Monitor

System Monitor is a utility found in Start | Programs | Accessories | System Tools. You can use System Monitor to chart and log various processes performed by your computer. With System Monitor, you can view specific areas of performance and identify components that are not performing in a satisfactory manner. System Monitor can help you determine such things as your processor performance, RAM usage and need, and a variety of other information.

17

If you don't see System Monitor or the other utilities discussed in the remainder of this chapter in System Tools, you may need to install them using Windows Setup in Add/Remove Programs in Control Panel.

When you open System Monitor, you see an empty grid, as shown in Figure 17-6. By default, System Monitor charts processes in a line chart format. You can change this option by clicking the View menu and clicking either Bar Charts or Numeric Charts.

You can dynamically change the type of chart you want to see by clicking chart-type button on the System Monitor toolbar.

Of course, you get the same information, regardless of what type of chart you choose to use. The following sections show you how to set up your charts and explore the options available.

Adding and Removing Chart Items

To begin using System Monitor, just add items to the chart so you can watch their progress. You can easily add items to the chart by following these steps:

1. In System Monitor, click Edit | Add Item.

2. In the Add Item window that appears, shown in Figure 17-7, select a category that you want to monitor. The possible monitor options appear in the Item window.

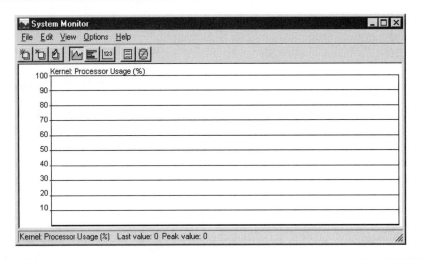

FIGURE 17-6   System Monitor

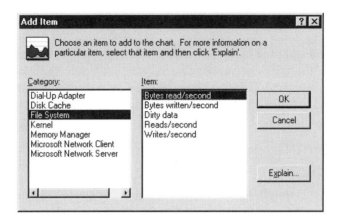

FIGURE 17-7   Select a category and an item you want to chart

Select the option you want to monitor, then click OK. If you want more explanation about the item, click the Explain button.

3. You can add other items to the chart by repeating steps 1 and 2. Each item appears in its own small chart where you can monitor its activity.

4. To remove an item from the chart, click Edit | Remove Item. Select the chart item you want to remove and click OK.

Changing Charting Speed

By default, the chart is updated every five seconds. However, you can increase or decrease this value. The question is, should you? As a general rule, a five-second chart update value gives you the best information to determine if a system resource is performing well. If you want to monitor the resource for a longer period of time, you may choose to increase this value to 10 or 15 seconds, but as a general rule, the default setting is best. To change the charting speed, click Options | Chart. Adjust the slider bar to the desired speed and click OK.

NOTE   *If you are charting a lot of items and you move the speed option to one second, you may notice that the system performance slows down because Windows Me must devote extra resources to keep up with the charting process.*

17

Using the Logging Option

If you are convinced that your system is having problems, you can use System Monitor to create a log file of the activity. Obviously, you should not create logs just for the fun of it, but they can be used to study chart data, and you can even e-mail that data to a technical support person. By default, any log you create is stored in C:\ and is called "Sysmon." To start logging, click File | Start Logging. To stop logging, click File | Stop Logging.

Resource Meter

Another utility in your System Tools folder is Resource Meter. You can't perform any configuration with Resource Meter, but it is a great way to watch major portions of your system to determine how your computer is handling the workload placed on it.

When you click Resource Meter in System Tools, a dialog box appears, shown in Figure 17-8, telling you that Resource Meter monitors all system resources, including itself.

When you click OK, an icon appears in your System Tray. To see what's going on, right-click the icon and click Details. A window appears, shown in Figure 17-9, showing you the percentage of resource usage in major categories.

Of course, these readings do not give you a lot of data, but if Resource Meter shows very high readings for long periods of time, this is a clue that your system components, such as processor and RAM, are probably being taxed by the demands of Windows Me and the programs you are running. In other words, you need to get rid of some programs that are hogging the computer's system resources or upgrade your hardware. As a general rule, most of the items you see in your

Log Files and Gibberish

To a normal computer user, System Monitor log files aren't particularly helpful. You have to know a thing or two about how System Monitor records data to make much sense of the log. For this reason, don't log a process unless you have a specific reason to do so or a technical support person has requested that you create the log.

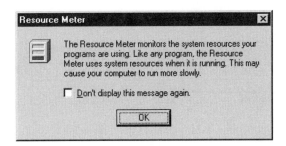

FIGURE 17-8   Click OK to view Resource Meter

System Tray are taking up CPU cycles. You may simply need to lose some of them in order to free up resources.

To exit Resource Meter, just right-click the icon in the System Tray and click Exit.

Net Watcher

Are you on a network or do you have a home network? Want to know who is using resources on your computer? You can! In System Tools, you'll find a utility called Net Watcher. Net Watcher lets you see who is connected to your computer and what they are doing there, as shown in Figure 17-10.

Net Watcher gives you information about who is connected to your computer, what shares they have open, and how long they have been connected. You can

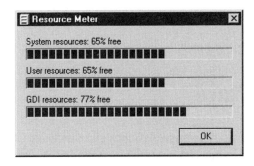

FIGURE 17-9   Resource Meter

17

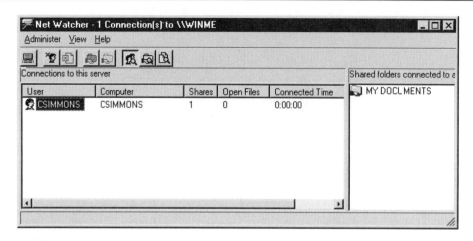

FIGURE 17-10   Use Net Watcher to see who is accessing resources on your computer

also click the View menu in Net Watcher to see connections by shared folders or open files.

Aside from seeing who is connected to your computer and what shares or files are in use, you can perform the following actions, depending how you are viewing the connections. Choose these options by clicking on the buttons on the toolbar:

- Share A New Folder—Create a new shared folder directly from this utility.

- Stop Sharing A Folder—Remove a share folder.

- Close A File—If a user is reading a file that you don't want them to read, you can close the file so the user can't read it.

- Disconnect A User—If someone should not be accessing your computer or has been connected to it for too long, you can forcefully disconnect the user from your computer.

Maintenance Wizard

Maintenance Wizard is similar to Scheduled Tasks. You can use Maintenance Wizard to automate several processes so they run automatically at specific times when you are not using your computer. The tasks include defragmentation (Disk Defragmenter), disk cleanup (Disk Cleanup), and error-checking (ScanDisk).

Rather than configuring these to run individually, you can use the Maintenance Wizard to set them up automatically. Maintenance Wizard is in Start | Programs | Accessories | System Tools. The opening screen, shown in Figure 17-11, enables you to run either an express or custom setup. The following two sections explore both of these options.

Express Setup

To use the Express setup feature, just follow these steps:

1. In Maintenance Wizard, click the Express radio button, then click Next.

2. Select a time that you want the wizard to run. Your computer must be turned on when the tasks are performed, but you should select a time when your work or play will not be interrupted. You are given three options: Midnight to 3:00 AM, Days—Noon–3 PM, or Evenings—8:00 PM–11 PM. Click the radio button next to the option you want, then click Next.

3. The next window tells you that Disk Defragmenter, Disk Cleanup, and ScanDisk will perform during the hours you specified. Click Finish.

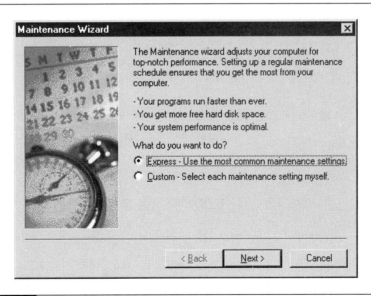

FIGURE 17-11   Maintenance Wizard welcome screen

17

Custom Setup

You may want to customize the maintenance tasks that are performed on your computer. To use Custom setup, just follow these steps:

1. On the Maintenance Wizard welcome screen, click the Custom radio button, then click Next.

2. Select the time you want the tasks to run by clicking the desired radio button, then click Next.

3. In the Start Windows More Quickly screen, shown in Figure 17-12, clear the check mark next to any items you do not want to run when Windows starts up. This action helps Windows start faster. Make your selections, and then click Next.

4. The next window prompts you to enable Disk Defragmenter, which optimizes Windows Me performance. Click the check box if you want to enable this feature, and then click the Schedule button to pick dates/times you want Disk Defragmenter to run. Click the Settings button to adjust which disks are defragmented. Click Next.

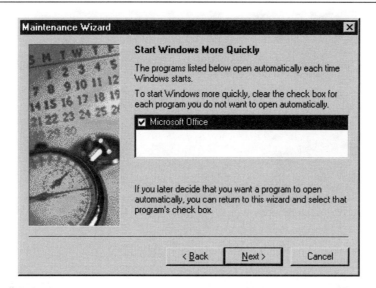

FIGURE 17-12   Deselect any unneeded items to help Windows start faster

5. The next window prompts you to enable ScanDisk to run. Click the Settings buttons to schedule when ScanDisk will run. Click Next.

6. The next window prompts you to enable Disk Cleanup, as shown in Figure 17-13. Select the items you want to clean up and adjust the schedule as desired. Click Next.

7. The final window gives you a summary of your settings. Click the Finish button.

Once you have completed the settings, you can always return to the wizard and run through the options in order to change your settings.

Using System Properties to Optimize Windows Me

You already know that you can use System Properties in Control Panel (or by right-clicking My Computer and clicking Properties) to access Device Manager, but you should also know that there is a Performance tab on the System Properties page, as shown in Figure 17-14.

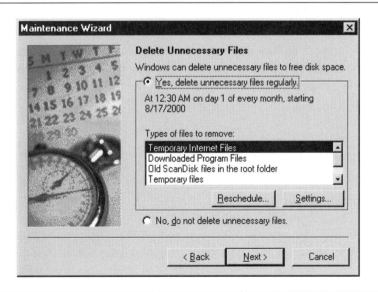

FIGURE 17-13   Select the items you want Disk Cleanup to manage

17

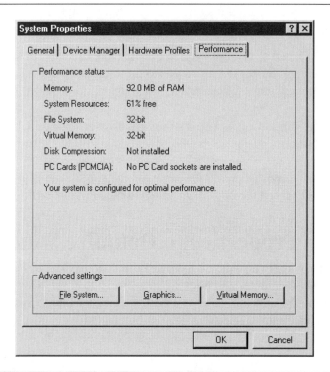

FIGURE 17-14
Performance tab in System Properties

A basic summary of your system's performance is presented on this tab. You also see some buttons at the bottom of the page where you can access different system component performance configurations. The following sections explore these options.

File System

File System Properties affect how storage devices, such as a hard disk, CD-ROM, or Zip disk, are used. As you can see in Figure 17-15, you are provided a standard interface with several different tabs.

Windows Me automatically configures these settings, so you should not change any settings on any of these tabs unless you are having specific performance problems with a certain device. Even then, changing settings on these tabs is usually not a solution. However, as a part of your monitoring and troubleshooting skills, it's good for you to know these File System Properties are available to you.

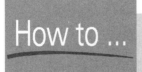 **System Resources**

Notice in Figure 17-14 the System Resources setting, which shows that 61 percent of my system resources are free. This is a good setting—it indicates that my computer does not have too many unnecessary processes running. What if you examine this setting and it shows 80 percent usage and above? This is a good indication that too many programs are running on your computer. The likely culprits are your startup programs. Depending on your computer manufacturer, you may have many different programs and utilities that start when you start Windows. You can change this process by removing some the unneeded programs. This frees up more system resources for needed applications to use so they can work faster. See the following sections for more information about cleaning out your Startup folder. To do so, just follow these steps:

1. Click Start | Run, type **MSCONFIG**, and click OK.

2. In the System Configuration utility, click the Startup Tab.

3. All items listed are started when Windows starts. To prevent some items from starting, just clear the check box next to them. Generally, you can read the name of the startup item and know what it is and whether you need it to start or not. If you are not sure what an item is, simply leave it checked. You can learn more about MSCONFIG in Chapter 18.

NOTE   *Do not change settings on the General tab that affect System Restore. This may prevent System Restore from functioning properly. (You can learn more about System Restore in Chapter 18.) Also, make certain that you do not select any of the check boxes on the Troubleshooting tab unless you are instructed to do so by your computer's manual or a technical support person.*

17

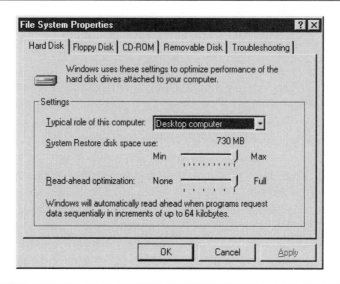

FIGURE 17-15   File System Properties

Graphics

The Graphics option provides you a single window with a slider bar to adjust graphics hardware acceleration. This setting is set to Full by default, and you should leave it there unless you are having problems with your graphical display. Even then, you should consult your video card documentation first.

Virtual Memory

Windows Me, like other Windows operating systems is configured to use virtual memory. Your computer has a certain amount of memory installed, such as 64MB, 98MB, and so forth. When you use your computer, open applications, surf the Net, or whatever, memory is used to hold the programming information that your computer needs to run the programs. When you have too many open programs, RAM begins to run low. In this case, Windows can use a portion of your hard disk to temporarily store information. This is called *virtual* memory because it is not real RAM; it's storage room borrowed from the hard drive. Windows Me is programmed to set its own Virtual Memory settings, as you can see in Figure 17-16.

You can change this option and configure the virtual memory settings yourself, but this is not highly recommended. Your best performance option is

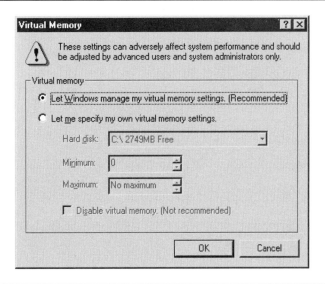

FIGURE 17-16   Virtual Memory settings

to allow Windows to continue using its own virtual memory settings—believe me, they are the best!

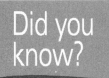

"Hey Man, I Can Get More Power Using My Own Settings"

Many people who learn a few things about virtual memory think they can configure their own settings to make Windows use more hard disk space—a replacement for physical RAM. This simply is not the case. Windows Me can handle these settings, and overriding Windows' settings is normally a bad idea. Virtual memory is used for "overflow" information—it is not designed in any way to be a replacement for physical RAM chips. If you need a RAM upgrade, tinkering with virtual memory will not solve the problem—in fact, it may create more. My final advice: leave this setting alone. If your system needs more RAM, your best bet is to part with a few hard-earned dollars and have more RAM installed.

17

Chapter 18

Solving Windows Me Problems

How To…

- ■ Use CTRL+ALT+DEL

- ■ Use Windows Help and Support

- ■ Boot into Safe Mode

- ■ Use System Restore

- ■ Access additional security tools

What? Windows Me isn't perfect? Well…not exactly. As with any operating system, you may have problems with Windows Me from time to time. Fortunately, I am very happy to tell you that Windows Me is the easiest system to fix that Microsoft has ever created—in fact, you may never need to call technical support. That seems like quite a claim, but Windows Me includes a number of very helpful tools so you can fix Windows Me without help from anyone else. In this chapter, I'll show you how to make use of those features and resolve typical problems you are likely to encounter.

Troubleshooting 101

Before we get into the tools and options, I'm going to get on my soap box for just a moment and give you some quick, easy, and important tips about troubleshooting Windows. When you experience a problem in Windows, there are some positive actions you can take; there are also some panic-driven actions you can take that are usually not very wise. So, without getting into the murky details of troubleshooting, here's my list of troubleshooting trips you should always follow:

- ■ Relax—If Windows Me experiences a problem, don't get in a hurry. Your system will not self-destruct or leak poisonous gas into the room and kill you. In other words, a problem with your system does not mean that it needs to go the computer E.R.—don't get in a hurry.

- ■ Think—What were you doing when the problem occurred? Consider grabbing a piece of scratch paper and writing down exactly what you were doing, including what applications were open when the problem occurred. If there are serious problems with Windows Me, you may need this information later.

■   Act—Try one thing at a time to resolve the problem. With each action you take, write down what you did. Do not randomly press keys—do one thing at a time in an organized manner.

Now, you may think, "but that's just it—what action should I try?" The rest of this chapter answers that very question.

Using CTRL+ALT+DEL

A common problem you may experience from time to time with Windows Me is a system lockup. A system lockup occurs when an application is naughty and doesn't behave the way it should. The application can interfere with Windows Me functionality and cause the application to lock. This means that you can't click any buttons or do anything with the application. In some cases, two applications that are open can interfere with each other and cause them both to lock.

In the case of a system lock, you should use your keyboard and press CTRL+ALT+DEL once. This action will open a Close Program dialog box in which you can select the name of the program and click End Task. In the Close Program dialog box, you will see the name of the program and a (Not Responding) note next to it. Clicking End Task forces the task to end so you can get control of your computer. If you have any unsaved data in your application at the time it locked up, I'm afraid you will lose that data (save data frequently when working to avoid loss).

TIP   *If you press* CTRL+ALT+DEL *twice, your computer will restart.*

In some cases, CTRL+ALT+DEL will not give you control of the computer. This problem occurs when errors occur within Windows Me, possibly caused by an application that, in turn, causes the operating system to hard lock. In this case, pressing CTRL+ALT+DEL doesn't do anything. Neither does pressing any key on your keyboard, and your mouse pointer is gone. In this case, the only way to get control of Windows Me is to turn off the computer using your computer's power switch. Just crawl under your desk, turn off the switch, wait at least 10 seconds, then turn the switch back on so your computer can begin rebooting. ScanDisk will automatically run during the reboot, and you should let it finish its check for file system errors.

18

Why Wait 10 Seconds?

As a general rule, you should never reboot your computer using the power switch—always use the Shut Down/Restart option in Windows Me. However, if your system locks up, you have no choice but to use the power switch. In this case, turn the switch off, wait at least 10 seconds, then turn it back on. Why wait, you might ask? The power switch simply cuts the power to the computer. Ten seconds gives your computer enough time to dump all of the data in RAM and stop the hard disk from spinning. If you turn the switch off and on too quickly, you could damage your computer's components.

Using Windows Help and Support

Windows Me has the best help files that have ever been produced by Microsoft. They are easy to use, attractive, and contain a wealth of information both locally on your machine and on the Internet. You can easily access Windows Help and Support by clicking Start | Help and Support. The Windows Help and Support interface appears, as shown in Figure 18-1.

There are four major parts of the Windows Help and Support program. Aside from using these four major parts, you can also perform text searches to find the information you need. The following sections address these issues.

Help and Support Home

When you first open Help and Support, you find yourself in the Home section, as shown in Figure 18-1. Home is the starting point of accessing Help and Support, and as you can probably guess, it mimics a Web page because the Windows Help and Support files are HTML-based, just as a Web page is. As you use Help and Support, you'll notice hyperlinks that enable you to jump from the help files to an additional help resource on the Internet.

In the left side of the Home window, you'll see some generic categories that can help you get moving in the right direction, such as Home Networking; Games, Sound & Video; etc. You also see the Fix A Problem and More Resources sections.

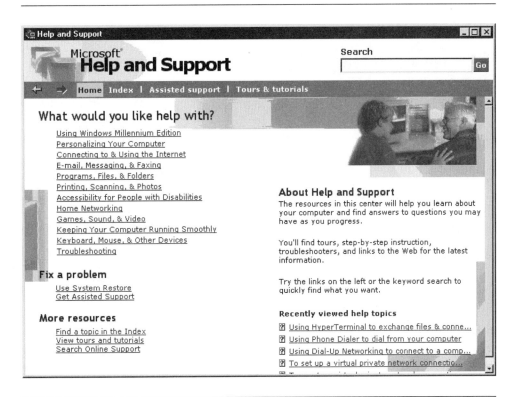

FIGURE 18-1   Windows Help and Support

If you have used the help files before, there will be a Recently Viewed Help Topics listing in the lower-right of window. This feature enables you to return to recently visited help topics more quickly.

Index

The Index option in Help and Support is just like any other index—the only difference is this one grabs the information for you instead of your having to look it up, as shown in Figure 18-2.

In the left side of the window, you see the entire index displayed in alphabetical order. Just use the scroll bar to locate a topic you want, select it, and then click the Display button. The information about that topic appears in the right pane. You can read the information, click the Print button to print a copy (which is

18

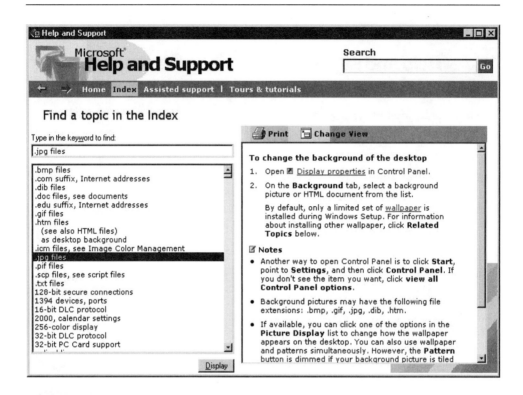

FIGURE 18-2 Help Index

a really nice feature!), and even reorganize the window by clicking the Change View button.

If you don't want to scroll down the list of index topics, you can just type something you want in the Search dialog box above the index. The closest matches to your search request will appear.

Assisted Support

If you are having serious problems with Windows Me that you can't seem to resolve, you can access the Assisted Support option of Windows Help and Support so you can get help from one of two different places—from either MSN or directly from Microsoft, as shown in Figure 18-3.

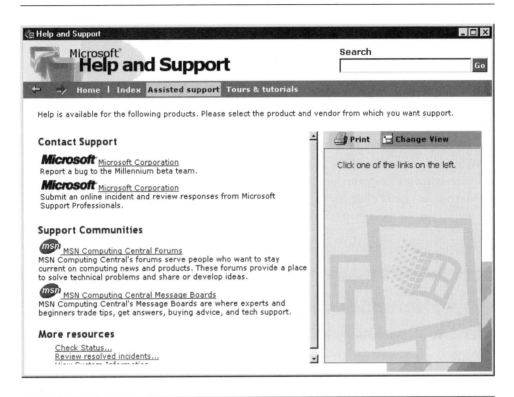

FIGURE 18-3   Assisted Support

By choosing the first option under Contact Support, you can use the Internet to report a bug directly to Microsoft. The Windows Me Web response team receives your report and will attempt to communicate with you via the Web to resolve your problem. To use this option, click it and an Internet connection will be launched. Microsoft's support site appears in the Help window, where you can begin filling out information to get help from Microsoft.

Your second option is to get help from MSN's forums and discussion boards. You do this by submitting an online incident and checking to see if there are any responses to that particular problem already listed. These options are obviously not one-on-one solutions, but you might be surprised by the answers you can get from these sites. You can learn all about problems and solutions other people have experienced, and you may find the answer to your problem right before your eyes!

18

 *Before choosing the first option and reporting a bug directly to Microsoft, you should visit the Microsoft Support Professionals responses to see if you can find the answer to your problem there. Again, it may be right before your eyes, and you will be able to fix your computer much faster if it is.*

Tours and Tutorials

The final section of the Help files is the Tours and Tutorials section. This section provides you with a number of "tours," or brief walk-throughs, that are designed to help you use various components of Windows Me. As you can see in Figure 18-4, all you have to do is click the tour or tutorial you want to view in the left pane. Movie files open their own windows to play, and tutorials appear in the right

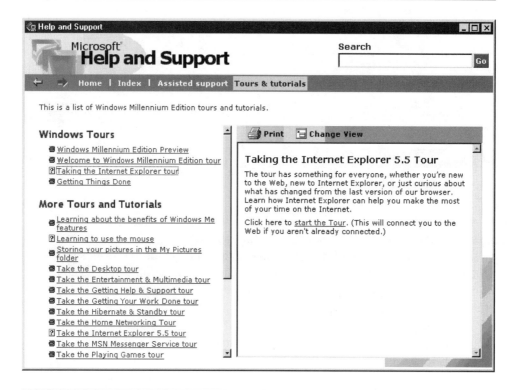

FIGURE 18-4   Tours and Tutorials

window on this screen. You can click on any of them you want to see. Some of them are good, some are kind of corny, but this is a place you can explore if you want more information about a particular subject.

Searching Windows Help and Support

One of the primary ways you will use Windows Help and Support is to search for topics. You use the Search option to find information about a certain topic or to troubleshoot a problem you are having. The Windows help files support text searches, which means that you can type a keyword or keywords into a search dialog box. Windows Me will try to find topics that match your request. The Search dialog box is in the upper right-hand corner of the Help and Support window. Just type the subject you want and click Go. Windows Help will return all possible matches for your subject. For example, I have searched for the word *network* in Figure 18-5. The results are displayed in the left side of the window. I can double-click any of them to see the information in the right side of the window.

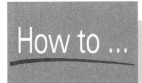 **Make Your Search Count!**

The Search feature of Windows Help is very useful, but you should follow some basic rules to make sure your search requests return the information you want. As you are searching, keep these points in mind:

- Searches are not case-sensitive—*NETWORK* and *network* are the same to Windows Me.

- You can use operator words such as *and*, *or*, and *not* to increase the odds of finding what you want—for example *home and network* or *protocol not TCP/IP*.

- Keep your search focused on keywords. For example, if you want to learn about home networking, just search for *home networking*, not *I want to learn about home networking*.

Make your primary search keyword the first word in a search.

18

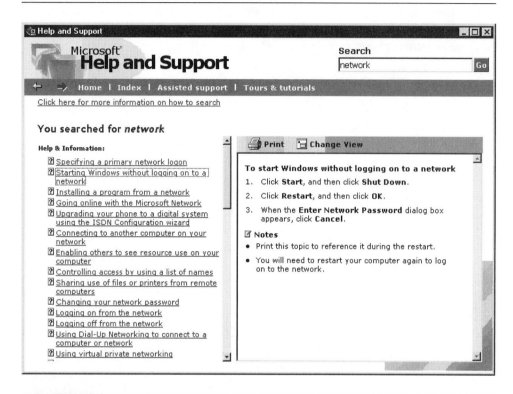

FIGURE 18-5 Use the Search feature to find topics of interest

Using Windows Troubleshooters

Within the Windows Help and Support interface, you can access a very handy and helpful component called a *troubleshooter*. A troubleshooter is an HTML interface that appears on the help window. The troubleshooter asks you a series of questions and instructs you to try different actions in order to attempt to resolve a problem you are having. There are many troubleshooters available in the Help files, and they are very easy to use. Just follow these steps:

1. Click Start | Help and Support.

2. In the Help and Support Search box type the kind of troubleshooter you want. For example, you might type **modem troubleshooter**, **ICS troubleshooter**, or **sound card troubleshooter**.

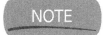 *Obviously, a troubleshooter does not exist for every possible problem you might experience with Windows, but there are troubleshooters for most hardware devices.*

3. Begin the troubleshooter by clicking an appropriate radio button, then click the Next button to continue, as shown in Figure 18-6.

4. Continue following the troubleshooter to attempt to solve the problem.

 Do not skip steps of the troubleshooter—this may prevent you from solving the problem!

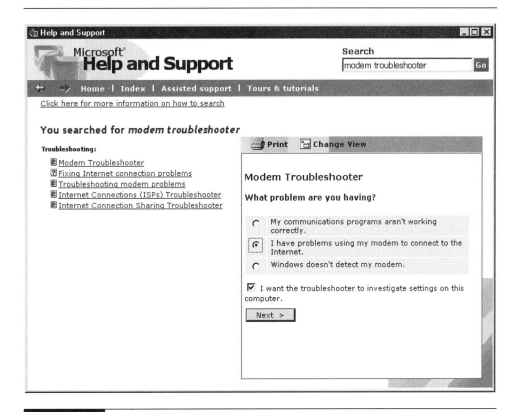

| FIGURE 18-6 | Answer the troubleshooter's question and click Next |

18

Using Safe Mode

Safe Mode is a Windows Me feature that enables you to start Windows with a minimal number of drivers. Safe Mode is used in instances where you cannot start Windows normally, and it's used to fix problems with your system. It essentially gets Windows up and running, but that's about it. While in Safe Mode, you cannot use a network, the Internet, your CD-ROM drive, or even Windows Help and Support.

So, why would you use Safe Mode? Let's consider an example. Let's say you install Fly-By-Night's Most Excellent Video Card (OK, it's just an example). You install the card and driver for the card. When you restart Windows Me, it boots, but then you get a "fatal exception" blue screen just before your desktop appears. You try this over and over with the same result. More than likely, the video card's driver is not working correctly with Windows Me. You can boot the computer into Safe Mode, and Windows will load a basic VGA driver to use with the card. Once booted, you can use Device Manager to remove or update the bad driver.

A number of other repair tools (which we'll explore later in this chapter) also require you to boot your computer into Safe Mode in order for them to work. Before I show you how to boot into Safe Mode, let me mention that there are some additional boot options you can choose. You can access all of these options by using the Windows Startup menu, which you'll see if you hold down the CTRL key on your keyboard when you turn on your computer (you can also press F8 on some computers). The Startup Menu gives you the following options:

1. Normal—Boots Windows Me normally.

2. Logged (BOOTLOG.TXT)—Creates a log file of the startup process. This feature can be helpful to technical support personnel who are trying to analyze boot problems with your computer.

3. Safe Mode—Boots in Safe Mode.

4. Step-by-step Confirmation—Prompts you to answer Yes or No to every portion of setup. You can skip over the loading of certain devices and services this way. Step-by-step configuration is normally used to identify boot problems or determine where a boot failure is occurring.

Now that you know what Startup Menu options are available, the following steps tell you how to boot into Safe Mode:

1. Turn on your computer and hold down the CTRL key (or press F8 on some computers).

2. When the Startup menu appears, press 3 on your keyboard and then press ENTER.

3. Windows Me boots into Safe Mode. The Windows Safe Mode Help and Support window automatically opens, as shown in Figure 18-7. Click Next to continue getting help from Help and Support, or close the window if you want to try to solve the problem on your own.

4. When you are ready to leave Safe Mode, simply reboot your computer without accessing the Startup Menu (or if you do, choose the Normal option).

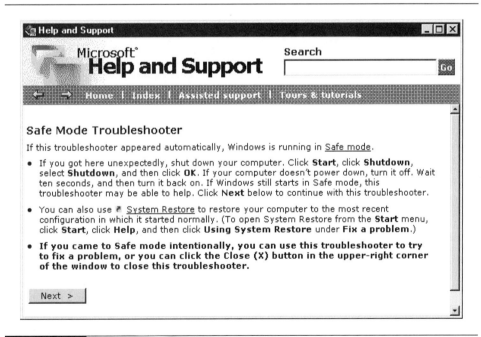

FIGURE 18-7   Windows Safe Mode Help and Support

18

Using System Restore

As you learn to use Windows Me, you will no doubt find several of its new features very helpful and fun. However, I can emphatically say that System Restore is the best new feature of Windows Me and can get you out of all sorts of trouble. What if your computer won't start? What if you install a bad application that wrecks your computer? What if little Johnny decides to delete C:\Windows? No problem: just use System Restore and put your computer back just as it was before the problem/tragedy/accident happened, with only a few mouse clicks from you.

Are you intrigued? If you have ever worked with Windows, I know you are because bad configuration problems can be a serious troubleshooting problem. System Restore leaves that legacy behind because you can easily restore your computer to a previous configuration. The following sections show you how to use System Restore.

System Restore Requirements

System Restore is automatically installed and configured on Windows Me if your computer has at least 200MB of free disk space after Windows Me is installed. If your computer does not have 200MB of free disk space, System Restore is installed, but it is not set up to run. System Restore functions by saving information about your system so that it can be restored in the event of problem. In order to function correctly, 200MB of free disk space is required, and in reality, System Restore may need much more. Fortunately, if you are using a newer computer, you most likely have plenty of free disk space and System Restore is already operational on your computer.

Enabling System Restore

If your computer did not have 200MB of free disk space upon initial installation, but you have made 200MB or more of free disk space available, you can enable System Restore so that the additional space begins functioning on your Windows Me computer. To enable System Restore, just follow these steps:

1. In Control Panel, double-click System, or right-click on My Computer and click Properties.

2. Click the Performance Tab, then click the File System button.

3. Click the Troubleshooting tab and clear the check box from the Disable System Restore option, as shown in Figure 18-8.

4. Click OK and OK again on the System Properties window.

Creating Restore Points

System Restore functions by creating *restore points*. A restore point is a "snapshot" of your computer's configuration that is stored on your hard disk. If System Restore needs to be used, System Restore accesses a restore point to reconfigure your computer. This brings your computer back to a stable state—a place where it was when the system was stable. Restore points enable your computer to travel back in time and be configured in the manner it was when it was stable.

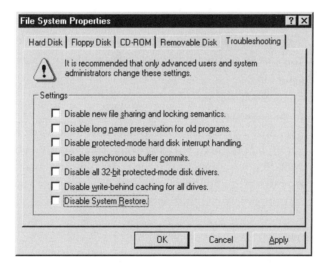

FIGURE 18-8   Clear the Disable System Restore check box

18

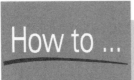

How to ... Adjust System Restore Disk Usage

By default, System Restore is given 12 percent of your hard disk space when you install Windows Me, assuming that 12 percent is at least 200MB. If you access System Properties and click the Performance tab and then click the File System button, you see a slider bar indicating the total amount of disk space System Restore is allowed to use on the Hard Disk tab. You can raise or lower this amount by moving the slider bar. However, keep in mind that System Restore must have at least 200MB, and if you want System Restore to function really well, you should leave this 12 percent setting at its default level.

NOTE   *It is very important to note here that System Restore restores your operating system and applications only. It does not save and restore any files. For example, let's say you accidentally delete that Great American Novel you are working on. System Restore cannot be used to get your novel back. Incidentally, System Restore does not affect other files, such as e-mail and Web pages. Performing a System Restore does not make you lose new e-mail or files—it only configures your system settings and application settings.*

System Restore automatically creates restore points for you, so in general, there is no need to manually create a restore point. However, what if you are about to try some configuration option or configure some software that you know may be risky or that has caused you problems in the past? You can manually create a restore point so you can restore your system to the exact present state that you want. To create a restore point, just follow these easy steps:

1. Click Start | Programs | Accessories | System Tools | System Restore.

2. In the System Restore window, click the Create A Restore Point button, then click Next, as shown in Figure 18-9.

3. In the window that appears, enter a description. You may want to include information that will help you identify this restore point over others. The

date and time of the restore point are added automatically so you don't need to include those. Click Next.

4. The restore point is created. Click OK and you're done.

Running System Restore

The eventful day finally arrives and you (or someone else) has done something to your computer, and now it doesn't boot, or it acts erratically. Whatever the problem, you can use System Restore to bring your computer back to an earlier

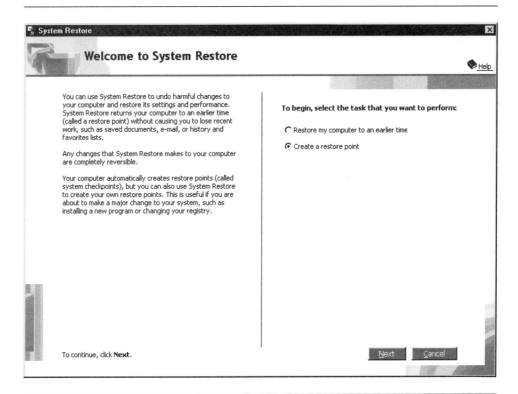

FIGURE 18-9   Click the Create A Restore Point button, then click Next

18

time when it was functioning appropriately. The following two sections show you how to use System Restore.

If You Can Boot Windows

If you can boot into Windows, follow these steps:

1. Click Start | Programs | Accessories | System Tools | System Restore. (If you cannot boot your computer, refer to the next section.) The System Restore Welcome screen will be displayed.

2. Click the Restore My Computer To An Earlier time radio button, then click Next.

3. A calendar and selection list is presented to you, as shown in Figure 18-10. You can select different days to find a desired restore point. If you did not create a restore point, you should choose the latest one available, which will be listed first in the current or previous day window. Select a restore point and click Next.

4. A message appears telling you to save all files and close all open applications. Do this, then click the Next button.

5. Restoration takes place on your computer. Your computer automatically reboots once the restoration is complete. Click OK to the restoration message that appears after you reboot.

If You Cannot Boot Windows

If you cannot boot Windows, follow these steps to run System Restore:

1. Turn on your computer and hold down the CTRL or the F8 key until you see the Startup Menu options.

2. Press 3 for Safe Mode, then press the Enter button.

3. Once Windows boots, the Help and Support screen that appears gives you the option to restore your computer. Click the System Restore link, which you can see in Figure 18-7.

4. Click the Restore My Computer To An Earlier Time radio button and then click Next.

5. A calendar and selection list is presented to you, as shown in Figure 18-10. You can select different days to find a desired restore point. If you did not create a restore point, you should choose to use the latest one available. The latest one will be listed first in the current or previous day window. Select a restore point and click Next.

6. A message appears telling you to save all files and close all open applications. Do this and then click the Next button.

7. Your computer automatically reboots once the restoration is complete. Click OK to the restoration message that appears after booting has taken place.

Current documents, files, e-mail, etc., are not affected during a restoration. However, if you installed an application after the last restore point was made, you will need to reinstall that application.

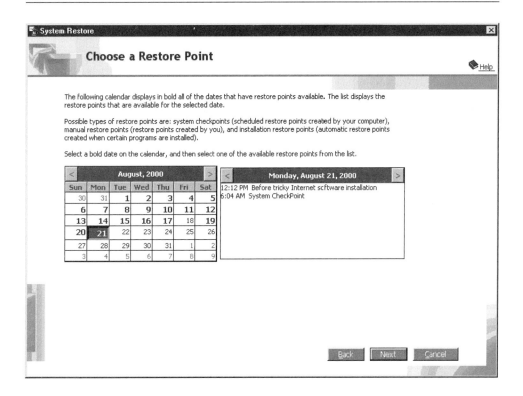

FIGURE 18-10 Select a restore point and click Next

Undoing a Restoration

As I have mentioned, I think System Restore is the best new feature of Windows Me. It can save you a world of pain and agony. But what happens if the restore doesn't go so well? What if there is a problem with the restore that leaves Windows Me in worse shape, or even unbootable? Good news: restoration is completely reversible, and the following two sections show you how to reverse a restoration.

Reversing Restoration If You Can Boot Your Computer

To reverse a restoration if you can boot your computer, follow these steps:

1. Click Start | Programs | Accessories | System Tools | System Restore.

2. In the System Restore window, click the Undo My Last Restoration radio button and then click Next.

 *The Undo My Last Restoration option does not appear unless you have previously run a restoration.*

3. Close any open files or applications, click OK, and then click Next.

4. The previous restoration is removed and your computer reboots. Click OK to the restoration message that appears after reboot.

Undoing a Restoration If You Cannot Boot Into Windows

If you cannot boot into Windows and you need to undo a restoration, just follow these steps:

1. Turn on your computer and hold down the CTRL or the F8 key until you see the Startup Menu options.

2. Press 3 for Safe Mode, then press the ENTER button.

3. Once Windows boots, the Help screen that appears gives you the option to restore your computer. Click the System Restore link.

4. Click the Undo My Last Restoration radio button and then click Next.

5. A message appears telling you to save all files and close all open applications. Do so at this time and then click the Next button.

6. Your computer is rebooted once the restoration has been removed.

Reverting a Restore

What happens if you run a restore, and now your computer will not start even in Safe Mode? No problem—you can revert the restore by using a Startup disk. The trick to this option is that you must *have* a startup disk. One may have shipped with your Windows Me installation CD, or you can make one by double-clicking Add/Remove Programs in Control Panel and then clicking the Startup Disk tab. Once you have a startup disk, you can revert a restoration on a completely unbootable Windows Me computer. Just follow these steps:

1. Insert the Startup disk into the computer and turn on the computer.

2. When the boot menu appears, choose the Start Computer With CD-ROM Support option.

3. Once the startup disk loads, a message appears so you can Revert The Restore Changes Made. If a restore caused your computer to become unbootable, type **1** to revert the changes. This will put your computer back to pre-restoration mode.

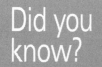
Did you know?

Wrong Restoration Point

What should you do if you run a restoration, but you selected the wrong restoration point? Let's say you run a restoration to solve a problem, but the restore point was not early enough. In other words, Windows Me created a restore point while the current problem existed. What now? No problem. Simply undo the last restoration, then run the restoration again, but select an earlier restore point to fix the problem.

18

 *If you bypass the revert option now, it will not be presented to you again!*

Problem Solving Tools

If you read Chapter 17, you learned about System Information, a great tool that gives you all kinds of information about hardware, applications, and settings on your computer. You can also use System Information to access a number of tools that can help you solve problems Windows Me may be experiencing. You can access these tools by clicking Start | Programs | Accessories | System Tools | System Information | Tools menu. The following sections point out the major tools and show you what you can do with them.

Faultlog

Faultlog, shown in Figure 18-11, is a simple text file log that records all system faults, such as invalid page faults. In general, you don't need to do anything with Faultlog, but if something keeps locking up your system, check out this log—it may give you some clues to the culprit.

```
Faultlog - Notepad
File  Edit  Search  Help

***********************************************************************
Date 07/17/2000 Time 15:06
RUNDLL32 caused an invalid page fault in
module KERNEL32.DLL at 016f:bff8e68b.
Registers:
EAX=02e2fe38 CS=016f EIP=bff8e68b EFLGS=00000287
EBX=816c661c SS=0177 ESP=02e2fc88 EBP=02e2fe38
ECX=00000177 DS=0177 ESI=000000ec FS=44ef
EDX=02e2fe28 ES=0177 EDI=00000200 GS=0000
Bytes at CS:EIP:
cc a1 f0 bc fb bf 8b 00 66 64 f7 05 1c 00 00 00
Stack dump:
79f10000 816c6668 00001021 816d7780 816d3728 c15c5000 ffffffff 00000000
ffffffff 00000001 02e2fccc bff6b8dc bff613e2 0000016f bff8a129 00000002
***********************************************************************
Date 07/18/2000 Time 11:25
EXPLORER caused a general protection fault
in module KRNL386.EXE at 0003:000023a8.
Registers:
EAX=00000000 CS=015f EIP=000023a8 EFLGS=00000246
EBX=bff64db4 SS=4b3f ESP=0000b56c EBP=0000b59e
ECX=00000000 DS=189f ESI=00000658 FS=14ef
```

FIGURE 18-11 Use Faultlog to examine Windows Me faults

Network Diagnostics

Network Diagnostics, shown in Figure 18-12, is a very cool tool that examines the state of your network and Internet connections. After the examination is complete, Network Diagnostics reports the state of your network and your computer's networking hardware and software configuration. Use this tool if you are having problems with Windows Me on a network and you can't seem to identify the problem. This tool may gather and report that information for you!

DirectX Diagnostic Tool

DirectX is a graphics technology that enables you to play those really cool games. However, you can have problems with various versions of DirectX and its operation with your system components. The DirectX Diagnostic Tool gives you an easy interface with a bunch of tabs, shown in Figure 8-13.

The DirectX files, media files, and drivers tabs of this tool report a variety of information to you. The Display, Sound, Music, Input, and Network tabs give you information about how DirectX is interacting with these system resources. Each of these tabs also contains a Test button so you can directly test how DirectX is interacting with the hardware. This is a great tool that can help you exactly identify what incompatibilities are occurring with DirectX and your hardware.

Signature Verification Tool

In order to protect Windows Me, files that are in use by the operating system are signed by Microsoft to ensure compatibility and security. You can use the Signature Verification Tool to make certain that files that are not signed are not in use on your system. When you open Signature Verification, just click the Start button to run the verification scan. Once the scan is complete, you see a report showing all of the unsigned files on your system, as shown in Figure 18-14. Generally, you don't need to use this tool, but if you have installed some programs on your computer that are giving you problems, you can run this utility to check for signatures.

 *By default, Windows Me gives you a warning message before you install unsigned files.*

18

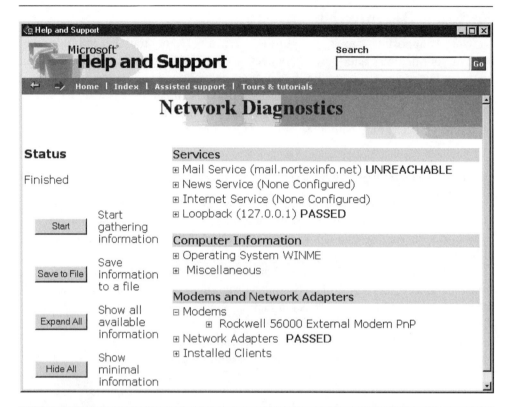

FIGURE 18-12   Use Network Diagnostics to find problems with Windows Me networking

Registry Checker

Windows Me, like all Windows operating systems, contains a *Registry*, which is essentially a big database of information about your computer. Every configuration on your computer is stored in the Registry, and Windows uses the Registry to learn how to set up and configure Windows when you boot it.

The Registry can become corrupt or there can be problems in the Registry that cause Windows Me to not act correctly. You can use the Registry Checker tool to find out if there are any problems. The simply utility runs and gives you a report. If there are Registry problems, you should run System Restore.

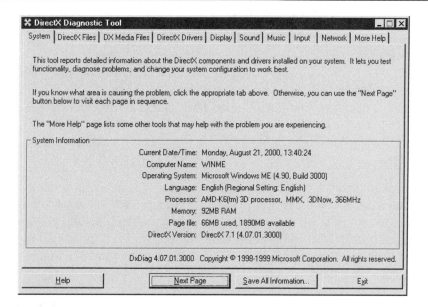

FIGURE 18-13 Use the DirectX Diagnostic Tool to solve compatibility problems with DirectX

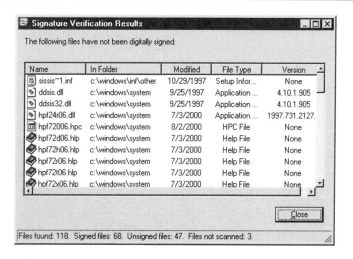

FIGURE 18-14 The Signature Verification tool reports signed and unsigned files

Automatic Skip Driver Agent

This tool functions in the background on your computer, and there isn't anything you can directly do with it. Automatic Skip Driver (ASD) Agent detects bad drivers. Once it finds one, ASD skips the driver the next time Windows Me loads. For example, if a bad driver causes a boot failure, ASD can flag the driver and not load it the next time you start Windows Me so that a driver does not prevent Windows Me from running.

Dr. Watson

Dr. Watson is a Windows tool that can inspect your system and generate a detailed report after a system fault has occurred. Dr. Watson can tell you what went wrong and sometimes suggest what can be done to fix the problem. Should you ever need to contact technical support, they may have you run Dr. Watson in order to take a "snapshot" of your system. Once the snapshot is taken, as shown in Figure 18-15, the report can potentially be used to solve the problem.

 *You can run this tool yourself, of course. The results are usually easy to understand. If you see a particular application or device listed, you may need to try reinstalling the application or device in question—or just remove it from Windows Me altogether.*

Did you know?   Checking Out the Registry

Windows Me includes a Registry editor that you can access by typing **regedit** at the Run line. You can use the Registry editor to browse the Registry database, and experienced users can even make direct changes to it. However, let me offer a stern warning: this is the easiest way to cause major problems with your computer! Changes to the Registry are automatic and can stop Windows Me from booting. If you do accidentally change something that causes problems, you will need to use System Restore to recover Windows Me. As I tell all users and even inexperienced IT professionals—stay out of the Registry unless you are sure you know what you are doing.

System Configuration Utility

The System Configuration Utility is a very useful feature of Windows that can help you manage various aspects of your computer, as shown in Figure 18-16. You can also access the System Configuration Utility by just accessing the Run line and typing **msconfig**.

System Configuration Utility lets you manage how Windows Me boots, what files are processed, and what options are enabled. As a general rule of thumb, the System Configuration Utility is an advanced tool that you do not need to use without technical support help. You can use the Startup tab to remove unneeded applications from your Startup menu (which makes Windows Me run faster—see Chapter 17 for more information), but other than this feature, you should not change any of the settings found in the System Configuration Utility unless otherwise instructed to do by technical support personnel.

NOTE   *Incorrectly changing settings in the System Configuration Utility can stop Windows Me from booting.*

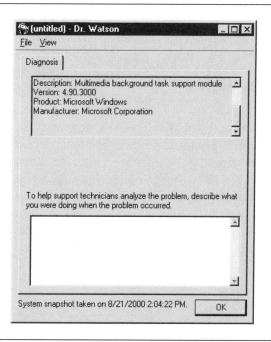

FIGURE 18-15   Dr. Watson takes a snapshot of your system

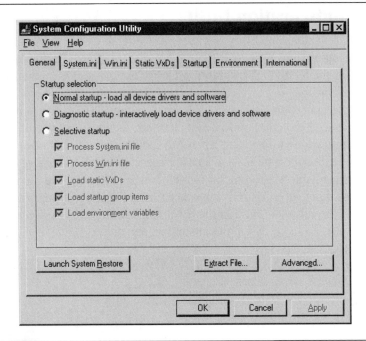

FIGURE 18-16   System Configuration Utility

Pulling it all Together

Troubleshooting is just one part of your work, play, and management with
Windows Me. Keep in mind that Windows Me is the most user-friendly operating
system Microsoft has ever produced. It plays better, works better, and it is easier
to fix when a problem occurs. As you are working with Windows Me, no doubt
things will happen from time to time that give you a raised eyebrow. That's
OK—remember, this book is your companion, so use it over and over again for
reference, and should a problem ever occur that you can't solve, Microsoft help
is just a few clicks away. Good luck with Windows Me! Have fun and enjoy!

Appendix A

Installing Windows Me

How To...

- ■ Prepare for a Windows Me Upgrade
- ■ Upgrade Windows 95/98 to Windows Me
- ■ Get a Computer with No Operating System Ready for Installation
- ■ Clean-Install Windows Me

Are you familiar with the cold chill? You know, those little goose bumps that work their way up your back and make the hair on your neck stand up? You normally associate the cold chill with a good horror movie, but installing an operating system can be just as frightening. If you are still holding that Windows Me CD-ROM in your hand and thinking, "Am I sure I want to take the risk..." you are certainly not alone. After all, you may have Windows 95 or 98 on your computer and all is well in the world—changing it may cause your world to end (well, not really, but it will feel like it). In any case, this appendix is your installation friend. It shows you how to install Windows Me as either an upgrade to an existing operating system, or as a "clean install" on a computer that does not currently have an operating system. Use this appendix to make your journey into the land of Windows Me installation quick and painless.

Upgrading to Windows Me

Most home users who purchase Windows Me will do so to upgrade their existing home PC. This means that you currently have a computer that runs Windows 95 or 98 and you want to upgrade that system to run Windows Me. To do this, you purchase a Windows Me upgrade CD so you can have the latest and greatest from Microsoft.

In a perfect world, upgrading your home PC would be a piece of cake. You'd pop the installation CD-ROM into your CD drive, answer a few questions from the setup program, and Setup would install Windows Me without any problems. When you find that perfect world, let me know so I can move there too.

The reality is that any number of problems can arise when upgrading to Windows Me. However, if you upgrade "smartly," the likelihood of encountering installation failure or problems is low. The trick is to do a bit of homework before installing Windows Me to make sure your existing PC and operating system are ready. It is all too tempting to start the installation and hope for the best, but in order to upgrade smartly, you need to first play detective for a few minutes and make certain all is well in your computer's environment. Upgrading smartly will

A

help you prevent a number of potential problems and help you find issues with installation before you ever begin.

So, how do you upgrade smartly? The following sections explore the tasks you should perform before attempting an upgrade to Windows Me.

Check the System Requirements

One big mistake computer users often make when attempting an upgrade or install is not checking the system requirements. Every piece of software, whether it be an operating system or an application, has certain requirements that must be met before the software can be installed or will function reliably. Again, an operating system is no exception. Your computer must have hardware that can handle Windows Me, so before attempting the installation, check out your computer to see if there are any potential problems. The following sections can help you make sure your computer is ready for Windows Me.

Processor

A computer's processor can be thought of as the computer's brain. The processor, well, *processes* information that the operating system or an application needs. For example, if you want your computer to multiply 467 and 345, that request is sent to the processor for completion. Once the processor performs the computation, it is returned to the requesting application (such as your system's calculator). In the past,

Did you know?   What About Windows 3.*x*?

Interestingly enough, concerning upgrading, Microsoft seems to have ignored Windows operating systems prior to Windows 95. Can you upgrade a Windows 3.*x* computer directly to Windows Me? Not really. Microsoft assumes you are running either Windows 95 or 98, so if you are still using Windows 3.*x*, there are a few problems. First, Windows Me works very differently and does not really *upgrade* 3.*x*—it needs to replace it. The other problem is hardware. If you are using Windows 3.*x* on an older computer, the odds are very good that your computer's hardware will not be able to handle the demands of Windows Me. If you still want to try it, I recommend a clean install (described later in this appendix). Make certain to carefully check your computer's hardware. See the following sections for more information.

processors were not very fast because operating systems and applications were not terribly complicated. However, with today's operating systems and applications, your computer's processor will have to be fast enough to handle Windows Me and all of the many tasks it can perform. For a Windows Me installation, you need a processor that is at least a Pentium (or equivalent) 150MHz. The megahertz number is the speed at which the processor can run. By today's standards, 150MHz is pretty slow. Most new PCs today contain a 400 or 500MHz processor, and 1GHz (gigahertz, or 1000MHz) processors are even available now. It is important to note here that 150MHz is the bare-bones minimum. Windows Me will run on this processor, but it will not run fast. In reality, you always want the fastest processor you can afford because you will see the best performance with it.

If your computer currently runs Windows 98 and your system works well with Windows 98 (in other words, if the computer does not slowly limp along), your computer will be able to handle Windows Me just fine.

If you check your computer's processor and find that it is not at least a 150MHz processor, what should you do? You have two options. First, you can upgrade by buying a new processor for your computer and paying someone to install it (unless you know a thing or two about hardware). In some cases, this

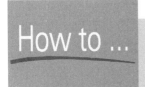
Finding Your Processor's Speed

Don't know what processor is hidden inside your computer? Here are two easy ways to find out:

1. Dig around and find the documentation that came with your computer. It should tell you the processor speed (along with all kinds of other information you'll need).

2. If you can't find your computer documentation, then in Windows 95/98, right-click the My Computer icon with your mouse and then click Properties. You'll see a System Properties window. Look on the General tab. It should tell you the manufacturer of your computer's processor and (hopefully) the speed.

is a great solution, but be careful. In many cases, you can purchase a new computer for not much more than a processor, so think carefully and shop smartly before deciding to upgrade your computer's processor. Because the technology is growing and changing so rapidly, your best bet is quite often to simply purchase a new computer—you'll gain the speed you need plus many new advantages.

> **TIP** *If your processor is too slow for Windows Me, the odds are good that other components are too old as well. In most cases, upgrading your processor usually means you'll have to upgrade other components, such as RAM. This is why buying a new computer is usually the best option.*

Random Access Memory (RAM)

You have probably heard the term RAM plenty of times, even if you do not have your head stuck in the computer world. Random Access Memory is the amount of memory your computer contains for current application and processes. RAM enables you to work with a Microsoft Word document while also surfing the Internet, it lets you draw pictures and run programs—anything that you do on your computer requires RAM. Simply put, the more RAM you have the faster and better your computer will run, and the happier you will be. For a Windows Me installation, you need at least 32MB (megabytes) of RAM. As with your processor, this is a bare-bones minimum. Most computer systems today are sold with at least 64MB of RAM and many contain 128MB or more. If you only have 16MB of RAM (which you may have if you are running Windows 95), you will need to upgrade your RAM before you can install Windows Me. As with the processor, think carefully before upgrading your RAM. Check your other system components and make certain they do not need to be upgraded as well. The odds are good that they do, and you may be able to buy a new computer with the same money you would spend on upgrades.

Hard Disk Space

Windows Me will need some of your hard disk space during and after the installation. Your computer's hard disk stores any data that you choose to save as well as your operating system itself. In order to upgrade to Windows Me, you must have between 320 and 430MB of free hard disk space. This means that you must have this much "spare room" on your hard disk so Windows Me can store its files. If you choose to install additional Windows Me components during Setup, you may need even more disk space—up to 550MB or so.

To check your computer's hard disk space, double-click the My Computer icon on your desktop. You see your C drive in the window. Right-click the C drive icon, then click Properties. The General tab of the Properties window shows you the amount of used and free space your disk contains. In Figure A-1, you see that my disk has 5.4GB of hard disk space available, so I have plenty of room for a Windows Me upgrade.

What if you do not have enough free disk space? Then you need to free up some disk space by removing data from your hard disk. This can include files, Internet pages, and even applications that you no longer use. You'll need to make some decisions about what you want to remove, but you must free up enough disk space for installation to be successful.

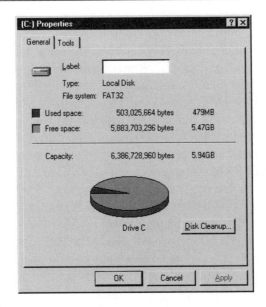

FIGURE A-1   Check the General tab on your disk's Properties window to make sure you have enough free disk space for installation

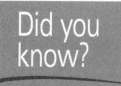

Compressed Drives

There are several drive compression utilities on the market today that essentially shrink the information on your hard disk in order to save space. Although these utilities are great, they can cause you some problems during an upgrade. As a safety precaution, uncompress any compressed drives. Also, note that Windows Me is not compatible with Stacker 4.1 or earlier. If you are using Stacker 4.1 or earlier, uninstall it before attempting to install Windows Me. Check the README file on your installation CD-ROM for late breaking news about upgrade incompatibilities; also check **www.microsoft.com/windowsme** for more incompatibility information.

In Figure A-1, notice the Disk Cleanup button. If you are using Windows 98, click this button and your system will help you remove old and unwanted items from your hard disk.

Other Requirements

Your processor, RAM, and disk space requirements are of utmost importance, but there are some other system requirements that should be met in order to make the most of Windows Me. These three requirements are virtually a given (unless your computer was built in the '70s), but make sure you have them anyway:

- VGA or higher resolution monitor
- CD-ROM or DVD-ROM drive (Windows Me isn't fussy about the drive speed)
- A mouse or similar pointing device

I told you those were easy. Now, you may also want to check a few other items. These are not required for a Windows Me installation, but they may impact how well your system works with Windows Me and how happy you will be with its functionality:

- If you plan on accessing the Internet (and I hope you do), you need at least a 28.8Kbps (kilobits per second) modem. Remember, 28.8 is the absolute minimum—and it will be ridiculously slow. The standard speed is 56Kbps, and you now have a number of broadband options available, including ISDN, DSL, cable, wireless, and satellite. None of these are required, of course, but while you are upgrading your system, this is an excellent time to look at your Internet connectivity speed and consider upgrading to a faster service if necessary.

- To make use of all Windows Me has to offer, you should have a good sound card, speakers (or headphones), a good video card, and so forth. There is a plethora of video and sound card products that are compatible with Windows, so check your local computer store for information and pricing.

- You may consider adding other components to your system, such as a DVD drive so you can run DVD games and movies on your computer. You can also use Windows Me to watch TV on your computer through a TV tuner card. You can always add these options to your system after installation, but now is a good time to consider them.

Back Up Your Data

From painful past experience, I have learned to always back up any data that I do not want to lose before ever tinkering with my operating system—and that includes an upgrade. If everything goes well during your upgrade, the computer will preserve all of your data and settings and you will not need to use your backup because the original data will still reside on your computer. However, if things do not go so well, you will desperately need a backup of your "critical" data—data that you cannot afford to lose. This includes documents, spreadsheets, Internet information, you name it. Spend some time on your computer finding everything you can't live without, then back that data up.

You can back up your data in a number of ways. First, Windows 95/98 includes a Backup utility in Accessories that you can use to create a backup file. You must then save this backup file to another location, such as a tape drive or even the hard drive of another computer. You may have other backup programs

A

and backup media you have purchased as well. Even if you don't, backing up your data doesn't have to be difficult. Simply copy any files you want to make certain you don't lose to a floppy disk or to a Zip or Jaz drive if your computer has one. If you only have a floppy drive, you may need several disks to make sure you save all of your data, but your time and effort will be well spent if something should happen during the installation.

Check Out Your Device Drivers

Every device attached to your computer, such as your printer, scanner, modem, etc. has a *driver.* A driver is a piece of software code that enables your computer to interact with the hardware device. Think of a driver as a car's steering wheel. In order to interact with your car and make it do what you want, you use a steering wheel to communicate with it, along with other controls like the brake and gas petal. In order for your computer to communicate and control a device, a driver must be installed. When you install a device, you normally use a floppy disk or CD-ROM that comes from the factory with your device. This installation media installs a driver that Windows can use. Windows also has its own driver database, and in many cases, Windows can install and use one of its drivers to manage a device.

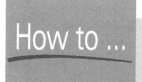 **Copy Items to a Floppy Disk**

You can easily copy items to a floppy disk by following these steps:

1. Insert a formatted floppy disk into your disk drive.

2. Right-click on the item you want to copy to the floppy, point to Send To, then click 3-1/2 Floppy. Or, you can open the floppy disk by double-clicking its icon in My Computer, then dragging the desired files or folders into the floppy disk window.

This action copies the files or folders to the floppy but does not remove them from your computer.

Drivers are always changing. When a new device is released, for example, a printer, the driver ships with it. However, as operating systems change, new drivers are developed so your printer can work with a new operating system. Before upgrading to Windows Me, you should visit the manufacturers' Web sites for your computer's devices. Look for new drivers for your particular model and see if there are any you can download. Download the drivers to a floppy disk and keep them. You may need these new drivers when you install Windows Me to ensure that your hardware works well with Windows Me. Check your device manufacturer's documentation for more information about downloading updated drivers. Even if you do not need to get any updated drivers, you do need to round up your floppies and CDs so you have access to your existing drivers in case you need them during installation.

Check for Viruses and Disable Antivirus Software

Before upgrading to Windows Me, you should run a full virus check on your computer system using an antivirus program, such as one from McAfee or Norton. You may currently have one of these programs, or you may need to buy one. If you use the Internet, you should certainly have virus detection software to make sure you

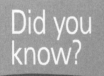

Did you know?   **Driver Problems**

Drivers, although quite necessary, can cause problems in Windows Me. Due to operating system conditions, a driver may become corrupt so that the device does not work correctly, or a driver may not interact with the operating system as it should. Any time a device is not working properly, always take a look at the driver first. The odds are high that the driver may be causing the problem. See Chapters 6 and 7 to learn more.

can both detect and disinfect your computer in the case of a virus. Antivirus software is normally under $50 and well worth your investment. If you do not have antivirus software, you can purchase it on the Internet, at any computer store in your area, or from many department stores.

Refer to your owner's instructions and run a complete virus scan of your system. Make sure your software has current virus definitions so it can detect the presence of a virus. Current definitions can be downloaded from the manufacturer's Web site. Once the virus scan is complete and you have removed any viruses, you need to disable your antivirus software before running Setup. Antivirus software will interfere with Windows Me installation, so make certain you check the antivirus documentation and disable the software accordingly.

Shut Down All Programs

Before running Windows Me Setup, make certain that you shut down all programs that are running and that you disconnect from the Internet. Also, if you have any programs that protect your Master Boot Record (MBR) by encrypting it, you need to uninstall that application. Some applications on the market today help protect your computer against sabotage or data theft by encrypting certain portions of your operating system so that unauthorized persons cannot read them. This software is not normally installed as a part of a purchase package, but do check your original documentation and make certain you do not have any applications like this installed. If you do, uninstall them before attempting to run Setup. These applications will cause the Windows Me upgrade to fail if they are running.

Upgrading Your Computer

Finally, after doing your detective work, you are ready to begin the upgrade to Windows Me. Before you get started, make sure you have everything gathered that you will need. First, you'll need the Windows Me CD-ROM and the product key. You should be able to find the product key on a sticker on the back of your CD-ROM jewel case. You should also have handy any disks or CD-ROMs containing drivers for your hardware in case Windows Me cannot install one of the devices. Finally, you need a 3.5 floppy disk that is blank and formatted.

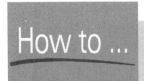 **Format a Floppy Disk**

You may have a floppy disk that you want to use for the Windows Me Startup disk that has been previously used for other purposes. That's OK, but before you can use it, you have to make certain the disk is formatted and blank. Just follow these steps:

1. Using My Computer, open the floppy drive and take a look at any information on the disk. If you want to keep the information, copy it to your computer and then move it to a different hard or floppy disk.

2. Click Edit | Select All.

3. Right-click one of the selected icons, then click Delete. Click OK to the message that appears.

   Or:

1. You can also remove data or format an empty disk by right-clicking the 3.5 floppy disk icon in My Computer and then clicking Format.

2. A Format window appears. Click the Start button to format the floppy disk and then click the Close button when the completion message appears.

   Now that you have your materials and you have taken some time to check out your computer and make certain it is ready for the upgrade, you are now ready to begin. The following steps walk you through the upgrade and describe each piece of the upgrade process to you.

1. Insert your Windows Me CD-ROM into your computer's CD-ROM drive. A message appears telling you that the CD-ROM contains a newer version of Windows and asks if you want to upgrade now. Click Yes. Window Me

A

is able to provide this message due to an auto-launch program on the CD-ROM. If the message does not appear, this just means that your computer is having problems reading the auto launcher, which is no big deal. Just open My Computer then double-click your CD-ROM drive icon. Your computer opens the CD-ROM and you see an icon called Setup. Double-click this icon to start the installation.

2. Setup begins by checking your system and preparing the Setup Wizard. This will probably take less than one minute.

3. The Windows Me installation Welcome screen appears, shown in Figure A-2. The Welcome screen tells that installation will take between 30 and 60 minutes, depending on what options you select and the speed of your computer. Click the Next button to continue.

FIGURE A-2   Click Next on the Welcome screen

4. The Licensing Agreement window appears, which gives all the laws and rules about using your new software. It's not very interesting to read (yawn), but you should read it. You must click the I Accept The Agreement radio button for installation to continue. Click this button, then click the Next button.

5. The Product Key window appears. Locate your product key on your CD-ROM jewel case and type the key into the dialog box just as it appears on the CD-ROM case. Click Next when you're done.

You don't have to worry about typing capital letters when you type your product key. The product key is not case-sensitive.

6. At this point, your computer checks your hard drive for any problems and prepares a directory, or storage location, for Windows Me to store its installation files on your computer.

7. Next, a window appears asking if you want to save your system files. You should choose to save your system files, as shown in Figure A-3. If you have a problem with Windows Me, you will be able to recover your

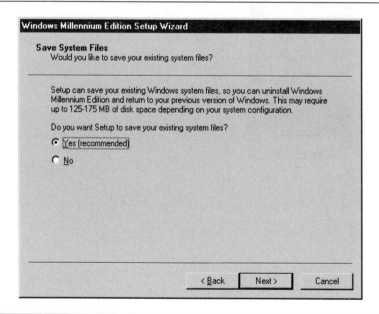

FIGURE A-3   Choose Yes to save your system files

previous operating system because you kept your system files. This process requires about 150MB of hard disk space. Choose Yes to save your system files, then click the Next button.

CAUTION   *If you do not save your system files, you will not be able to recover your previous operating system in the event of an installation failure. I strongly urge you to save your system files!*

As you can see in Figure A-4, Setup scans your computer and then saves your system files. This process may take a few minutes to complete.

8. Next, your computer prompts you to create a startup disk, as shown in Figure A-5. This is where you need that formatted, blank floppy disk that you made before you started Setup. Insert the disk into your computer's floppy disk drive, then click the OK button. When Setup finishes making the floppy disk, a message appears telling you to remove the disk from your computer. Remove the disk, then click OK to the message.

9. A completion window appears. Click the Finish button.

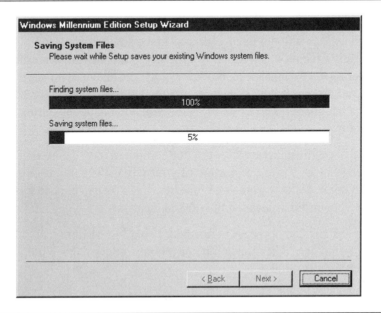

FIGURE A-4   Setup saves your existing system files

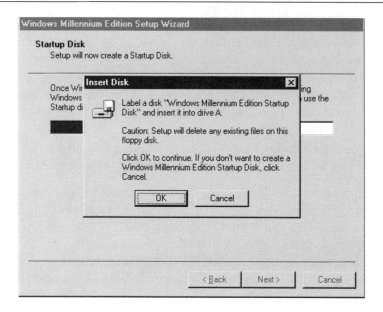

FIGURE A-5 Insert a formatted, blank floppy disk and then click OK

10. At this point, the interactive part of Setup is over. This means that Windows Me will not need your assistance any longer to complete Setup. The only exception is if Windows Me needs a hardware driver from you. Under most circumstances, however, you don't have to do anything else and you can leave your computer unattended for the next half-hour or so. The remainder of the steps simply tell you what happens during the rest of Setup.

11. Setup copies installation files to your computer. You can see the file copy progress in the lower left portion of your screen. The main screen tells you about some of the features of Windows Me. You can choose to sit and read these screens, or you can simply take a nap.

12. Once the file copy process is finished, Windows Me automatically reboots your computer. When the computer reboots, you see the Windows Me logo screen for first time.

A

13. Windows Me completes the upgrade of your configuration files and begins the hardware detection and setup phase. Windows looks for and installs your hardware devices, such as your keyboard, mouse, modem, monitor, and so forth. Your screen may flicker a few times, which is fine. However, if Setup stops doing anything for a long time, it means it has had problems with one of the hardware devices. Just turn the power to your computer off, wait ten seconds, then turn it back on. Setup will continue.

14. Setup may reboot your computer during hardware detection. If it does, hardware detection continues until it has finished, and then the computer is rebooted again. You don't have to do anything during this entire process.

15. After reboot, Setup finalizes installing by configuring items such as Control Panel and your Start menu. Once this is complete, Windows Me reboots.

16. This is your first real boot of Windows Me. A dialog box appears asking if you want to use a password to log on to your system. If you do, enter the password; if you don't, click Cancel.

17. Windows Me finishes loading and you see your desktop for the first time.

Did you know?

How About a Nap?

Do you like the fact that Setup collects all the necessary information from you at the beginning, and then leaves you alone? It is no accident that Setup works this way. During the days of Windows 95, Setup required you to baby-sit the computer during installation. It might work for some time, then ask you a question, or wait for you to click a button so it can reboot. This was all changed with Windows 98 due to customer requests. Windows Me, like Windows 98, does not require you to baby-sit Setup. Once it has the necessary information from you, it can take care of installation all by itself, including all of the reboots!

 *If installation does not go so well and you have problems starting Windows Me, see Chapter 18 for helpful troubleshooting tips.*

Installing Windows Me on a Computer with No Operating System

You may need to install Windows Me on a computer that does not have an operating system. For example, let's say you purchase a computer from a supplier or even over the Internet. These machines are often sold unformatted and without an operating system. Or, perhaps your Windows 95/98 computer has too many goofy system problems you don't want to contend with and you want to clean-install Windows Me so that it does not use and keep all of those older operating system files. No matter what your reason, you can install Windows Me on a computer that has no operating system.

This discussion brings up an important question. Should you format an existing hard drive and "blow away" your old operating system so you can clean-install Windows Me? Not usually. It is best if you upgrade your existing operating system to Windows Me in order to preserve your system and hardware settings. However, in some cases, you may wish to clean-install in order to get away from problems in your older operating system. This is, of course, fine, but as a rule of thumb, always choose an upgrade over a clean installation for Windows Me.

Preparing for a Clean Installation

Just as with an upgrade, you need to spend a little time preparing for the clean installation. This means that you need to examine your computer's hardware and make certain the computer meets at least the minimum hardware requirements. You also need to locate floppy disks and CD-ROMs that contain drivers for your computer's hardware. The first section of this appendix examines these issues, so refer to that section for specific information.

Create a Startup Disk

In order to install Windows Me on a computer with no operating system or to remove an old operating system from a computer, you will need a Startup disk. The Startup disk is a floppy disk that contains boot and program information to start your computer. Once you start the computer, you can perform some configuration so that you can begin the installation. You can create a Startup disk using a computer running either Windows 98 or Windows Me. For example, if you currently have Windows 98, you can use your current operating system to create the Startup disk. If your friend down the street already has Windows Me installed, you can use that machine to make your Startup disk. You will need a blank, formatted floppy disk to create the Startup disk. See the How To box earlier in this chapter for instructions on how to format a floppy disk. To create the Startup disk, follow these steps:

1. On a Windows 98 or Windows Me computer, click Start | Settings | Control Panel.

2. Double-click the Add/Remove Programs icon.

3. Click the Startup Disk tab, as shown in Figure A-6.

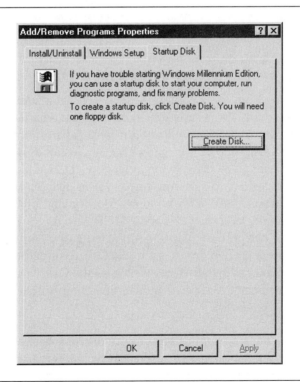

FIGURE A-6   Access the Startup Disk tab to create a Startup disk

4. Insert the blank, formatted floppy disk into the floppy disk drive and then click the Create Disk button on the Startup Disk tab.

5. Click OK when the completion message appears and then click the Close button on the Startup tab. Remove the floppy disk from the disk drive.

Once the Startup disk is created, you can start the computer on which you want to install Windows Me by turning off the computer, inserting the floppy disk into the disk drive, and then turning the computer back on. Your computer should start from the floppy disk and a menu appears that enables you to start setup from the CD-ROM and start the computer with or without CD-ROM support.

NOTE   *If your computer does not start from the floppy disk, you will need to edit the computer's CMOS (Complementary Metal Oxide Semiconductor), which basically tells your computer how to operate, such as booting from the floppy or not. Check your computer's documentation for instructions. In most cases, however, typical computers will boot from their floppy drives without any problems.*

Using FDISK to Partition Your Hard Disk

Windows Me (or any Windows operating system, for that matter) cannot use a hard disk that is not ready for installation. In order to use a hard disk, Windows Me expects to find one or more hard disk *partitions.* A partition is a physical segment of the hard disk on which Windows Me can install its operating system. Hard disk partitions are given drive letters, such as C, D, E, and so forth. For example, you could create two partitions on your hard disk (called the primary partition and logical partition). With Windows Me, you don't have a partition size limitation. For example, let's say you have a 12GB hard drive. You can use the entire hard drive for one primary partition (drive letter of C), or you could split it so that the disk becomes two drives, such as a C drive of 6GB and a D drive of 6GB. This way, you can install Windows Me on the C drive and use the other drive for storage. You can even install another operating system if you want (this is called a *dual boot scenario*).

NOTE   *It is beyond the scope of this book to explore dual boot scenarios. You need to know a few advanced configuration issues in order to establish a dual boot system, but if you are interested in learning more, search the Microsoft Web site or the Web itself for more information.*

In order to partition your hard disk so that Windows Me can install on it, you use a program called FDISK, which can be found on your Startup disk. Before you move any further, you do need to know a big warning. FDISK completely destroys all data on your hard disk. If you have data that you do not want to lose, or if you do not want to lose your current operating system, then stay away from FDISK. You cannot recover data or an operating system if you remove it using the FDISK utility.

The following sections show you how to perform some common tasks using the FDISK utility. You can learn more about using FDISK by consulting your Windows Me documentation found on your Windows Me CD.

Removing Partitions

If you want to perform a clean install of Windows Me on a computer that currently has an operating system, then you must remove or delete the existing partitions on the disk in order to repartition it.

CAUTION   *Deleting a partition removes all of the data on that partition. That data cannot be recovered.*

In order to remove any existing partitions, use FDISK to first remove any extended partitions, then any logical partitions, and then, finally, the primary partition. Once these partitions are removed, you can create new partitions for your Windows Me installation. To use FDISK to remove partitions, follow these steps:

1. Boot your computer using the Startup disk, then choose the Without CD-ROM Support option (since you don't need your CD-ROM at this time).

2. Your computer boots and presents you with an A:\ prompt. Type `fdisk`, then press ENTER. The FDISK program begins.

3. You are asked if you want to enable large drive support. If you enable large drive support, your computer must use the FAT32 file system, which is supported and desirable for Windows Me. The only reason you would not use large drive support is if you wanted to set up your computer to run Windows Me and an older operating system, such as Windows 95 or Windows 3.x (which you probably do not want to do). Type Y, then press ENTER.

4. From the menu, choose the fourth option so that you can inspect your computer's partitions, then press ENTER.

5. Take note of any partitions that are listed, then press the ESC key.

6. Now you are back at the main menu. Press 3 to delete a partition or logical drive and press ENTER.

7. Follow the instructions that appear on your screen so that you are deleting your extended partitions, logical drives, and your primary partition.

 *At any time when using FDISK, simply press* ESC *on your keyboard to return to the previous screen or menu.*

Creating a Partition

Once you have removed any existing partitions, you must then create a new partition on which Windows Me will install. You can create a primary partition and a logical partition if you desire, or you can create just a primary partition. There's no right or wrong here—it is just a matter of what partition design will work best for you.

What about NTFS?

NTFS is the file system of choice for Windows NT and Windows 2000 computers. NTFS provides superior system and file security and is most often seen in Microsoft networks where Windows NT and 2000 computers and servers are used. Windows Me, like 95 and 98, does not support NTFS because NTFS is *not* designed for home use. If you want to install Windows Me on a computer that was once formatted with NTFS, you must use FDISK to repartition it so you can remove NTFS.

NOTE *You cannot dynamically change partitions once you have established a partition scheme and installed Windows Me. In order to change your partitions, you must reinstall Windows Me, unless you have some additional partitioning software, like PowerQuest's Partition Magic. Windows 2000 operating systems do, however, allow you to dynamically alter partitions (called volumes in Windows 2000).*

To use FDISK to create partitions in Windows Me, follow these steps:

1. Boot your computer using the Startup disk, then choose the Without CD-ROM Support option (since you don't need your CD-ROM at this time).

2. Your computer boots and presents you with an A:\ prompt. Type **fdisk**, then press ENTER. The FDISK program begins.

3. You are asked if you want to enable large drive support. If you enable large drive support, your computer must use the FAT32 file system, which is supported and desirable for Windows Me. The only reason you would not use large drive support is if you wanted to set up your computer to run Windows Me and an older operating system, such as Windows 95 or Windows 3.x (which you probably do not want to do). Type **Y**, then press ENTER.

4. On the menu that appears, select number 1, Create DOS Partition Or Logical DOS Drive.

5. You are asked if you want to use the maximum space for the primary partition. If you choose Yes, then your entire hard disk will be used for the primary partition. If you choose a smaller size, your remaining hard disk space can be used for an extended partition. Make your selection and follow the instructions that appear.

6. When you finish, you will be prompted to mark the primary partition as Active if you created more than one partition (if not, you won't get this message). Press ESC to return to the menu, then select number 2, Set Active Partition. On the window that appears, choose your primary partition to set it as the active partition.

7. Press ESC. You are prompted to reboot your computer for the changes to take effect.

Formatting the Hard Disk

Once you have created a partition for the hard disk, you need to format it so that Windows Me can store data on the disk. Formatting a disk divides the disk into sectors and places a file system on the disk that Windows can use. Think of your unformatted hard disk as an empty filing cabinet. Without any kind of order, information will not be stored in a logical way and you will not be able to easily find and use your files. It's the same with Windows Me. In order to use the hard drive, Windows Me must be able to store data in a logical manner, and formatting your hard drive provides this order that the operating system needs.

To format a hard disk, you use the Startup disk. Follow these steps:

1. Start your computer with the Startup disk. When the menu appears, choose to boot the computer without CD-ROM support (since you do not need your CD-ROM at this time).

2. At the A:\ prompt, type **dir x:**, where *x* is the drive letter you want to format. For example, if you created only one drive using FDISK, then type **dir C:**.

3. If your C drive is unformatted, you will receive the following message (if it is not unformatted, see the previous section to use the FDISK utility. Make sure you are not examining the wrong drive. Formatting a drive that contains data will destroy the data):

```
Invalid media type reading drive C
Abort, Retry, Fail?
```

4. Press A to abort. You can now format the drive by typing **format x:** where *x* is the drive letter. For example, if you are formatting your C drive, you would type **format C:** and press ENTER.

5. Give the drive a name if you want and press ENTER.

6. The drive is formatted—this may take several minutes to complete.

Installing Windows Me

Once you have partitioned your computer with no operating system and formatted the drive, you are all set to begin the installation of Windows Me. Because you have no operating system, you must, once again, use your Startup disk to begin the install. Also, Windows Setup will need more information from you because there are no existing files from which to copy information. All of this is easy, however. Just follow these steps to install Windows Me on your newly formatted hard drive:

1. Start your computer with your Startup disk. When prompted select the Start Computer with CD-ROM Support option, then press ENTER.

    INSERT ME CD

2. When an A:\ prompt appears, enter the letter of your CD-ROM drive followed by a colon. Typically, your CD-ROM drive letter is D, so you would type **D:**.

    E:\ setup

3. The prompt changes to D:\. Type **setup**, then press ENTER.

4. Setup runs Scandisk to check your drive. This process enables Windows Me to check your file system and configuration. Once your drive checks out, Setup then begins the interactive portion of Setup.

5. Setup prepares the Installation Wizard and then a Welcome screen appears.

6. The Welcome screen tells you that installation will require 30 to 60 minutes. Click Next on the Welcome screen.

7. You see the Windows Me licensing agreement. This agreement tells you what you can legally do (and can't do) with your operating system. Click the I Accept The Agreement radio button, then click the Next button.

NOTE   *Setup will not continue unless you accept the licensing agreement.*

8. The next window prompts you to fill in your CD-ROM product key, which is on the back on your CD-ROM jewel case, usually on a sticker. Enter the product key exactly as it appears on the jewel case. You do not, however, have to enter uppercase letters as the key is not case sensitive.

9. Windows asks you to select a directory in which to install Windows Me. The default location is C:\Windows. Under normal circumstances, you should select this default and click Next, but you can select another directory location if necessary. Make a selection, then click the Next button.

10. Installation now checks for installed components (there are none, since you are installing on a clean hard drive) and checks the available disk space.

11. Setup asks you to choose a Setup option. You have the following choices:

   ■ Typical—Installs the most common Windows components used by most PC owners.

   ■ Portable—Installs the basic Windows components. This option is typically used for laptop computers in order to conserve resources and hard disk space.

   ■ Compact—Installs no optional Windows components. This option is best used when hard disk space is low.

12. Enter your name and company, if necessary. Click Next.

13. The Windows Components window appears. Choose either to install the most common components, or you can select the custom option and choose the components you want to install from the list that appears. Make your selection, then click Next.

14. Windows Me assigns a default computer name, workgroup, and computer description. You can change these if you want by entering new information in the available dialog boxes. Make your selections, then click Next.

15. Select your country or region from the list and click Next.

16. Select your time zone and click Next.

17. The Create Startup Disk window appears. To make a Startup disk, place a formatted, blank floppy disk into your floppy disk drive and click OK. When the disk is made, click OK to the completion message, then remove the disk from the drive.

Since you already have a Startup disk used to FDISK and to the format of your computer, you don't need to make one now. However, if you used a Windows 98 Startup disk, go ahead and make a new Windows Me Startup disk. If you used a Windows Me Startup disk created from another computer, just click OK to this message, then click Cancel when you are prompted to insert a floppy disk. This saves you the time it would have taken to create the floppy disk, since you don't need one.

A

18. At this point, the interactive part of Setup is over. This means that Windows Me will not need your assistance any longer to complete Setup. The only exception is if Windows Me needs a hardware driver from you. Under most circumstances, however, you don't have to do anything else and you can leave your computer unattended for the next half-hour or so. The remainder of the steps simply tell you what happens during the rest of Setup.

19. Setup copies installation files to your computer. You can see the file copy progress in the lower left portion of your screen. The main screen tells you about some of the features of Windows Me. You can choose to sit and read these screens, or you can simply take a nap.

20. Once the file copy process is finished, Windows Me automatically reboots your computer. When the computer reboots, you see the Windows Me splash screen for the first time.

21. Windows Me completes the installation of your configuration files and begins the hardware detection and setup phase. Windows looks for and installs your hardware devices, such as your keyboard, mouse, modem, monitor, and so forth. Your screen may flicker a few times, which is fine. However, if Setup stops doing anything for a long time, it means it has had problems with one of the hardware devices. Just turn the power off to your computer, wait ten seconds, then turn it back on. Setup will continue.

22. Setup may reboot your computer during hardware detection. If it does, hardware detection continues until it has finished, then the computer is rebooted again. You don't have to do anything during this entire process.

23. After reboot, Setup finalizes installing by configuring items such as Control Panel and your Start menu. Once this is completed, Windows Me reboots.

24. This is your first real boot of Windows Me. A dialog box appears asking if you want to use a password to log on to your system. If you do, enter the password; if you don't, click Cancel.

25. Windows Me finishes loading and you see your desktop for the first time.

Appendix B

Keyboard Shortcut Quick Reference

How To...

■ Use Keyboard Shortcuts

Are you tired of using your mouse so much? Then how about a few helpful keyboard shortcuts? Windows Me, like previous versions of Windows, includes a number of helpful keyboard shortcuts to save you time and energy. Many of your applications have keyboard shortcuts as well. Check your applications' documentation for details about those shortcuts.

OK, here they are—in a few nice, easy-to-read tables.

To Do This...	Press This...
Copy a File	Hold down CTRL while dragging the file to the desired location
Create a Shortcut	Hold down CTRL+SHIFT while dragging the file to the desired shortcut location
Tab through pages in a Properties sheet	CTRL+TAB
Close a folder	SHIFT and click the Close ("X") button
Bypass a CD-ROM's autorun	Hold down SHIFT when you insert the CD-ROM
Switch between opening a new window and closing an existing window	Press CTRL and double-click a folder
Copy a file	CTRL+C
Open a file	CTRL+O
Print a file	CTRL+P
Save a file	CTRL+S
Cut a file	CTRL+X
Paste a file	CTRL+V
Undo	CTRL+Z
Select All	CTRL+A
Show "What's This?" Help	SHIFT+F1
Show Help window	F1
Cancel	ESC
Select an item	SPACEBAR
Show pop-up menu	SHIFT+F10
Activate or inactivate menu bar mode	ALT
Display next primary window	ALT+TAB

TABLE B-1   Shortcuts for Windows, Objects, and Folders

To Do This...	Press This...
Display next window	ALT+ESC
Show drop-down menu for active window	ALT+SPACEBAR
Show drop-down menu for active child window	ALT+HYPHEN
Show Properties	SHIFT+ENTER
Close active window	ALT+F4
Switch to next window within an application	ALT+F6
Capture window	ALT+PRINT SCRN
Capture desktop	PRINT SCRN
Activate Start menu	CTRL+ESC
Rename an item	F2
Find an item	F3
Delete an item	DELETE
Delete an item without putting it in recycle bin	SHIFT+DELETE
Explore an item	SHIFT+double-click

TABLE B-1   Shortcuts for Windows, Objects, and Folders *(continued)*

To Do This...	Press This...
Cancel current task	ESC
Click a button	SPACEBAR
Select or clear a check box	SPACEBAR
Carry out a following command	SPACEBAR
Click a selected button	ALT+underlined letter
Move forward through options	CTRL+SHIFT+TAB
Move backward through options	ENTER
Move forward through tabs	TAB
Move backward through tabs	SHIFT+TAB
Open a folder one level up	CTRL+TAB

TABLE B-2   Shortcuts Within Dialog Boxes

B

To Do This...	Press This...
Display Combo box	F4
Refresh	F5
Move focus between panes	F6
Go To command	CTRL+G
Go to parent folder	BACKSPACE
Expand everything under a selection	Press * on keypad
Expand selection	Press + on keypad
Collapse selection	Press - on keypad
Expand current selection	RIGHT ARROW
Collapse current selection	LEFT ARROW
Move backward	ALT+LEFT ARROW
Scroll without moving selection	CTRL+ARROW
Close folders	SHIFT+Close ("X") button

TABLE B-3   Windows Explorer Shortcuts

To Do This...	Press This...
Activate a selected link	TAB+ENTER
Show a shortcut menu for a link	SHIFT+F10
Go to next page	ALT+RIGHT ARROW
Go to previous page	ALT+LEFT ARROW
Go to a new page	CTRL+O
Move forward between frames	CTRL+TAB
Move back between frames	SHIFT+CTRL+TAB
Move to beginning of page	HOME
Move to end of page	END
Start a new window	CTRL+N
Print	CTRL+P
Refresh	F5
Scroll to beginning of page	UP ARROW
Scroll to end of page	DOWN ARROW
Scroll to beginning in page increments	PAGE UP
Scroll to end in page increments	PAGE DOWN
Stop downloading	ESC
Save	CTRL+S

TABLE B-4   Helpful Internet Explorer Shortcuts

Appendix C

Windows Media Player Keyboard Shortcut Quick Reference

How To...

■ Use Media Player's Keyboard Shortcuts

Are you becoming a Windows Media Player guru? There's a lot you can do with Windows Media Player (see Chapter 14), but you can speed up your work and play by using these helpful keyboard shortcuts!

Media Player Menu Shortcuts

You can use a variety of keyboard shortcuts to access items in the Media Player menus. The following tables show you these shortcuts.

To Do This...	Press This...
Open	CTRL+O
Open URL	CTRL+U
Close	CTRL+W
Exit	ALT+F4

TABLE C-1   File Menu

To Do This...	Press This...
Full Mode	CTRL+1
Compact Mode	CTRL+2
Toggling between window and full screen	ALT+ENTER

TABLE C-2   View Menu

To Do This...	Press This...
Play/Pause	CTRL+P
Stop	CTRL+S
Skip Back	CTRL+B
Skip Forward	CTRL+F
Shuffle	CTRL+H
Repeat	CTRL+T
Volume Up	F10
Volume Down	F9
Volume Mute	F8

TABLE C-3   Play Menu

To Do This...	Press This...
Search Computer For...	F10
Help Topics	F1

TABLE C-4   Tools Menu

Media Player Feature Shortcuts

For some Media Player features, there are additional shortcuts you can use to make your work and play easier. The following tables list these options.

To Do This...	Press This...
Copy Music	ALT+C
Stop Copy	ALT+S
Get Names	ALT+G
Album Details	ALT+A
Back	ALT+B

TABLE C-5   CD Audio Features

To Do This...	Press This...
New Playlist	ALT+N
Add to Playlist	ALT+A
Search	ALT+S
Media Details	ALT+M
Back	ALT+B
Add	TAB+ENTER
Add Currently Playing	TAB+ENTER+T
Add File	TAB+ENTER+F
Add URL	TAB+ENTER+U
Delete	TAB+ENTER
Delete from Playlist	TAB+ENTER+P
Delete from Library	TAB+ENTER+L
Delete Playlist	TAB+ENTER+A

TABLE C-6   Media Library Features

Skin Shortcuts

When you apply a skin to Media Player, there are several keyboard shortcuts you can use. See the next table for details.

To Do This...	Press This...
Access Shortcut menu	SHIFT+F10
Navigate through Menus	SHIFT+F10, ARROW KEYS, ENTER
Close Shortcut	ESC
Open	CTRL+O
Open URL	CTRL+U
Shuffle	CTRL+H
Repeat	CTRL+T
Volume Up	F10
Volume Down	F9
Mute	F8
Play/Pause	CTRL+P
Stop	CTRL+S

TABLE C-7   Skins Shortcuts

Glossary

Application   A loose term describing a type of program that is often used for some business or production purpose. For the most part, the term *application* and the term *program* are used interchangeably. Microsoft Word is an example of an application.

Browser   A program that enables your computer to download and interpret HTML pages. Browsers, such as Internet Explorer, enable you to surf the World Wide Web.

Capture   In Windows Movie Maker, the process of gathering film data that is converted from analog to digital media format.

Components   Typically, pieces of an operating system or application that perform some specific purpose. Window Me includes a number of components that are not installed by default. These components can be installed using Windows Setup found in Add/Remove Programs

Compression   The act of reducing the size, in terms of kilobytes or megabytes, of a file. Compression helps reduce disk storage space per file or folder. Windows Me supports folder compression natively. WinZip and Stuffit are examples of compression applications.

Control Panel   Located in My Computer, Control Panel gives you a number of features that enable you to configure Windows Me.

Desktop   The primary area of your Windows Me computer where you work. The desktop contains standard icons, such as My Computer, Recycle Bin, and so forth.

Dial-up   A type of networking in which your computer uses a telephone line to dial a connection number to another computer. Dial-up connections are used for both Internet connectivity and private networks.

Driver   A piece of software that enables Windows Me to interact with a hardware device. Windows Me contains an extensive database of drivers that can be used for Plug-and-Play devices.

Download   The process of receiving Web content from a Web server to your computer. The browser you are using then interprets the Web content and displays it to you.

E-mail   Electronic mail. Enables you to communicate with people all over the world by sending e-mail messages and attachments over the Internet.

E-mail client   A program that enables you to send, receive, and manage e-mail and e-mail addresses. Outlook Express is an e-mail client.

Explorer   A Windows component that enables you to manage files, folders, and network connections. Due to Windows Me Web integration, Explorer is now considered an "accessory" in Windows Me.

File   Any saved item, such as documents, pictures, videos, etc. Various programs and applications are used to open files.

File system   A method of hard disk organization used by Windows Me that enables it to read and write data to the disk. Windows Me can read the File Allocation Table (FAT) or File Allocation Table 32 (FAT32) file systems.

Folder   In Windows Me, a folder essentially looks and works as a paper folder you would find a filing cabinet. Folders are used to store programs and files.

Fragmentation   Over time and with usage, data on hard disks is written in a noncontiguous format, which causes slower disk performance. A file can be composed of different segments beginning in a block in one physical location on the hard drive, and ending in a completely different location. This process is known as *fragmentation*. Disk Defragmenter in Windows Me is used to correct the problem.

Hardware   Any device found in your computer is considered hardware, as are other devices that may connect to it. Common examples are video cards, keyboards, hard drives, printers, game controllers, etc.

HTML   HyperText Markup Language. Web pages are written using HTML and are downloaded and interpreted by browsers.

HTTP   HyperText Transfer Protocol. HTTP is the protocol that transfers HTML pages from Web sites to users' computers.

Icon   A symbol that appears on your computer, usually in the form of a picture that represents some file, folder, application, or other component.

ICS   Internet Connection Sharing. A Windows Me feature that enables you to share an Internet connection from one computer and have other computers use the share on your home network.

Internet   A vast public computer network that enables people all over the world to freely exchange ideas and information.

Internet Connection   A type of connection that enables your computer to connect to the Internet. This may include dial-up, DSL, ISDN, or other connection options.

ISP   Internet Service Provider. Although the Web itself is free, you must pay an ISP a fee in order to access and use the Web. MSN, AOL, and CompuServe are just a few examples of ISPs.

Media Player   A Windows Me application that lets you listen to CDs and play virtually any multimedia file on your local machine or on the Internet.

Movie Maker   A Windows Me application that enables you to record, edit, and manage home movies.

MSN   The Microsoft Network. MSN is both a Web search engine and an ISP. Visit MSN at **www.msn.com**.

Operating System   Computer code that operates a computer's hardware. Operating systems are used to run applications and programs and manage a computer. Windows Me is an operating system.

Plug and Play   A technology that enables a computer to detect when a new hardware device has been installed or when one has been removed. This feature enables the computer to automatically manage hardware and adapt to changes. Windows Me is a Plug-and-Play compliant system.

Program   A loose term that refers to some kind of computer code used for a specific purpose. Applications, games, and utilities are all programs.

Properties   Most features and programs within Windows Me have Properties pages. Properties pages often enable you to configure various components for the specific feature or program.

Protocol   A communication behavior rule that computers use to communicate with each other. A very common protocol today is TCP/IP.

Registry   A Windows database that contains all of the information about your Windows configuration and hardware. Windows operating systems read and write to the database to configure your system and adapt to changes.

Restore point   A place in time to which System Restore can save your configuration settings to the hard disk so that the system can be restored to that time in the event of a failure.

Safe Mode   A Windows Me feature that lets you boot Windows using a minimal number of drivers. Safe Mode is used to repair Windows Me when you cannot boot normally due to some system or hardware problem.

Share   A folder, printer, application, drive, or some other item that is available to other users on a network.

Skin   An overlay graphic that enables programs that supports skins, such as Media Player, to look a certain way. The skin changes the graphical appearance of the program's interface.

Split   In Movie Maker, the process of breaking a film clip into more manageable pieces.

Start menu   Your gateway to Windows Me. Found on the taskbar, the Start menu gives you access to virtually all of the Windows Me components as well as any programs you install.

System Restore   A Windows Me feature that enables Windows Me to reconfigure your computer to an earlier time in the event of some configuration, application, startup, or other system error.

Taskbar   A thin bar that runs along the bottom of the desktop. The taskbar contains the Start menu and a number of other program options.

Trimming   In Windows Movie maker, the process of cutting unwanted movie footage out of a movie.

TCP/IP   Transmission Control Protocol / Internet Protocol. TCP/IP is the most common computer protocol today. TCP/IP is used on the Internet and in private networks for communication between computers. TCP/IP is considered a "suite" of protocols because it combines over 100 communication protocols that give you the vast functionality you find on the Internet.

Web TV for Windows   An additional Windows Me component that enables you to receive television signals over the Internet and watch them on your Windows Me computer.

World Wide Web   A part of the Internet that displays HTML pages that users can download with a browser. Most Internet traffic and usage is Web-based.

Index